"Fresh, interesting, and sure to delight"

For those with food allergies, eating the wrong food can be life-threatening. *The Whole Foods Allergy Cookbook* is one mother's response to the news that her infant son had severe dairy and soy allergies. That Cybele Pascal is such a gifted chef ensures this book a strong following beyond allergy sufferers. In fact, she chose to develop her recipes for those with allergies to eggs, wheat, peanuts, tree nuts, fish, and shellfish, in addition to dairy and soy, covering 90 percent of all food allergies. Her dishes are fresh, interesting, and sure to delight.

Foreword Magazine

"A culinary wealth of dishes"

Eliminating all eight of the allergens responsible for 90 percent of food allergies, the two hundred gourmet and homestyle recipes comprising *The Whole Foods Allergy Cookbook* by hypoallergenic cooking expert Cybele Pascal offer a culinary wealth of dishes that would serve any dinning occasion from simple family meals to festive celebratory occasions for anyone with a common food allergy. With easy-to-follow, step-by-step recipes . . . *The Whole Foods Allergy Cookbook* will prove one of the most popular additions to any cookbook collection in general, and the kitchens of food allergy sufferers in particular.

Midwest Book Review

"A wonderful assortment of delicious recipes"

Those of us who deal with food allergies every day, both as patients and as allergists, owe a big thanks to Cybele. I am happy to have a great cookbook to recommend to parents and people with food allergies. This book provides a wonderful assortment of delicious recipes that are allergy-safe. Right now, since avoidance is all we have for prevention, it's nice to know that low-allergy meals can taste so good.

Christine Fusillo, MD

Chief of Pediatric Allergy
Westchester Medical Center, New York Medical College

The Whole Foods ALLERGY COOKBOOK

SECOND EDITION

Two Hundred Gourmet & Homestyle Recipes for the Food Allergic Family

Cybele Pascal

SQUAREONE
PUBLISHERS

The information contained in this book is for educational purposes only. It is not provided in order
to diagnose, prescribe, or treat any disease, illness, or injury, and the author, publisher, printer(s), and distributor(s) accept no responsibility for such use. Those individuals suffering from any disease, illness,
or injury should consult with their physician or qualified primary care provider. This book eliminates
all "major food allergens" as identified by the US Food and Drug Administration (FDA). The FDA
identifies the eight most common allergenic foods as milk, eggs, fish (e.g., bass, flounder, cod), crustacean shellfish (e.g. crab, lobster, shrimp), tree nuts (e.g., almonds, walnuts, pecans), peanuts, wheat, and soybeans. These
foods account for 90 percent of food allergic reactions. They, and any ingredient that contains protein derived
from one or more of these foods, are designated as the "major food allergens." This book does *not* eliminate
gluten, and is not intended for use by people with Celiac Disease.

COVER DESIGN: On the Dot Designs
INTERIOR DESIGN: Cathy Lombardi

Square One Publishers
115 Herricks Road
Garden City Park, NY 11040
(516) 535-2010 • (877) 900-BOOK
www.squareonepublishers.com

Library of Congress Cataloging-in-Publication Data

Pascal, Cybele.
  The whole foods allergy cookbook : two hundred gourmet and homestyle recipes
for the food allergic family / by Cybele Pascal. — 2nd ed.
      p. cm.
  Includes bibliographical references and index.
  ISBN-13: 978-1-890612-45-0
  ISBN-10: 1-890612-45-6
  1. Food allergy—Diet therapy—Recipes. I. Title.
  RC588.D53P368 2009
  641.5'631—dc22

CONTENTS

For Lennon and Montgomery,
with all my love

ACKNOWLEDGMENTS

First and foremost, I'd like to thank my entire extended family for their endless support and willingness to be tasters for the better part of three years. I'd like to express deep appreciation to my husband, Adam, for his encouragement and enthusiasm (I know he married me for my cooking).

In addition, I'd like to thank the following people: Julie Barer at Sanford J. Greenburger Associates for her belief in this project; Beth Berger, my attorney; and Howard Bostwick, M.D., the pediatric gastroenterologist who was so supportive back in the beginning of this journey when we were so very worried about our son Lennon's sick little tummy.

Thanks to Judith Weinraub for her keen journalist's eye and savvy; to Dan Barber and Michel Nischan, two brilliant chefs, for their votes of confidence; to Lynda Schneider, M.D., and her staff of nutritionists at Children's Hospital in Boston for looking over the manuscript; and to Mary Jo Widmer and the review staff at *Food Allergy and Anaphylaxis Network* (FAAN) for their support and guidance.

Tremendous thanks to David Richard and Heather Flournoy at Vital Health Publishing for their help and willingness to bring me on board.

I am especially thankful to Eric Chivian, M.D., for his tireless efforts to help others stay healthy, and to my mother, Susanna, and my grandmother, Catherene, for teaching me to cook at such a young age.

I am forever indebted and grateful to Christine Fusillo, M.D., my sons' allergist, for all her guidance. And lastly, but most importantly, thank you to my two wonderful sons, Lennon and Montgomery, without whom I never would have written this book.

FOREWORD

Alexander could not eat peanuts. All of his friends could. But if Alexander ate just one peanut, he could get so sick he could end up in the hospital.

Alexander's peanut problem is the subject of an amusing and informative video for children. Why amusing? Alexander is an elephant; an elephant who couldn't eat peanuts. Why informative? Because it is full of important information and demonstrates to children, in language and pictures they can understand, that they are not alone in having allergic reactions.

If it appears to you that there are a lot more food-allergic children than before, you are right. Food allergies are increasing at an alarming rate. The rate of peanut allergies alone has doubled in the last five years. In fact, allergies in general are increasing. That means that there are more people today with nasal allergies, eczema, asthma, and food allergies than ever before. Why is this happening, and is there anything we can do to stop it? Before we can answer these questions, we need to understand what causes an allergy.

The cause of an allergy is an overactive immune system. The immune system is our defense system, and most parts of this system are helpful and protective. Having a properly functioning immune system is vital to good health, because without it we would be prone to infection.

The immune system is composed of a variety of different cells and proteins. Some of the cells of the immune system manufacture *antibodies*, which travel around the body through the bloodstream. Antibodies are able to recognize foreign particles that could harm us, such as viruses and bacteria.

The antibodies attack these infections and limit how much damage they might otherwise cause us. When it functions properly, the immune system is an exquisite, beautifully orchestrated system.

One of the antibodies we make is called *antibody E*. Antibody E is found in all humans. In nonallergic people, it is found in very, very small amounts. In allergic people, however, it can be found in very large amounts. In fact, it is this ability to make large amounts of antibody E that distinguishes the allergic person from the nonallergic person.

The ability to make lots of antibody E is a genetic trait. This means that, in your DNA (the code which makes each of us a unique individual), you are "programmed" either to produce large amounts of antibody E or not. Please note that you are not born with a specific allergy, but with the genetic trait that determines whether or not you produce large amounts of antibody E. You can inherit that tendency. If one parent is an antibody-E producer, there is a 40 percent chance the children will be antibody-E producers. If both parents have that trait, their offspring have an 80 percent chance of carrying the same trait. If neither parent has the trait, there is about a 20 percent chance the children will be antibody-E producers.

If this tendency to produce antibody E is what makes us allergic, and if the rate of allergy is rising, why is this happening? Is something going on in our genes that is making us more allergic, or is there another explanation? In fact, there is probably not just one explanation, but many. One of the many theories for why the rate of allergy is rising is called the *hygiene hypothesis*. To understand this theory, we must go back to the immune system.

As mentioned earlier, antibody E circulates in the bloodstream. In allergic people there is a lot of it. It is also found on certain cells of our body called *mast cells* (see Figure 1).

Let's look at Alexander the Elephant's problem. Alexander makes too much antibody E against peanuts. His antibody E is in his bloodstream, and it is also attached to his mast cells. If Alexander eats a peanut, the peanut protein is "grabbed" up by the antibody E. When this attachment takes place, a message is sent to the mast cell to open up and release chemicals to defend the body against harm. The most well-known of these chemicals is histamine.

Histamine's action on the body depends on where it is released. Histamine can make your eyes and nose itch; it can make you feel nauseous and throw up; it can make it hard for you to breathe; it can give you hives or eczema. It can also do all of these things all at once. This is the strongest and scariest reaction, called *anaphylaxis*. Anaphylaxis only occurs from allergy to foods, and to certain foods in particular—namely, peanuts, tree nuts, and fish/shellfish. Other foods, such as milk, eggs, wheat, and soy, can also cause anaphylaxis, but they do so less often. More commonly, they cause less severe reactions such as reflux, hives, and eczema.

In fact, 90 percent of food allergies are caused by eight foods: *milk, eggs, wheat, soy, peanuts, tree nuts, fish,* and *shellfish*. People who are anaphylactic to these foods make too much antibody E against them.

Now back to the hygiene hypothesis as to why allergies are on the rise. It turns out that the pro-duction of antibody E needs some help from cells in our body. These cells are called *helper T cells*. There are two kinds, *TH1* and *TH2* (see Figure 2). TH2 helps our bodies make antibody E; TH1 helps the other part of our immune system, the defend-

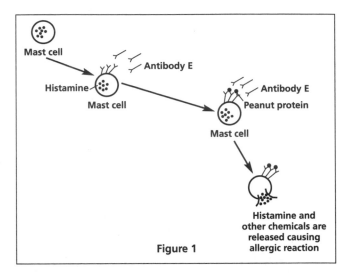

Figure 1

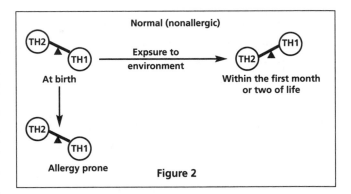

Figure 2

ing part. Babies are born as TH2 creatures. As they are exposed to germs and bacteria after birth, their bodies gradually shift to the TH1 type.

These days, babies receive many vaccinations, so they do not get as sick as in the past. Today, we have powerful antibiotics to protect them if they do get sick. We have also become a less rural society, with more people living in urban and sub-urban settings. Our homes are cleaner; we do not have dirt floors. All of this means that infants are being exposed to fewer germs, which is good. As a result, however, infants are not shifting to the TH1 type, but are remaining as type TH2. Remember,

TH2 helps our bodies make antibody E. So the hygiene hypothesis suggests that there are more allergies because we are becoming more TH2-like.

Now *please* do not stop having your children vaccinated in order to expose them to more germs because of this theory. And there is no need to pack up and move to a farm. The hygiene hypothesis simply offers one explanation for why we are seeing more food allergies, more nasal allergies, and more allergic asthma.

Now to the most difficult question: Is there something we can do to change this trend? Researchers are looking at a number of possible ways to achieve this goal. One approach involves the development of vaccines against substances such as peanut pro - tein that trick the immune system. Results from this strategy are likely a decade away. Another strategy involves the use of probiotics. Probiotics are harmless bacteria that, if introduced early enough into the intestinal tract of the infant or the breast-feeding mother, may cause a shift from the TH2 to TH1 subtype in the baby. Some preliminary studies are promising. Another novel treatment being investigated now involves the use of a good antibody to block antibody E (see Figure 3). This strategy is currently available for the treatment of moderate to severe asthmatics, twelve years of age and older. It is currently being studied for the treatment of severe food allergies and is likely to be approved within the next five years.

In the meantime, what can we do? We can certainly raise awareness about common symptoms in children that strongly indicate the possibility of food allergy. The two most notable conditions are eczema and gastro-esophageal reflux. I see many infants and children with chronic eczema who are receiving only topical creams; often no one has mentioned the possibility that food allergy may be the cause of the eczema. I also frequently see children with gastro-esophageal reflux, many of whom require daily medication to control the excessive spitting up often caused by food allergy. Early identification of the possible relation between these conditions and an allergy to food could reduce the duration and severity of the symptoms in these children.

Sadly, our only current strategy for people with food allergies is avoidance of the food or foods they are allergic to. This means paying strict atten - tion to ingredients and reading every food label carefully, with particular attention to the alternate names of food allergens (such as casein and whey for milk proteins and albumin for egg). Food-allergic people and their families are keenly aware of how meticulous you must be when trying to avoid exposure to the food allergen.

As far as prevention, what can we do now? In 2000, the American Academy of Pediatrics (AAP) and the American Academy of Allergy, Asthma, and Immunology issued some recommendations to help prevent the development of food allergy. One is that breast-feeding should be encouraged for at least six months. Also, mothers should keep highly allergenic foods (tree nuts, peanuts, and shellfish) out of their diets while breast-feeding. Some researchers also suggest that mothers keep highly allergenic foods out of their diets during pregnancy. Certainly, if an infant is showing signs of any food

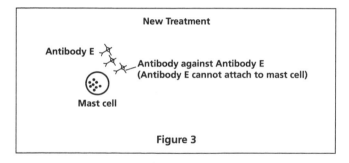

New Treatment

Antibody E

Antibody against Antibody E
(Antibody E cannot attach to mast cell)

Mast cell

Figure 3

allergy, it is advisable for the breast-feeding mother to keep that culprit food out of her diet. It is rec-ommended she keep other highly allergenic foods out of her diet as well (the above-mentioned tree nuts, peanuts, and shellfish, as well as dairy, eggs, soy, fish, and sometimes wheat). No solids should be introduced to the child until six months of age. Wheat and eggs should not be given until twelve months. Children should avoid highly allergenic foods (nuts, peanuts, and all fish) until they are three years old. If a child has at least one allergic parent, some experts recommend waiting longer before introducing these foods—for example, waiting eighteen months before introducing eggs, and until age five before adding nuts or fish to the diet.

Some newer recommendations drawn from a study on peanut allergy suggest measuring the blood allergy levels in siblings of peanut-allergic children *before* they try eating peanuts. It appears that siblings of peanut-allergic children have about a 15 percent chance of being peanut-allergic themselves. Perhaps we should also be thinking about applying these recommendations more broadly, measuring blood allergy levels for other foods (like tree nuts, eggs, milk) in a child with a food-allergic sibling before exposing them to the food.

While these recommendations are helpful and may, over time, reduce the incidence of food allergy, limiting exposure to these foods is difficult. Parents and patients become afraid to experiment and try new things. Children who try to avoid foods that made them sick tend to become "picky" eaters. That is why I think this book is such a great help. I first met the author, Cybele Pascal, through her son Lennon. Lennon was an infant when I met him as a patient. He had eczema, reflux, and chronic bloody diarrhea, despite being exclusively breast-fed. A variety of creams were being used for the eczema, and he was taking medicine to control the excessive spitting up. I helped identify the foods he was allergic to, and put mom on a low-allergy diet. Lennon improved dramatically. His parents, however, had mixed emotions about Lennon's food allergies. On the one hand, I know they were glad that a cause of his symptoms had been identified. On the other hand, like most parents of allergic children, they did not relish the prospect of reading labels and avoiding these foods. And since Cybele was breast-feeding, she had to avoid these foods too. She and Lennon's dad, Adam, had spent many years enjoying a variety of cuisines, and perhaps for this reason, it was particularly frustrating for Cybele to restrict her diet. But Cybele is a cook, and over time she was able to turn the restrictions in Lennon's and her diet into something very positive—a slew of delicious recipes for her family to enjoy, free of the most common food allergens.

Those of us who deal with food allergies every day, both as patients and as allergists, owe a big thanks to Cybele. I am happy to have a great cookbook to recommend to parents and people with food allergies. This book provides a wonderful assortment of delicious recipes that are allergy-safe. Right now, since avoidance is all we have for prevention, it's nice to know that low-allergy meals can taste so good.

Christine Fusillo, M.D.,
Chief of Pediatric Allergy,
Westchester Medical Center,
New York Medical College,
Board Certified in Pediatrics and
Allergy, Asthma, and Immunology

INTRODUCTION

If you're reading this, either you or someone close to you has probably already been suspected of, or diagnosed with, food allergies. And if you're reading this, you probably already know that it's tough finding foods you *can* eat. At times, it may seem difficult to eat out at restaurants, or at friends' houses, or even at school. And cooking up meals for the food-allergic family may seem downright impossible. A severe food allergy can make you or your child feel isolated and self-conscious—just think of the peanut-free tables in school cafeterias, Medi-alert bracelets, the ever-present Epi-pens, special instructions for teachers, school nurses, baby-sitters, other parents, and relatives . . . and then, of course, the "special" meals at breakfast, lunch, and dinner. It's enough to take the joy out of the whole eating experience for anybody. How tragic, given that food is one of life's greatest pleasures.

But having food allergies *doesn't* have to mean not enjoying food. I'm here to tell you, you don't have to feel deprived! In fact, with a little recipe revision, you can eat just about anything you want. You can have multiple food allergies and still enjoy wonderful meals with incredible variety—meals that really are delicious and satisfying for the whole family. So to those of you already enduring the restrictions of a hypoallergenic diet, I would like to stress that this is a *real* cookbook with scrumptious foods that everyone in your household will want to eat. Some are adaptations of old recipes I used to make before food allergies came into my life and others are things I've always made, which luckily are still okay. But all are delicious foods that I would still eat with pleasure, even if I weren't being forced to by a little troublemaker called "allergic response."

Though hypoallergenic cooking is relatively new to me, I am not a novice cook. This doesn't mean I was trained at a culinary institute, or that I have my own show on the Food Network. What it does mean is that I have a lifetime of experience cooking easy home-style meals. I've been cooking for as long as I can remember. Some of my fondest childhood memories are of standing alongside my grandmother as we kneaded bread and flipped pancakes on the griddle. During my teens, I went to a boarding school that stressed the value of labor and was given the job of cooking the nightly vegetarian meal for the school's fifty vegetarians. I learned then and there that simpler is better, especially when you're thrown into the trenches. But simple does not have to mean tasteless. Simple does not mean buckwheat noodles with kelp and a few sesame seeds. Simple to me means easy to prepare, which is the goal of every one of us raising families or juggling busy careers.

The recipes in this book are an eclectic mix, as my culinary influences are varied. In addition to an ancestral hodgepodge that includes Southern, Italian, and Jewish food, I have worked at many wonderful restaurants over the years, learning the cuisines of France, the West Indies, traditional New England, eclectic Nouvelle-America, and Japan. I love food, and I have always loved to cook. So when it came time to revise my menus, I knew I could make it fun.

Sadly, the idea for this cookbook came to me out of necessity several years ago when my then four-month-old son Lennon was diagnosed with severe dairy and soy allergies. My poor baby had a stuffy nose and had been spitting up, burbling, hiccupping, and having chronic bloody diarrhea for two months. He also had rashes, eczema behind his ears, and hives. I was breast-feeding—supposedly the best thing for him—but whenever he nursed, things only got worse. I tried formula, both dairy and soy, both of which resulted in projectile vomiting. His pediatrician first put him on antibiotics, "just in case," then stopped the treatment and suggested that maybe the baby was intolerant to the lactose in my breast milk. When I suggested that maybe Lennon was allergic to something I was eating, he said he'd never heard of such a thing.

My husband Adam and I were at our wits' end, and little Lennon was unhappy, to say the least. After testing for bacterial infections and viruses, and ruling out lactose intolerance, we finally arrived at the food allergy diagnosis, first through the research we did ourselves on the internet, and then through the expert advice of several wonderful physicians. I was put on a strict "Ma-ternal Avoidance Diet" and, lo and behold, Len-non's bloody diarrhea stopped. It was miraculous. All of a sudden I realized what a normal baby diaper looked like. And this wasn't all—the spitting up, the hiccupping, the audible stomach rumblings, the stuffy nose, the rashes—*all* of it stopped.

I was so relieved at first, I didn't even notice that I was subsisting on nothing but fruit and chicken. But after a couple of weeks, it suddenly dawned on me as I scanned the cupboards in hungry desperation: "What in God's name am *I* supposed to eat?!" Lennon was blissfully nursing, but I was dropping dress sizes.

You see, for those of you new to this, when you have a food-allergic child whom you're breast-feeding, the AAP recommends that you stay away from *all* the foods that the child is allergic to, as well as potentially dangerous allergens (as specified by your allergist and/or pediatrician) because exposure to the proteins from the trigger foods can wreak havoc on the baby's already susceptible immune system. So, to avoid creating additional allergies, it is often suggested that the breast-feeding mother steer clear of all the major allergenic foods. This means no dairy, eggs, wheat, soy, peanuts, tree nuts, fish, and shellfish. Additionally, your little one may very well be on this diet for his or her first three to five years. On top of this, if you have a family history of allergies, especially on both sides, you may be advised to cut out several of these allergenic foods while you're pregnant, too. So, this potentially means *many* years of cooking without dairy, soy (which goes by many names and is used as a filler everywhere), eggs, peanuts, tree nuts, shellfish, fish, wheat, and then whatever other allergens you have been told to cut out of your diet.

If you're anything like I am, this sounds like living hell. I'm one who reads cookbooks in bed at night. I have subscriptions to *Cook's Illustrated* and *Saveur*. I grew up tugging at my mother's apron strings as we baked apple pies and discussed the merits of Chicken Marsala. And though I'm a writer, I was very happy cooking for a living after graduating from college, and sometimes secretly wish I'd followed that other path. On top of all this, I make a homemade meal (albeit often a very simple one) every single night for my husband who returns home late and likes nothing better than a steaming plate of homemade cheese manicotti. "This is going to be impossible," I thought to myself. "What a horrible, horrible thing. . . ."

Or was it? I'll admit I found it daunting at first, but I rose to the challenge for the love of my child. Of course there was a period of adjustment, of much trial and error. There was even a period of denial in the beginning. I thought that maybe Lennon's system was just immature, and that it had somehow matured coincidentally at the same time I had stopped these foods—and God did I miss my morning latte. "Maybe just a quarter cup of milk won't hurt," I thought to myself, and against the advice of our doctors, I tried milk in my coffee. Within a couple of hours, Lennon's stomach was in a terrible uproar. I learned my lesson and stopped experimenting. This doesn't mean I didn't slip up once in awhile, but it was always when I was eating out or at somebody else's house and the waiter or cook or friend just didn't realize that when I said, "no dairy, no soy, no . . ." I meant it. And I always knew when there was a slip-up, because Lennon suffered the consequences.

Figuring out what's happening to you or your loved one may take time. It certainly did for me. It was only after close observation, and some real digging into our family histories, that I began to put the pieces together.

First, I discovered that I had been prone to rashes and hives as a child. Then my mother revealed that she had developed horrible rashes on her hands while working as a tomato picker on a kibbutz in Israel years ago; she was told it was an allergy. I remembered that my grandfather was said to be "intolerant" to many foods, which caused him to shy away from eating anywhere but at home (I realized he probably had food allergies), and my brother swells up like a balloon from bee and wasp stings.

My husband Adam comes from a family where it seems just about everybody suffered from chronic diarrhea for the first year of his or her life. While his sister was purportedly raised on iced tea and Jell-O until she was twelve months old because she couldn't tolerate formula and her mother wasn't breast-feeding, his cousin is allergic to eggs, nuts,

dairy, and cat dander, and has had chronic intestinal problems her entire life.

After thinking about all these factors, it finally dawned on me that Adam and I, without realizing it, both had family backgrounds with a high incidence of food allergies.

Now that I know this, it's clear that my children have a higher chance of developing allergies, and I need to take precautions, such as practicing prevention. My experience with my first child led me to eliminate shellfish, tree nuts, and peanuts while I was pregnant for the second time. But when my son Montgomery developed colic, eczema, and reflux in his first couple weeks of life, I realized it was once again time to take the plunge. Our family allergist said, "Colic, eczema, reflux? Sounds like allergy." I was instructed to cut out dairy, soy, eggs, and fish, in addition to the shellfish, tree nuts, and peanuts I'd already omitted. The colic stopped, the reflux stopped, and the eczema is gone.

Had I realized years ago that it could be so easy to provide relief for my infant by modifying my diet, I would have tried it when I first began nursing Lennon. So, I encourage you to inform yourself if you suspect that you or your children may have a predisposition to allergies. Ask family members some key questions, such as, has anyone had asthma? Is anyone seemingly intolerant to certain foods? And remember, seasonal allergies count here too. If you find a lot of affirmatives, you may wish to try this diet.

Looking on the bright side, and I promise there is one, following this diet has given us some wonderful rewards. I'm not going to lie; it's hard to go out to dinner sometimes when all you can order is the chicken breast ("without the sauce, please"). But I've discovered that eating this way has been really great in many respects. First of all, I lost my thirty-five pregnancy pounds by Lennon's sixth month. Second, my own occasional bouts of eczema disappeared, I stopped getting migraines, and the mysterious red rash that would appear on the sides of my nose on a fairly regular basis has been completely gone ever since I started this diet. I feel great! Additionally, my husband lost five unwanted pounds and lowered his cholesterol. He says he doesn't even miss the Parmesan on his pasta anymore. In fact, the lack of cheese lets you really taste the other ingredients.

Do not be discouraged if it takes you a little while to navigate the grocery store or think up a good dessert. It takes time to adjust your eating habits. I've spent years figuring out what I can and can't eat. So after all this trial and error, I've written down what I've learned in the hope that I may spare you some of the hassle.

In the beginning, I looked to cookbooks for guidance myself, but they all seemed specific to a certain food allergy—for example, how to bake without eggs or make desserts without dairy. And then I'd find books supposedly for dairy-allergic people that listed butter as an ingredient. Books purported to be allergen-free were full of recipes with nuts and fish. Additionally, most of the books were geared toward feeding your food-allergic child—a wonderful thing, but what about the rest of the family? I just couldn't find a comprehensive cookbook for those of us out there (and we are many, I assure you) who can't eat *any* of a long list of foods, but who want to eat together.

Over 12 million Americans have food allergies, and that number is rising rapidly. There are many questions about why this is occurring, but this book is not intended to answer those questions. Rather, this book is about all the wonderful healthy and delicious foods you *can* eat. After a couple of months, you'll hardly notice that you've been on a special diet.

This book is not intended to diagnose, treat, cure, or prevent disease, so please check with your doctor before trying this diet, and with a dietitian about balanced nutrition. However, if you suffer from food allergies, or if you are breast-feeding, and you come from a family with a history of food allergies (or any allergies), I strongly advise you to follow this plan (as personalized by your physicians). It can spare you a lot of heartache and protect your child from potential illness. I also recommend you use it for an allergic child and any other allergic members of your household. Additionally, it can be used by people who are following an elimination diet to find out what they're allergic to. Food-allergic or not, *The Whole Foods Allergy Cookbook* has been designed to be enjoyed by the entire family.

HOW TO USE THIS BOOK

First of all, these recipes taste good and are simple and easy to prepare. They have been formulated so that nobody feels deprived, and they are designed to be made on an everyday basis. Second, I've created these recipes without using any of the known major allergic trigger foods: *dairy, eggs, soy, wheat, peanuts, tree nuts, fish,* and *shellfish.* These foods are the ones that experts generally agree are the most likely to cause an allergic response, including anaphylactic reactions, and are therefore the most important to avoid.

Of course there are a myriad of other allergenic foods; in fact, people can be allergic to any food. So use your common sense. If you're allergic to corn, for example, then don't make the cornmeal Jammy Surprise Muffins. I have included berries, seeds, legumes (including peas and green beans), but don't give them to your child if your doctor has told you not to. And, of course, if you *can* tolerate one or more of these omitted foods, by all means add it or them back in. I encourage you to use these recipes as they suit your particular food needs, reincorporating ingredients that are safe for you. Different people will be instructed to avoid different key allergens. I happen to like barley flour and oat flour, but if you can eat wheat and you prefer it, you're more than welcome to make your baked goods with all-purpose flour. If you prefer to use rice milk instead of oat milk, or vice-versa, go ahead.

Use your judgment; the lists of ingredients are merely guidelines. As any cook knows, recipes are *never* exact, and the best guide is taste. Follow your palate, because it knows what it likes better than any cookbook-writing mom of a food-allergic family. And, I forgot to tell you, my dog is food-allergic also. I'm not kidding. So, although she's on a special diet prescribed by her vet, I can still give her table scraps because they're *hypoallergenic.* My recipes are good for the whole food-allergic family, and that means doggie, too.

NOTE

You should know that there is a difference between a food intolerance (such as a gluten intolerance, which might apply to all glutens found in barley, oats, spelt, wheat, etc.) and a food allergy. A food intolerance means that the body lacks the ability or the enzymes to digest that particular food, whereas a food allergy involves an immune-system response.

With a true food allergy, the immune system mistakenly identifies a food as harmful, and then creates specific antibodies to that food. The next time the individual eats the food, the immune system releases massive amounts of chemicals, including histamine, in an attempt to "protect" the body from what it perceives as an invader. The chemicals released by the immune system trigger a variety of allergic symptoms that can affect the respiratory system, the gastrointestinal tract, the skin, or the cardiovascular system.

Currently, there is no cure for food allergies, and avoidance is the only way to prevent a reaction. This cookbook avoids foods that cause food allergies, but does not address food intolerances.

Additionally, this book is not a nutritional guide. Please speak to your doctor if you choose to follow this diet. Your doctor can help advise you on which foods are the right ones for you to eliminate. You should also consult a dietitian about balanced nutrition. Women on Maternal Avoidance Diets while breast-feeding will need to take calcium supplements (sometimes up to 1500 mg a day while nursing) as well as other vitamins and minerals. You should also consult your child's pediatrician about nutrition, weaning, and giving hypoallergenic formula to your baby, when that is appropriate.

The Whole Foods
Allergy Cookbook

WHOLE FOODS

This is a whole foods cookbook, so first, let's talk a little bit about whole foods. What are "whole foods"? They are foods in their most natural state, which means they are not processed or are minimally processed. They are unrefined and unadulterated, without additives or preservatives, the way nature made them—that is, *whole*. Good examples of whole foods and whole foods products are fruits and vegetables; whole grains like brown rice, quinoa, oats, and barley; beans and seeds; cold-pressed olive oil and organic coconut oil; unrefined sweeteners like honey

and maple syrup; organic or grass-fed beef, free-range organic chicken, and wild or free-range game. Whole foods are hormone-free, additive-free, pesticide-free unprocessed foods that are as close to their natural state as possible.

Why eat this way? Because processing food removes its nutrients, and it is especially important for people with food allergies who are on restricted diets to get the most nutritive value from every bite they eat. Whole foods are better for you and better for the planet. Optimally, you want to get your food straight from the farm to the table—the fresher the better—because it will have more flavor, but more importantly, because it maintains the integrity of its nutrients. Whole foods like fruits, vegetables, and whole grains are packed with anti-oxidants, vitamins, minerals, flavonoids, and fiber, all of which help to ward off disease. And our bodies process these nutrients much better when ingested from whole foods than in supplement form.

But why eat "organic"? Because if your goal when eating a whole foods diet is to eat foods in their most natural state, then logically the most natural food is best of all. Organic foods are the most natural foods you can possibly find.

None of the recipes in this book are complicated or excessively time consuming. They are all simple to follow and easy to prepare. And they are all made from whole foods ingredients, so that my family and yours can get the most complete nutrition possible.

Where can you buy these whole foods? Farmers markets, natural and health food stores, co-ops, and more and more often these days at your local supermarket or grocery store. The more you buy them, the more demand increases, and the easier they'll be to find!

Tips for a Whole Foods Diet

- Shop farmers' markets if possible.

- Buy the freshest produce you can find.

- Buy organic or free-range chicken and meats that are raised without antibiotics, hormones, or animal byproducts.

- Eat a wide variety of fruits and vegetables as well as whole grains.

- Vary your diet; don't eat the same things every day.

- Eat healthy monounsaturated fats, free of trans-fats, like cold-pressed olive oil.

- Read labels—if a product has a long list of ingredients, it's probably not that close to its original form and potentially poses a higher risk for allergic reaction.

- Most importantly, make your own meals whenever possible. It takes a little longer than opening a can and sticking it in the microwave, but the payoff is huge.

BASIC SUPPLIES

The following foods and food products are staples of a whole foods, allergen-free diet. Most basic supplies are available at supermarkets, health food stores, and natural foods stores like Whole Foods Market. You can also go online to organic, vegan, vegetarian, and allergy-free food Web sites (a helpful list is provided in the Resources at the back of the book) and have the items sent to you. Or you can ask your local grocer to order them. I realize some products will seem foreign at first, but once you've stocked your kitchen, it will be smooth sailing.

Because each person's food sensitivity and reaction is unique (ranging from mild intolerance to life-threatening and severe food allergies) it is up to you, the consumer, to monitor manufacturing conditions and ingredients. If manufacturing conditions, potential cross contact between foods, and ingredient derivatives pose a risk for you, please re-read all food labels and contact man-ufacturers to confirm potential allergen concerns before consumption. Be aware that ingredients and manufacturing practices can change overnight and without warning.

THE PANTRY

GRAINS/GRAIN PRODUCTS

Amaranth Flour—high in protein, calcium, fiber, and B vitamins; works well for baking, particularly when mixed with other flours such as oat flour.

Barley Flour—a mild-flavored flour, excellent for baking.

Buckwheat Flour—an Old-World flour, good for baking and for coating; can be mild to strong in flavor; despite its name, it is not a form of wheat.

Corn Flour—finer-grained than cornmeal.

Cornmeal

Grits

Millet—a fine-grained, quick-cooking cereal eaten all over the world as porridge or prepared like rice; has a consistency similar to polenta; available both prepackaged and in bulk.

Millet Flour—a mild-flavored flour; excellent for baking, especially when mixed with oat flour.

Oat Bran

Oat Flour—a mild flour; great for coating and thickening, and excellent for baking.

Oats

Pearled Barley—the oldest cultivated cereal in the Near East and Europe; eaten like rice or in soups; available both prepackaged and in bulk.

Polenta—a fine to coarsely ground, slow-cooking cornmeal; also available ready made.

Quinoa—a quick-cooking, high-protein grain; eaten as a breakfast cereal or in place of rice or other grains; available both prepackaged and in bulk.

Quinoa Flakes—a gluten-free hot cereal that can be used just like oats.

Quinoa Flour—a high-protein flour with a distinctive taste that works well for baking.

Rice—long- and short-grain brown, brown basmati, arborio, wild, etc.

Rice Flour—made from either brown or refined white rice; when mixed with other flours, adds a mild, light, silky texture to baked goods.

Rye Flour—a strong-flavored flour that is good for baking bread.

Tapioca Flour—a mild, starchy flour that works well as a binder.

OILS

Canola Oil—a mild oil that is great for baking.

Olive Oil—choose regular or extra virgin varieties from various regions; go wild, it will be one of your best friends.

Vegetable Shortening—use dairy/soy-free types like Spectrum Naturals Organic Shortening.

SWEETENERS

Agave Nectar—a wholesome natural sweetener that is low on the glycemic index and considered suitable for diabetics. Light agave nectar is mildest and best for baking.

Date Sugar—a whole foods sugar made from ground dates; can be used in place of brown sugar.

Honey—a great substitute for refined sugar; must be cooked for infants under one year old because of the potential risk of botulism.

Maple Chunks—small crystallized bits of maple syrup.

Maple Sugar—an excellent sugar substitute for baking; available both prepackaged and in bulk.

Maple Syrup—good for baking or as a topping.

Molasses—a rich-flavored sugar substitute.

Palm Sugar—a nutritive whole foods sugar that is low on the glycemic index; suitable to use as a refined white sugar substitute. As an added benefit, it is relatively inexpensive.

BAKING/COOKING PRODUCTS

Baking Powder—common leavening agent for baked goods; make sure it is albumin-free (because albumin is made from eggs). The double-acting type has twice the rising power, which is sometimes needed without eggs.

Baking Soda—common leavening agent.

Chocolate, Unsweetened

Chocolate Chips—choose dairy-free, soy-free varieties. Enjoy Life brand is my favorite.

Cocoa Powder

Cornstarch

Ener-G Egg Replacer—an egg substitute used in baking; made from potato starch, tapioca flour, hypoallergenic leavening, cellulose gum, and carbohydrate gum.

Tapioca, Minute

Vanilla Extract—avoid those made with a wheat-based alcohol; McCormick's brand is fine.

MILK SUBSTITUTES

"Better Than Milk" Rice Powder

Oat Milk—fortified with calcium and vitamins D and B; slightly richer than rice milk (my personal savior because it's great in coffee).

Rice Milk—fortified with calcium and vitamins D and E.

HERBS/SPICES

Dried Herbs—cilantro, oregano, parsley, rosemary, thyme, etc. (keep as many on hand as you can store).

Pepper—black, cayenne, chili, etc.

Salt, Kosher

Salt, Sea—High-quality like Fleur de Sel, and super-fine for baking.

CONDIMENTS/FLAVORINGS

Hot Sauce

Ketchup

Mustard—deli, Dijon, etc.

Pickles

Salsa

Sherry, Dry

Vinegar—balsamic, red, white, cider, rice wine.

Wine—Madeira, Marsala, red, sake, white.

CANNED/BOTTLED GOODS

Artichoke Hearts—in water or olive oil (avoid soy oil).

Beans—black, white, chick peas, kidney, etc.

Broth, Regular and Low-Salt (chicken, beef, vegetable)—check labels for soy and Monosodium Glutamate (msg); I like Kitchen Basics brand.

Corn, Sweet

Fruit—peaches, pears, apricots, pineapple, pie cherries, fruit salad, etc. (for snacks, desserts, and baking).

Pumpkin

Sweet Potatoes

Tomato Paste, Puree, Sauce

Tomatoes—whole, diced, crushed.

PRODUCE

Garlic

Mushrooms, Dried—shiitake, porcini, etc.

Onions

Potatoes—fingerling, Idaho, new, red bliss, russet, Yukon gold.

Sweet Potatoes

Tomatoes, Sun-dried

Yams

SEEDS/SEED BUTTERS (IF PERMITTED)

Flax Seeds and Meal

Pumpkin Seeds and Butter

Sesame Seeds and Butter (Tahini)

Sunflower Seeds and Butter

PASTA

Brown Rice Pasta—a firmly textured pasta; available in a variety of shapes, but especially good as spaghetti or linguini.

Mung Bean Cellophane Noodles

Quinoa Corn Pasta—nice substitute for egg noodles or any other type of pasta; available in a variety of shapes.

Rice Stick Vermicelli

BREAD/BREAD PRODUCTS (ALLERGEN-FREE)

Bread, Rolls, Buns—gluten-free, allergen-free. Ener-G and Food for Life both offer many options.

Bagels—nut and gluten-free; Enjoy Life brand is recommended.

Brown Rice Bread Crumbs

CEREALS, READY-TO-EAT (ALLERGEN-FREE)

Amaranth Flakes

Corn Flakes

Nutty Flax, Nutty Rice, Perky O's—gluten-free, allergen free cereals by Perky's/Enjoy Life.

Oat Circles

Puffed Rice

SNACKS (ALLERGEN-FREE)

Cookies—Enjoy Life brand is recommended.

Corn Chips

Fruit, Dried—choose unsulfured types.

Oat Crackers

Pappadams—an Indian cracker typically made from lentil, chick pea, or rice flour.

Popcorn

Potato Chips

Rice Cakes and Crackers

THE FRIDGE

HERBS/SPICES/CONDIMENTS

Capers

Fresh Herbs—parsley, basil, and any others you like. (I also keep mint, thyme, sage, chives, and cilantro.)

Olives

Peppers, Marinated

Shallots

PRODUCE

Avocados

Broccoli

Carrots

Cauliflower

Cucumbers

Eggplant

Fruit, Fresh—all types.

Lemons/Limes

Lettuce

Spinach

Squash

Tomatoes

LUNCHEON MEATS (ORGANIC AND/OR NITRATE-FREE)

Bacon

Chicken breasts—grilled.

Ham

Hot Dogs

Prosciutto

Turkey—fresh roasted.

OTHER ITEMS

Cooking Wine

Jams, Fruit-Only with No Added Sugar—cherry, apricot, black currant, peach, etc.

Tortillas—brown rice and corn varieties.

Yogurt, Vegan—several types of soy-free vegan varieties are available (one made with rice milk, and one made with coconut milk).

THE FREEZER

MEATS (ORGANIC AND/OR FREE-RANGE)

Beef—steaks or ground (lean).

Buffalo (bison)—ground; good for burgers and chili.

Chicken—whole or parts.

Duck—breasts.

Lamb—chops, roasts.

Pork—chops, roasts (loin).

Rabbit

Sausage—chicken, turkey, Italian-style (nitrate-free)

Turkey—breast (split) or ground.

Venison

VEGETABLES

Broccoli

Corn

Peas

Spinach

Squash

DESSERT ITEMS

Fruits—mango, pineapple, berries, etc.

Rice Dream—vanilla, chocolate, etc
(a great substitute for ice cream).

Sorbets—be sure to check ingredients; some contain traces of dairy.

Substituting the Substitutions

If you wish to add back forbidden ingredients to your diet (with the permission of your allergist), use the following chart as a guide.

INGREDIENT	SUBSTITUTION
1 cup any alternative flour (except buckwheat)	1 cup whole wheat flour
1 cup any alternative pasta	1 cup whole wheat pasta
1 cup oat milk or rice milk	1 cup cow's milk or soy milk
1 Tbsp. vegetable shortening	1 Tbsp. butter or soy-based margarine
1 ½ tsp. Ener-G Egg Replacer mixed with 2 Tbsp. rice or oat milk	1 egg

NOTE: Use peanuts, tree nuts, fish, and shellfish at your own discretion.

BREAKFAST

- Pancakes
- Muffins
- Scones
- Biscuits
- Breads
- Cereals

When my son Lennon was nine months old, he decided he would no longer eat puréed baby food, or even cereal. He would only eat breakfast in chunks that he could feed to himself. Given that he was already deprived of so many foods, I decided to indulge him as much as he wanted, the good old-fashioned way. I made him breakfast from scratch.

Although it's pretty easy to find cereal that a food-allergic person can eat (amaranth flakes, oat circles, rice puffs, oatmeal), baked goods are another story. Almost all mixes have at least one forbidden ingredient, and prebaked goods usually include eggs, butter or soy-based margarine, whey (milk), and most often white or whole wheat flour. Breakfast is the only meal that our whole family eats together, so I needed to find foods that were delicious to all of us—to Lennon and me, who have extremely restricted diets, and to my husband, who can eat whatever he likes. I began to experiment, adapting my older recipes, and discovered that none of us missed the eggs, dairy, or wheat. In fact, we love our new lower fat, cholesterol-free, hearty country-style breakfasts.

NOTES

A few words about flour: Most of the recipes in this book contain oat flour and barley flour. I also occasionally use amaranth flour, rice flour, rye flour, buckwheat flour, millet flour, corn flour, and quinoa flour.

Though it may seem that I've overcomplicated the recipes that have more than one flour listed in the ingredients, you should know that these flours often don't do as well on their own in baked goods, and need the partner flour for rising or binding. A good reference book for flour combining is *My Kid's Allergic to Everything Dessert Cookbook* by Mary Harris and Wilma Nachsin (see p. 201). If you *can* eat wheat and prefer it, replace the listed flours with whole wheat or whole wheat pastry flour.

Peach Pancakes

When I was growing up, I always looked forward to my Grandmother Millie's visits from New Jersey because she'd take me out for pancakes, huge-heaping-plates-full slathered in syrup. These peach pancakes aren't quite as decadent as my childhood IHOP flapjacks with whipped cream and chocolate chips, but I promise, they're delicious. The peaches combine beautifully with the oat flour for a delicate sweet flavor. Drizzle a little maple syrup on top, and you've got a mouth-watering breakfast.

Blend oat flour and barley flour, baking powder, salt, and cinnamon in one bowl, and the egg replacer, rice/oat milk, honey, and canola oil in another. Make sure honey has been whisked in thoroughly. Whisk wet ingredients into dry. Add a little more flour if it seems too thin. Oat flour compacts differently on different days due to humidity levels. Add peaches and mix briefly. Cook the pancakes on a *lightly* oiled medium-hot griddle or skillet. When bubbles start to appear around the edges of the pancakes and have just popped, turn them.

MAKES 18 (4-inch) PANCAKES

1 cup oat flour
1 cup barley flour
3 tsp. double-acting baking powder
1/2 tsp. salt
1/2 tsp. cinnamon
3 tsp. Ener-G Egg Replacer mixed with
    4 Tbsp. enriched rice or oat milk
1 3/4 cups enriched rice or oat milk
2 tsp. honey
2 Tbsp. canola oil
1 cup diced fresh peaches (or drained
    canned peaches in their own juice)

Variations

For **Apricot Pancakes**: Substitute 1 cup drained canned apricots for the peaches. They are just as tasty.
For **Chocolate Chip Pancakes**: Add 1/2 cup dairy-free, soy-free chocolate chips.

Apple Pancakes

*These pancakes can be made year round, since good apples are always readily available.
The more flavorful the apple, the better they will taste. In the fall it's fun to try a good
old-fashioned variety like Winesap or Russet, but Granny Smiths will work just as well.*

2 small apples

1½ cups oat flour

1/2 cup barley flour

3 tsp. double-acting baking powder

1/2 tsp. salt

1/2 tsp. cinnamon

1 ¾ cups enriched rice or oat milk, warmed

2 Tbsp. honey

2 Tbsp. canola oil

3 tsp. Ener-G Egg Replacer mixed with
    4 Tbsp. enriched rice or oat milk

Peel, core, and chop apples. Blend oat flour, barley flour, baking powder, salt, and cinnamon in large bowl. Combine warm rice/oat milk with honey and canola oil. Add to dry ingredients and mix briefly until blended but still lumpy. Stir in egg replacer. Add apples. Cook the pancakes on a medium hot griddle. When bubbles appear and have just popped, turn the pancakes.

MAKES 18 (4-inch) PANCAKES

Variations

- For **Banana Pancakes**: Add 2 sliced bananas instead of apples.
- For **Blueberry Pancakes**: Substitute 1 cup fresh or frozen blueberries for apples and omit cinnamon.
- For **Plain Pancake**s: Omit fruit altogether.

Buckwheat Cherry Pancakes

I love the taste of buckwheat, but given its strong flavor, I've cut it here by half with barley flour. I think you'll enjoy this cherry spin on an old favorite.

Combine buckwheat flour, barley flour, baking powder, and salt in one bowl, and canola oil, egg replacer, rice/oat milk, cherries, cherry fruit-only jam, and honey in another. Let sit a few minutes so the dried cherries can reconstitute. Combine all ingredients. Cook the pancakes on a lightly oiled medium-hot griddle or pan. Please note that buckwheat pancakes take a little extra cooking, so really wait for bubbles to appear around the edges of the pancakes before you flip them.

MAKES 18 (4-inch) PANCAKES

1 cup buckwheat flour

1 cup barley flour

3 tsp. double-acting baking powder

1/2 tsp. kosher salt

2 Tbsp. canola oil

3 tsp. Ener-G Egg Replacer mixed with 4 Tbsp. enriched rice or oat milk

1³/₄ cups enriched rice or oat milk

1/2 cup dried cherries (or fresh if you have them, pitted and quartered)

2 Tbsp. cherry fruit-only jam

3 tsp. honey

Variation

For **Buckwheat Strawberry Pancakes**: Substitute 2 Tbsp. strawberry fruit-only jam for the cherry jam, and 1/2 cup fresh sliced strawberries for the cherries.

Basic Muffins

This is a simple unadorned muffin. It can be eaten any time of day, plain, with honey, or with fruit-only jam.

1/2 cup canola oil

1 cup light agave nectar

1 ½ cups unsweetened applesauce

1 tsp. vanilla extract

1 ¼ cups oat flour

1 ¼ cups barley flour

1 ½ tsp. baking soda

1/2 tsp. salt

Preheat oven to 350 degrees. Line a muffin pan with 12 muffin liners. Using an electric mixer set on medium, combine canola oil and agave nectar. Add applesauce and vanilla extract. Mix. In a separate bowl, combine oat flour, barley flour, baking soda, and salt. Add dry ingredients to wet and mix until just combined. Spray inside of muffin liners lightly with baking spray (or use a pastry brush to brush lightly with a little canola oil), and fill liners to the rim. Bake in center of oven 30–35 minutes until lovely golden brown on top, rotating the pan once when halfway through baking. Let muffins cool in pan 5 minutes before removing to a cooling rack.

MAKES 12 MUFFINS

Tip

Use Beyond Gourmet unbleached baking cups.

Variations

- For **Banana Muffins**: Replace applesauce with 1½ cups mashed banana, and add 1/2 tsp. cinnamon.
- For **Berry Muffins**: After you've combined the liquid and dry ingredients, fold in 1 cup berries.
- For **Carrot Muffins**: Add 1/2 tsp. cinnamon to the dry ingredients and fold in 1 cup shredded carrots and 1/2 cup raisins at end.

Applesauce Oat Raisin Muffins

This is a nice wholesome muffin that can be eaten for breakfast or as a snack.

Preheat oven to 400 degrees. Combine oat flour, amaranth (or barley) flour, baking powder, and cinnamon in a large bowl. Add the vegetable shortening and, using a wire pastry blender (or two knives), cut it into the dry ingredients until it's the texture of a coarse meal. Stir in raisins. Add the applesauce and honey to egg replacer, and then pour into dry ingredients, mixing until combined but still lumpy. Line muffin cups with liners. Fill each cup with batter. Bake for 25 minutes, or until golden brown on top. Serve with honey or fruit-only jam.

MAKES 12 MUFFINS

1½ cups oat flour

1/2 cup amaranth flour or barley flour

2 tsp. double-acting baking powder

1 tsp. cinnamon

4 Tbsp. vegetable shortening

3/4 cup raisins

1½ tsp. Ener-G Egg Replacer mixed with
   2 Tbsp. rice or oat milk

1 cup cold applesauce

1/2 cup honey

Jammy Surprise Muffins

My Grandmother Catherene was originally from Texas. She grew up in Amarillo and made fantastic cornbread. She had all sorts of molds for her cornmeal creations, and we ate them every which way—with butter and honey for breakfast, with fried fish or chicken for dinner, with jam for dessert—you name it, we ate it. So, to carry on a long tradition, albeit minus the buttermilk and butter, here is my addition to the family canon of corn muffins. The quinoa flour gives these muffins a higher protein quota than you'd normally get with white flour. Quinoa is an ancient grain and is excellent mixed with corn.

1 ¾ cups quinoa flour

3/4 cup corn flour (see Tip below)

1 ½ tsp. baking soda

1/2 tsp. salt

1/2 cup canola oil

3/4 cup honey

1 ½ cups plain vegan yogurt

2 tsp. cider vinegar

1/2 cup seedless fruit-only jam

Preheat oven to 350 degrees. Line a muffin pan with 12 liners. Spray inside of liners lightly with baking spray (or use a pastry brush to brush lightly with a little canola oil). Whisk together quinoa flour, corn flour, baking soda, and salt. In a separate bowl, mix canola oil and honey. Add yogurt. Mix well. Add vinegar, then immediately stir in flour mixture. Fill muffin liners halfway with batter. Spoon a heaping teaspoon of jam onto each one, then top with remaining batter. Bake in center of oven 20 minutes until golden brown, rotating the pan once when halfway through baking. Let muffins cool in pan 5 minutes before removing to a cooling rack.

MAKES 12 MUFFINS

Tip

Corn flour has a much finer grain than cornmeal. Look for it at your local health food store or Whole Foods Market.

Sweet Potato Cranberry Muffins

These muffins taste very New England to me—lending a little bit of
Thanksgiving to any morning of the year. If you or your child can't
eat berries, substitute dried cherries for the cranberries.

Preheat oven to 350 degrees. Line a muffin pan with 12 muffin liners. Using an electric mixer set on medium, combine canola oil and maple syrup. Add sweet potato, nutmeg, and cinnamon. Mix. In a separate bowl, combine oat flour, barley flour, baking soda, and salt. Add dry ingredients to wet and mix until just combined. Fold in cranberries. Spray inside of muffin liners lightly with baking spray (or use a pastry brush to brush lightly with a little canola oil) and fill liners. Bake in center of oven 30–35 minutes until lovely golden brown on top, rotating pan once when halfway through baking. Let cool in pan 5 minutes before removing to a cooling rack.

MAKES 12 MUFFINS

1/2 cup canola oil
3/4 cup maple syrup
1 ½ cups sweet potato puree (1 15oz can sweet potato)
1/4 tsp. nutmeg
1/2 tsp. cinnamon
1 ¼ cups oat flour
1 ¼ cups barley flour
1 ½ tsp. baking soda
1/2 teaspoon salt
1 ½ cups fresh cranberries or 1/2 cup dried

Oatmeal Raisin Scones

I used to cook at a restaurant in Cambridge, Massachusetts, owned by a great baker named Diane. It was called Pentimento, after the book by Lillian Hellman. The walls were covered with pictures of Sam Sheppard, and David Mamet would eat there. It was a very theatrical place. Pentimento was known for its baked goods, and on weekends there was a line around the block of people waiting to be seated for brunch. Diane's scones were amazing—so amazing that when she fed them to her dachshund Roxanne, she got so fat that the vertebrae in her neck fused. I took this as a sign to make a lower-fat healthy version. So here goes. This is the puritanical but still delicious oatmeal raisin scone.

1/2 cup oat flour

1/2 cup millet flour

1 cup barley flour

1/2 tsp. baking soda

3 tsp. double-acting baking powder

1/4 tsp. salt

1/4 cup + 2 Tbsp. palm sugar
   or maple sugar

1 cup rolled oats (not instant)

1/2 cup raisins

1/4 cup + 2 Tbsp. canola oil

1/2 cup oat milk

Preheat oven to 375 degrees. In large bowl mix together oat flour, millet flour, barley flour, baking soda, baking powder, salt, and palm or maple sugar. Stir in oats and raisins. Add canola oil, and mix until crumbly. Add oat milk and blend. The dough will not become smooth, so don't worry that it's coarse. Lay out a large sheet of wax paper. Turn out dough onto wax paper and use hands to mound dough into two circles. Flatten into disks about 1 inch thick. Use a knife to cut each disk into quarters and, using a spatula, slide them onto a lightly greased cookie sheet. Bake for 15 minutes until golden brown. Serve hot with fruit-only jam or honey.

MAKES 8 SCONES

Potato Scones

These scones are Scottish in origin. They are a great way to use up leftover mashed potatoes. They aren't what you'd usually think of as a scone, as they're flatter than most. Traditionally, they would be eaten with eggs and fried bacon or sausage. Since I've omitted eggs from this book, I'd suggest eating them with fried bacon or sausage and maybe some roasted tomatoes, or even a little fruit. They're also lovely slathered with a little honey or jam.

Mix the flours and salt into the potatoes. Add the canola oil. If you're not using leftover mashed potatoes with rice milk and oil already added, add a little extra canola oil and a splash of rice milk. The dough should be thick enough to turn out onto a floured board. Knead it a little with your hands until the ingredients are thoroughly combined. Add a little more flour if needed. Divide dough into two balls. Roll out one ball on a floured board to about 1/4 inch thick and then cut into quarters. Repeat with other ball. Cook in a heavy dry skillet (I prefer cast iron), about 3–4 minutes per side, until golden spots appear. The trick with these is to cook them at a low enough temperature that they cook evenly. If you cook them at too high a temperature, they'll burn on the outside and be underdone on the inside.

MAKES 8 SCONES

2 cups mashed potatoes
3/4 cup barley flour
3/4 cup oat flour
1/2 tsp. salt
4 tsp. canola oil

Basic Biscuits

Biscuits are extremely versatile, and can be eaten any time of day.
They are delicious either sweet or savory.

1 cup oat flour

1 cup barley flour

5 tsp. double-acting baking powder

1 tsp. salt

5 Tbsp. vegetable shortening

2/3 cup oat milk or rice milk

Preheat oven to 450 degrees. Line a cookie sheet with parchment paper. Whisk together flours, baking powder, and salt. Add vegetable shortening and cut in, using either a pastry blender or two knives, until the consistency of a coarse meal. Add oat/rice milk and combine with a wooden spoon, making sure to incorporate crumbs at the bottom of the bowl. If it seems too dry, add a little more oat/rice milk, starting with 1 tablespoon. Turn out onto a lightly floured board, and pat into a disk 1-inch thick, pressing in any loose bits. Use a floured 2-inch round biscuit cutter to cut out biscuits, cutting them as close together as possible. Gather up scraps and repeat. Bake in center of oven about 12 minutes until tops are golden brown. Serve hot with fruit-only jam or honey, or along with soup or salad for lunch.

MAKES ABOUT 8 BISCUITS

Tip

Roll leftover dough in a 1/4-inch-thick circle or square. Fill with a few Tbsp. fruit, a drizzle of honey, and a pinch of cinnamon, then fold over and seal edges. Bake along with biscuits for a yummy fruit turnover.

Variations

- For **Herb Biscuits**: Add 2 Tbsp. chopped fresh herbs such as dill, basil, or parsley to the dry ingredients before adding liquid. Serve with any meal.
- For **Currant Biscuits**: Add 1 Tbsp. palm or maple sugar, and 1/4 cup currants soaked in 2 Tbsp. dark rum, sherry, or Marsala to dry mixture before adding liquids.
- For **Orange Biscuits**: Add 1 Tbsp. palm or maple sugar, replace 1/3 cup of rice or oat milk with orange juice, and add zest of half an orange to dry ingredients.

Grandmother Catherene's Cornbread

Of course my Grandmother made this with butter, white flour, and buttermilk, but otherwise it's all the same. This cornbread can be eaten at breakfast, lunch, or dinner.

Preheat oven to 400 degrees. Preheat the pan; this will give you a nice crust. I use a 10-inch cast iron skillet (the traditional way), but you may also use a similarly sized baking pan, square or round, it doesn't matter. Combine flours, cornmeal, salt, baking powder, and baking soda. In another bowl, combine oat milk, lemon juice, honey, and egg replacer. Whisk well. Add to flour mixture. Add canola oil. Beat until smooth. Remove hot pan from oven and quickly spray with canola oil spray or other oil of choice. Pour in batter and set pan in center of oven. Bake 25–30 minutes at 400 degrees, then turn heat down to 300 degrees and bake another 10 minutes or so until set in the center. Remove from oven. Let cool about 15 minutes before slicing into squares or pie-shaped wedges.

SERVES 8

2/3 cup white rice flour
1/3 cup tapioca flour
3/4 cup yellow cornmeal
1/4 tsp. salt
2 tsp. double-acting baking powder
3/4 tsp. baking soda
1 ¾ cups oat milk or rice milk
2 Tbsp. lemon juice
2 tsp. honey
3 tsp. Ener-G egg replacer mixed with
    4 Tbsp. oat milk or rice milk
1/4 cup canola oil

Variations

- For **Corny Cornbread**: Add up to 1/2 cup either fresh or canned (drained) corn kernels.
- For **Jalapeno Cornbread**: Add half a chopped jalapeno pepper.
- For **Bacon Cornbread**: Add 1/4 cup crispy fried regular or turkey bacon.

Banana Bread

*I began making this recipe back in college when I needed an excuse not to study.
It was great comfort food at 1:00 AM before an exam, and a wonderful breakfast the next
morning before I went off bleary-eyed to take my test. I've adapted it here for the
hypoallergenic diet, but I think it's just as scrumptious. The amaranth flour gives
a lovely nutty flavor originally provided by pecans. Enjoy!*

1 cup oat flour

1 cup barley flour

1 cup amaranth flour

1 ½ tsp. baking soda

1/2 tsp. salt

1/4 cup canola oil

3/4 cup honey or light agave nectar

1 ½ cups mashed ripe banana (about
    3 bananas)

juice of 1/2 a lemon

1/2 tsp. nutmeg (nutmeg is not a nut)

3/4 cup flax seed meal

1/2 cup raisins

Preheat oven to 350 degrees. Combine oat flour, barley flour, amaranth flour, baking soda, and salt, and set aside. Using an electric mixer set on medium, combine canola oil and honey/agave nectar. Add bananas, lemon juice, and nutmeg. Once thoroughly mixed, add flax seed meal, then raisins. Add dry ingredients to wet, and mix until just combined. Grease a loaf pan, then sprinkle with a little flour, tapping out any extra. Transfer batter to the loaf pan. Bake in center of oven about 55 minutes, rotating once when halfway through, until golden brown on top. Let bread cool in pan about 5 minutes, before removing and transferring to a cooling rack. Let rest at least 30 minutes before slicing.

MAKES ABOUT 8 SERVINGS

Rye Bread with Dates

This is a delicious old-world type of quick-bread. My mother would have served it with a big slather of cream cheese, but it's much less sinful and just as tasty the way we eat it in my house.

Preheat oven to 350 degrees. Put dates in a large bowl. Mix molasses into warmed rice milk and then add to dates. Mix in egg replacer, canola oil, and vanilla extract. Combine rye flour with baking powder. Stir into liquid mixture. Pour into oiled loaf pan dusted with a little rye flour. Bake about 1 hour until top is browned and bread has begun to pull away from sides of pan. Let cool about 20–30 minutes before slicing. Serve with tart orange marmalade or just on its own.

MAKES ABOUT 8 SERVINGS

1 cup chopped dates
1/2 cup enriched rice or oat milk, warmed
1/3 cup molasses
3 tsp. Ener-G Egg Replacer mixed with
    4 Tbsp. enriched rice or oat milk
1/4 cup canola oil
1 tsp. vanilla extract
2 cups rye flour
2 tsp. double-acting baking powder

Cherry Vanilla Bread

*Cherry and vanilla are a perfect combination. This quick-bread
is delicate and lightly sweet with an enticing aroma.*

1¹/₂ cups oat flour

1/2 cup amaranth or barley flour

2 tsp. double-acting baking powder

1/2 cup maple sugar or palm sugar

1/4 tsp. cinnamon

1/2 cup enriched rice or oat milk

2 Tbsp. lemon juice

1/2 cup dried cherries (not freeze dried)

3 tsp. vanilla extract

1/4 cup canola oil

1/4 cup honey

3 tsp. Ener-G Egg Replacer mixed with
    4 Tbsp. enriched rice or oat milk

Preheat oven to 325 degrees. In large bowl combine oat flour, amaranth flour, baking powder, maple sugar/palm sugar, and cinnamon. Combine rice/oat milk, lemon juice, cherries, vanilla extract, canola oil, honey, and egg replacer. Add liquid ingredients to dry, stirring until just combined. Pour into a lightly oiled loaf pan dusted with a little oat flour and bake about 1 hour. Remove from oven and let cool in pan at least 15 minutes before slicing.

MAKES ABOUT 8 SERVINGS

Orange Zucchini Bread

*This quick-bread is a great way to get vegetable haters of all ages to eat
their greens. It's wonderful for breakfast, but also good with tea or as a snack.*

Preheat oven to 325 degrees. Combine oat flour, barley flour, baking powder, and cinnamon. Combine orange juice, canola oil, honey, and vanilla extract. Dilute honey by mixing thoroughly. Add liquid mixture to dry mixture. Stir. Add egg replacer. Then stir in shredded zucchini and oats. Pour into an oiled loaf pan lightly dusted with oat flour, and bake 1 hour. Remove from oven and let cool in pan about 15 minutes. Then turn out onto a rack. Let cool before slicing.

MAKES ABOUT 8 SERVINGS

1¼ cups oat flour

1¼ cups barley flour

4 tsp. double-acting baking powder

1 tsp. cinnamon

1/4 cup orange juice

1/4 cup canola oil

3/4 cup honey

1 tsp. vanilla extract

3 tsp. Ener-G Egg Replacer mixed with
   4 Tbsp. orange juice

2 cups loosely packed shredded zucchini
   (about 1 medium zucchini)

1/2 cup oats

Pineapple Banana Granola

Making your own granola is as simple as can be, and it tastes delicious. I started making my own because most store-bought granola, even at the health food store, contains nuts or seeds or some other forbidden ingredient. This granola is not just great for breakfast, you can bag some up and send it off to school with your little one for a snack.

2 cups rolled oats

1/4 cup canola oil

1/4 cup date sugar or maple sugar

1/4 cup maple syrup

1/2 cup freeze-dried banana chips crumbled (or chopped up regular dried banana, or fried banana chips, but check what kind of oil they've been fried in)

1/2 cup freeze-dried pineapple bits (or chopped up regular dried pineapple chunks)

1/2 cup golden raisins

Preheat oven to 300 degrees. In a bowl, mix rolled oats with canola oil, date sugar, and maple syrup. Spread on a greased cookie sheet. Cook on middle rack for 15 minutes, stir up a bit, cook another 15 minutes, stir again, and cook 5 final minutes. Put banana chips, pineapple bits, and raisins in the bottom of a large baking pan. Pour oat mixture over and gently combine. Let cool. Once cool, store in an airtight container in fridge. Serve with rice milk or oat milk.

MAKES 6–8 SERVINGS

Cinnamon Fig Granola

For a simple yet hearty breakfast, try the following granola recipe with a little enriched rice milk.

2 cups rolled oats

1/4 cup canola oil

1 tsp. ground cinnamon

1/4 cup date sugar or maple sugar

1/4 cup honey

1/2 cup dried figs chopped into small pieces

1/2 cup raisins

Preheat oven to 300 degrees. In a bowl, mix rolled oats with canola oil, cinnamon, date sugar, and honey. Spread on a greased cookie sheet. Cook on middle rack about 15 minutes, stir up a bit, cook another 15 minutes, stir again, and cook 5 final minutes. Put chopped figs and raisins in the bottom of a large baking pan. Pour oat mixture over and gently combine. Let cool. Once cool, store in an airtight container in fridge. Serve with rice milk or oat milk.

MAKES 6 SERVINGS

Sweet Grits

Grits are small, broken grains of corn, first eaten by Native Americans. They are a good source of calcium and iron and have no fat or cholesterol. Down South, grits are usually eaten like potatoes—salty. They're wonderful fried with cheese or bacon, or sprinkled with just a little salt and pepper and some bacon fat. However, I like my grits sweet and enjoy them as a hot breakfast cereal. The following recipe makes a warm, comforting meal or snack for any time of the day.

Bring water or rice milk to a boil in a medium saucepan. Slowly whisk in the grits. Stir well and reduce heat to low. Cook covered 15 minutes, stirring occasionally. Remove from heat and let sit 5 minutes. Stir in honey or maple syrup and serve.

SERVES 4

4 cups water or enriched rice milk
3/4 cup old-fashioned grits
4 Tbsp. honey or maple syrup

Muesli

Muesli is a low-fat heart-healthy breakfast. Eat it with fresh fruit and enriched rice milk or a little juice for a tasty breakfast that keeps you feeling full for hours.

Crumble oat bran flakes a bit. Toast sunflower/pumpkin seeds on cookie sheet in oven at 375 degrees for a couple of minutes until golden, shaking once or twice. Combine all ingredients. Store in an airtight container.

MAKES 8 SERVINGS

1½ cups oat bran flakes
1½ cups oats (not instant)
2 Tbsp. currants
1/4 cup dried apple, chopped
2 Tbsp. chopped dates
2 Tbsp. dried berries (freeze-dried raspberries or blueberries are great, but any kind will do)
2 Tbsp. date sugar or maple sugar
1/4 tsp. cinnamon
2 Tbsp. toasted sunflower or pumpkin seeds (optional)

LUNCH

- Soups
- Salad Dressings
- Green Salads
- Hearty Salads
- Spreads
- Sandwiches

Lunch is not a heavy meal at my house. It usually consists of soup, salad, a sandwich, or maybe leftovers from the previous night's dinner. I've included mostly soup and salad recipes here because I think most people can come up with good sandwich ideas on their own. However, I have included several recipes for spreads and made a few sandwich suggestions.

I've begun this section with soup recipes. *I love soup!* Having my big orange Le Crueset pot on the stove simmering with some lovely soup is my idea of a proper kitchen. And making up a big pot of soup is a great time-saver as well. It provides you with several days of lunch, or when supplemented with bread and a salad, a nice light dinner.

You might also pair up some of the lighter green salads with half a sandwich or a bowl of soup for lunch, or try one of the heartier dishes like Pasta Salad (p. 59) or Quinoa Tabouli (p. 56)—each a filling meal by itself.

Minestrone

*I made this soup when I was in college with whatever I had in my cupboards.
It's a hearty minestrone that really fills you up. It doesn't have to be exact. If you want
to throw in some other vegetables like zucchini, be my guest. If you or your child can't
eat legumes, you can supplement with extra pasta and/or vegetables.*

3 Tbsp. olive oil

1 large onion, chopped

3 or 4 cloves garlic, minced

2 bay leaves

2 tsp. dried oregano

1½ cups chopped celery

3 carrots, peeled, halved, and chopped

2 medium potatoes, peeled and chopped
   into small pieces

1 28-oz. can chopped tomatoes with
   their juice

6 cups chicken or vegetable broth

1 Tbsp. honey

1 Tbsp. balsamic vinegar

2 Tbsp. red wine (optional)

salt and pepper

chili pepper flakes (optional)

1/2 cup cooked black beans

1/2 cup cooked split peas or lentils

1 cup short pasta of some kind

1 tsp. dried basil

1/4 cup chopped fresh basil (or parsley)

In large pot, cook olive oil, onion, garlic, bay leaves, and oregano over medium-high heat until onion is translucent. Do not burn the garlic. Add celery, carrots, and potatoes. Cook about 3 or 4 more minutes, stirring. Add tomatoes, broth, honey, balsamic vinegar, wine, salt, pepper, and chili pepper flakes (if using), and bring to a boil. Reduce heat to medium-low and simmer partly covered about 30 minutes. Add black beans, split peas, pasta, and dried basil. Cook about another 30 minutes. Add a little water or more broth to thin if necessary. Remove from heat, stir in chopped basil or parsley. Eat piping hot.

SERVES 6–8

Curried Pumpkin Soup

This lovely orange soup is as delightful to the eye as it is to the tummy.
Eat it during any season as a healthy lunch rich in beta-carotene.

Sauté first five ingredients together over medium-high heat in large heavy pot until carrots have begun to soften. Add cumin and curry powder. Cook another couple of minutes. Puree in food processor, adding a cup of the vegetable broth. Return to pot. Add rest of broth, pumpkin, wine, salt and rice wine vinegar. Bring to a simmer and reduce heat to low. Cook partially covered about 30–40 minutes, stirring about every 10 minutes. When done (flavors will bind and the soup will taste rich), remove from heat and grind in black pepper to taste. Serve piping hot with a sprinkle of scallions and crumbled crackers.

SERVES 8

1 onion, chopped (about 1½ cups)
2 tsp. fresh ginger, minced
2 cloves garlic, minced
3 Tbsp. olive oil
3 carrots, peeled and chopped
1/2 tsp. cumin
2 tsp. curry powder
6 cups vegetable broth
2 15-oz. cans pumpkin
3/4 cup dry white wine
1 tsp. salt
1 Tbsp. rice wine vinegar
fresh ground pepper
2 or 3 chopped scallions (green part only)
crispy crackers (whatever kind are allowed)

Tip

Try with Amy Lyn's Original Flax Thins in Baja Chili flavor.

Creamy Red Pepper Soup

This rich red soup is brimming with vitamin C.
It is wonderful for lunch, or as a starter with dinner.

2 medium potatoes, chopped into
   1-inch pieces
6 cups low-salt chicken or vegetable broth
4 red (or orange) bell peppers
1 large onion, minced
4 Tbsp. olive oil
1/2 cup canned tomatoes, chopped
   (or fresh ripe tomatoes)
2 Tbsp. oat flour or rice flour
1 cup enriched rice milk
1 scant Tbsp. honey
1/2 tsp. paprika
1/4 tsp. cumin
2 Tbsp. Port or dry sherry
salt and pepper
chopped parsley for garnish
crackers or blue corn tortilla chips
   for garnish

You will need two large pots. In one, cook the potatoes in 2 cups of chicken broth, loosely covered over medium heat. Meanwhile, wash, deseed, and cut up the peppers. Set aside. In other large pot, cook minced onion in 2 Tbsp. olive oil over medium heat until soft, but not browned. Add chopped peppers, chopped tomato, and 4 remaining cups of chicken broth. Cook until peppers become soft. When potatoes are cooked to very tender (you want them well cooked—otherwise you'll wind up with a gluey consistency in your soup), put potatoes and their broth in food processor and puree. Put back in pot. When peppers are soft, turn off heat and puree in batches, adding what's been liquefied to the pot with the potatoes. When all pepper/tomato mixture has been pureed, and pepper pot is empty, put remaining 2 Tbsp. of olive oil in pan, turn heat to medium-high, and stir in the flour. Cook, stirring for about 2 minutes, and then add rice milk. Cook, stirring, until the sauce thickens into a roux. Once it's thickened to a nice cream sauce, add back in the pureed pepper/tomato/potato mixture. Combine, and turn heat to medium-low, then stir in honey, paprika, cumin, Port (or sherry), salt, and a few grindings of fresh pepper. Cook at a simmer about 20 minutes, stirring occasionally. Serve very hot with a sprinkle of fresh chopped parsley, and crackers or blue corn tortilla chips. I like the blue corn tortilla chips myself because they look so pretty against the red/orange soup.

SERVES 8

Cream of Asparagus Soup

Cream of asparagus soup always reminds me of my childhood. My mother gave it to me for lunch on winter weekends, alongside a sandwich. This recipe is a great alternative to a dairy-based cream soup. It's creamy and hearty, even without the cream.

Break off tough bottoms of asparagus and steam stalks until just tender. Cut off tips and reserve about 10 for garnish. Put the rest of the tips in a bowl and add remaining asparagus, cut into 1/2-inch pieces. Make a roux by heating the olive oil in a pot over medium heat. Add 2 Tbsp. oat flour and cook, stirring, about 2 minutes. Add 2 cups of the chicken broth and cook about 10 minutes, stirring frequently until sauce thickens up a bit. Add remaining chicken broth and rice milk and bring to a simmer. Add chopped asparagus and simmer about 10 minutes until very tender. Take pot off heat and puree the asparagus by ladling it out with some of the broth into a food processor or blender. Once pureed, return to soup pot. Place back on low heat; add nutmeg, salt, pepper, and honey. Bring to a simmer. If you like a slightly creamier soup (which I do), combine 1 Tbsp. oat flour with about 1/4 cup soup in a little bowl, blending thoroughly, and then add back to pot. Cook at a slow simmer about another 10 minutes until soup is creamy. Remove from heat, stir in parsley and asparagus tips, and serve piping hot.

SERVES 6

1 bunch of asparagus (about 2 cups
   when chopped)
2 Tbsp. olive oil
2 Tbsp. oat flour (or other allowed flour)
4 cups low-salt chicken broth
2 cups enriched rice milk
pinch nutmeg
3/4 tsp. salt
fresh ground black pepper
1 tsp. honey
1 more Tbsp. oat flour (optional)
chopped parsley

Variations

- **Cream of Broccoli**: Substitute 2 cups lightly steamed broccoli, chopped small, for the asparagus.
- **Cream of Spinach**: Substitute one package frozen spinach for the asparagus.
- **Cream of Celery**: Substitute 2–3 cups steamed chopped celery for the asparagus.

Cauliflower Soup

Cauliflower soup is light and delicate. Eat it with
a sandwich, or as is, for a quick summer lunch.

1 head cauliflower

3 stalks pale celery

6 cups low-salt chicken broth

1 medium onion, diced

2 cloves garlic, diced

3 Tbsp. olive oil

2 Tbsp. flour (oat, rice, etc.)

1 cup enriched rice milk

1/2 cup white wine

3/4 tsp. salt

fresh ground pepper (white if possible)

1 tsp. Parisien Bonnes Herbes (check
   Resources, p. 197, for Penzeys Spices), or
   dried chervil, or dried chives

2 scallions, the green part only, chopped

2 Tbsp. dry sherry

Cook the cauliflower and celery in 5½ cups of the chicken broth in a large heavy pot. Meanwhile, cook the onion and garlic in 1 Tbsp. of the olive oil over medium heat in another large pot. Cook well, but do not brown. When soft, puree the onion garlic mixture with remaining 1/2 cup of chicken broth. Return to pot. When cauliflower and celery are very soft, puree in batches, returning puree to the pot with the onions. Be sure you don't overfill the food processor or it will spill out the bottom. Once you've pureed all the cauliflower, celery, and broth and you have an empty pot, turn the heat to medium-high, add the remaining 2 Tbsp. olive oil, let it get hot, add the 2 Tbsp. flour, and cook, stirring constantly, a couple of minutes. Add the rice milk and cook, stirring, until it thickens into a nice cream sauce. Add the puree back into the pot with the cream sauce, then add the white wine, the salt and a little pepper, and the dried herbs. Cook over low heat, simmering very gently about 15 minutes or so. At very end, add chopped scallions and sherry. Serve with crackers.

SERVES 8

Wild Mushroom Bisque

Top this lovely soup with a sprinkling of chopped chives for an elegant but hearty lunch.
When I don't have fresh chives, I use something called Parisien Bonnes Herbes, sold by
mail from Penzeys Spices. It's a dried blend of chives, dill weed, basil, French tarragon,
chervil, and white pepper. It's marvelous as a soup garnish.

Soak wild mushrooms in hot water for half an hour. Remove from water, wringing out by hand, and set aside in a bowl. Strain the soaking water into another bowl to use for cooking potatoes. Put chopped potatoes (peeled if thick-skinned potato like Idaho, but not if Yukon or Red), vegetable broth, and reserved mushroom-soaking water in a pot, cover, bring to a simmer, and cook until potatoes are tender.

Meanwhile, in large soup pot, combine olive oil, onion, shallot, and celery and cook over medium heat. Sauté until onion becomes slightly translucent. Add white mushrooms, wild mushrooms, and sea salt. Cook covered about 5 minutes. Then add thyme. Cook 5 more minutes. Then add 1 cup of the rice milk. Cover, reduce heat to low, and simmer 5 more minutes. Remove from heat and stir in sake, and several grindings of fresh pepper. Puree mushroom mixture in food processor, and then return to soup pot. Puree potatoes and their cooking broth in food processor and add to pureed mushroom mixture. Add last 1/2 cup rice milk (or more for a thinner soup) and heat over medium heat. Adjust salt and pepper, and serve piping hot, sprinkled on top with pretty chopped chives or crumbled crackers.

SERVES 6

1 oz. dried wild mushrooms

1 cup hot water

2 medium potatoes

2 cups vegetable broth

2 Tbsp. olive oil

1 medium onion, minced

1/2 shallot, minced

2 stalks celery, including leaves, chopped

12 oz. white mushrooms, roughly chopped

1 tsp. sea salt

1½ tsp. chopped fresh thyme (or 1 scant tsp. of dried)

1½ cups rice milk

1/2 cup sake (or Madeira or dry sherry)

salt and pepper to taste

chopped chives (optional, but great) or Parisien Bonnes Herbes

crackers (optional)

Mushroom Barley Soup

Mushroom barley soup has been a favorite in my family for generations.
My great-grandmother Dora would make it for my father when he was a little boy,
using a recipe from her childhood when she lived in Lithuania. When I was a child,
my father made it for me. And now I make it for my sons. And sometimes,
on occasion, I now make it for my father.

1 cup pearled barley (quick cooking)

3 cups water

1 oz. dried wild mushrooms,
    soaked in 1 cup hot water for
    at least 30 minutes

2 Tbsp. olive oil

1 onion, diced

2 carrots, chopped

3 stalks celery, chopped

2 bay leaves

1 Tbsp. fresh thyme leaves, or
    1 tsp. dried thyme

12 oz. fresh mushrooms, sliced

1 tsp. salt

8 cups vegetable broth

1/2 cup red wine

1/4 cup chopped parsley

fresh ground pepper

Cook barley until water is absorbed. The time on this varies from brand to brand, from between half an hour to 1 hour. Set aside. Meanwhile, soak mushrooms. Using your fingers, lift the reconstituted wild mushrooms out of the water, squeezing the liquid back into the bowl to be used later. Rinse mushrooms thoroughly and chop. Strain their soaking broth through a tight strainer or sieve, saving it for the soup. In large heavy pot, heat olive oil over medium heat. Add onion, and sauté a couple of minutes, then add carrots, celery, bay leaves, and thyme. Cook, stirring frequently, until the celery and carrots have softened a bit. Add the sliced fresh mushrooms and cook a couple of minutes until softened. Add the chopped wild mushrooms and salt and cook a few more minutes. Then add the cooked barley, the vegetable broth, the reserved mushroom broth, and the wine. Bring to a simmer, lower heat, and cover loosely. Cook, stirring frequently, about 1 hour more. Add the parsley, remove from heat, and grind in fresh pepper.

SERVES 8

Corn Chowder

*Corn chowder is a great alternative to clam chowder or fish chowder.
If corn is in season, use fresh. Otherwise, canned or frozen corn work just fine.
The bacon in this recipe really gives it zip, but if you'd rather have it completely
vegetarian, omit the bacon and just add a little more salt.*

Cook bacon in the olive oil over medium heat until crispy.
Add the onion and celery and cook about 5 minutes. Add
potatoes and broth. Cook at a simmer about 15 minutes
until potatoes are tender. Add the rice milk and corn.
Cook about another 20 minutes. If you desire a creamy
chowder (I do), combine 2 Tbsp. flour with some of the hot
soup in a little bowl, stirring until smooth. Add back into
the pot. Stir in well. Add salt and pepper, and cook a little
longer to thicken slightly. Serve garnished with a little
chopped parsley.

SERVES 8–10

2 Tbsp. olive oil

2 oz. organic nitrite-free bacon, diced

1 small onion, diced

2 stalks celery, cut up

3 medium red potatoes, cut into
half-inch cubes

4 cups vegetable broth (or low-salt
chicken broth)

3 cups rice milk

3 cups corn

2 Tbsp. allowed flour (optional)

salt and pepper

chopped parsley

Tortilla Soup

I first ate tortilla soup when I was living in Montreal (and wishing I was in Mexico). It's fantastic on a cold winter day to warm you up, and equally delicious with a nice frosty beer on a summer evening. And kids love it because of the tortilla chips.

3/4 lb. boneless chicken breast

1 28-oz. can of chopped tomatoes

2 tsp. minced fresh or dried jalapeno pepper (less if for little children)

3 large cloves garlic, minced fine

1 large onion, minced

juice of 1½ limes

1/4 tsp. salt

fresh ground pepper

4 cups low-salt chicken broth

tortilla chips—crumbled a bit—I like blue corn chips because they look pretty against the red soup

1/4 cup chopped cilantro

diced avocado (optional) for garnish

Steam the chicken breast about 10 minutes and set aside. Combine tomatoes, jalapenos, garlic, onion, lime juice, salt and pepper. Heat chicken broth. Cut up chicken into bite-sized pieces. Add tomato mixture and chicken to broth. Cook over low heat at a slow simmer about 30 minutes. Serve garnished with plenty of tortilla chips and chopped cilantro. Add diced avocado (if using) at the very end.

SERVES 4

Tip

Try with Garden of Eatin' Sesame Blues all natural tortilla chips.

Chicken Soup with Cornmeal Dumplings

I used to make great matzo ball soup, but had to revise it, since matzo is made from wheat, and matzo balls call for eggs. This delicious southern style alternative is true comfort food at its best.

Sauté carrots and celery in olive oil in large pot over medium heat. When softened, add chicken, broth, and salt. Bring to a boil, then reduce heat and cook at a slow simmer about 15 minutes. Meanwhile, make the dumplings. Mix cornmeal, oat flour, barley flour, baking powder, and salt. Add rice/oat milk and stir until moist. Add egg replacer. Stir well. Wet hands with water and mold dough into balls about 1½ inches in diameter. You will have about 16 dumplings. When soup has cooked about 15 minutes, drop in dumplings and parsley. Be sure that the soup is barely simmering, because if you boil it, the dumplings will fall apart. Cover pot, turn heat as low as possible, and cook about 15 more minutes. When done, adjust salt to taste, grind in fresh pepper, and serve, gently lifting out the dumplings with a large spoon.

SERVES 6–8

Soup:

2 carrots, chopped

2 stalks celery, chopped

2 Tbsp. olive oil

2 cups diced cooked chicken (leftovers are fine)

10 cups low-salt chicken broth (or better yet, homemade stock)

1 tsp. kosher salt

2 Tbsp. chopped parsley (or more to taste)

fresh pepper

Dumplings:

1/3 cup yellow cornmeal

1/2 cup oat flour

1/2 cup barley flour

1 tsp. double-acting baking powder

1/4 tsp. salt

1/2 cup enriched rice or oat milk

1½ tsp. Ener-G Egg Replacer mixed with 2 Tbsp. enriched rice or oat milk

Lemon Chicken Soup with Rice

This is a great soup for sick days. It's light and comforting.

1 cup chopped cooked chicken (leftovers are fine)

6 cups low-salt chicken broth

2 bay leaves

4 tsp. very finely minced onion

1 carrot, peeled, halved, and chopped into small pieces

1 stalk celery (including leaves), halved and chopped into small pieces

4 whole allspice (optional)

8 peppercorns (or a couple grindings of fresh)

1/2 tsp. salt

1 cup cooked rice (brown basmati, texamati, etc.)

2 tsp. olive oil

juice of 1–2 lemons

Combine chicken, chicken broth, bay leaves, onion, carrot, celery, allspice, peppercorns, and salt. Cook 10 minutes at a slow simmer. Add rice and simmer another 15 minutes. Remove from heat and stir in olive oil and lemon juice. Start with juice from 1 lemon and taste. Add more as necessary (lemons vary in juiciness so you'll have to do this one by taste).

SERVES 6

Portuguese Kale Soup

I grew up on Cape Cod where there's a large Portuguese population. One of my favorite Portuguese dishes is kale soup. My recipe uses garlic chicken sausage instead of the traditional chorizo or linguica, because I prefer to cut the fat and salt content. However, if you wish to use the original, go right ahead.

In large heavy pot, sauté onions and garlic in olive oil over medium heat until soft. Stir in the paprika and cayenne pepper and cook about 1 minute. Add potatoes and chicken broth and bring up heat to high. Bring to a boil, then reduce heat to low, cover loosely, and simmer about 15 minutes until potatoes are soft. Using a potato masher, mash them as much as possible. Add the tomatoes, kidney beans, and sausages. Simmer partially covered about 45 minutes. Stir occasionally. Bunch kale leaves together and cut into strips about 1/4 inch across. When soup has simmered about 45 minutes, add kale and cook another 15–30 minutes, stirring kale into it. Remove from heat, add freshly ground pepper, and serve.

SERVES 8–10

1 medium onion, diced (about 1½ cups)

2 large cloves garlic, minced fine

2 Tbsp. olive oil

1/2 tsp. paprika

1/4 tsp. cayenne pepper

2 large potatoes, peeled, quartered, and cut into half-moon-shaped pieces about 1/4 inch thick

8 cups chicken broth

2½ cups chopped tomatoes, canned or fresh

1 can (15.5 oz.) precooked kidney beans, drained and rinsed (about 1½ cups)

12-oz. package of precooked garlic chicken sausage (4 large links), cut into quarters lengthwise and then chopped into small pieces

8 cups tightly packed kale, washed and leaves stripped off the stems

freshly ground pepper

Turkey Noodle Soup with Spinach

*Personally, I think turkey soup works just as well for soothing a cold
as chicken soup (aka Jewish penicillin)—and if you add some pasta and spinach,
you've got a complete meal. When I make this soup, I sometimes add
leftover turkey gravy to the broth for added flavor.*

1/2 medium-sized onion

3 stalks celery, chopped

4 scallions, sliced (or 1 tsp. dried chives)

1 Tbsp. olive oil

2 cups cubed cooked turkey meat

8 cups low-salt chicken broth

pinch of thyme

1/2 tsp. salt (or to taste)

2 medium carrots, chopped

2 oz. pasta (I like tagliatelle, two nests broken in half, but you can use whatever shape you prefer—stars, noodles, etc.)

1 10-oz. package chopped frozen spinach

fresh ground pepper

1 tsp. hot sauce

Note: Pasta should be rice, quinoa, corn, or regular durum wheat if allowed.

Sauté onions, celery, and scallions in olive oil in a large heavy pot over medium heat until soft, about 5 minutes. Add the turkey, broth, thyme, salt, and carrots to the pot. Bring to a simmer, and cook about 25 minutes. Add the pasta and cook until just done, then add the spinach, pepper, and hot sauce. Serve piping hot.

SERVES 6–8

Variation

If you happen to have a leftover Roast Turkey Breast (p. 99), you can use the meat for this recipe. Just add the breast—bones and all—to the sautéed onion, celery, and scallions along with 8 cups water (rather than chicken broth). Let simmer about 25 minutes, then remove the pot from the heat and let the broth cool. Once cooled, remove the turkey meat from the bones, cut into bite-sized pieces (there should be about 2 cups), and return to the pot. Add the salt and carrots, and bring to a slow boil. Add the pasta, and proceed as above.

Vichyssoise

*Vichyssoise is one of those soups that professional chefs turn their
noses up at because it's so old-fashioned and has been done a million times.
However, there's a reason for its staying power. It has a wonderful
smooth texture and a delightful country French flavor.*

Cook onion, leeks, and celery in olive oil in large pot over medium-low heat. Cook, stirring frequently, until soft but not browned—about 20 minutes. Add potatoes, chicken broth, salt and pepper, and 1 Tbsp. of the sherry. Bring to a boil, then reduce heat to a simmer and cook until potatoes are soft—about 30 minutes. Remove from heat, and puree in food processor in batches, transferring puree to a bowl. When it's all been pureed, return to the pot, add in the cup of oat milk and the last Tbsp. of sherry, and about 1/2 tsp. salt and some more pepper. Warm until piping hot, but not boiling. Serve with chopped chives, or parsley or just as it is. This is great hot or cold, and is even better the second day.

SERVES 6–8

3 Tbsp. olive oil

1 large onion, diced

3 leeks, well washed and chopped
    (white part only)

1 stalk celery, chopped (include leaves
    if it has them)

2 large baking potatoes (Idaho), peeled
    and cut into thin slices

4 cups low-salt chicken broth

salt (a few shakes at first, and then about
    1/2 tsp. at the end)

black and white pepper (white optional)

1 cup oat milk or rice milk

2 Tbsp. dry sherry—divided

chopped chives or parsley for garnish
    (optional)

Gazpacho

This soup is great in summer when you can buy farm-fresh vegetables just picked.
It's pretty to look at and packs a major nutritional punch.

1 large sweet onion

3 cloves garlic

1 large unpeeled English cucumber, or
   2 medium cucumbers, peeled

1 red bell pepper (or color of choice)

2 medium ripe tomatoes

2 Tbsp. tightly packed fresh basil

3 cups tomato juice

3 Tbsp. olive oil

2 Tbsp. balsamic vinegar

1 tsp. honey

salt and pepper to taste

hot sauce or cayenne pepper to taste
   (optional)

chopped bell pepper, scallions, cucumber,
   or basil leaves for garnish (optional)

tortilla chips, crumbled for garnish
   (optional)

Combine onion and garlic in food processor. Puree. Add cucumber and bell pepper. Puree. Add tomatoes and basil. Puree. Add rest of ingredients. Blend. You may need to remove a little of the puree from the food processor before adding all the tomato juice depending on the size of your processor. If so, you can just combine it all in the bowl you'll use for chilling. Taste for seasonings. Chill at least 1 hour before serving, or even better, overnight.

SERVES 4–6

My Favorite Dressing

This salad dressing never wears out its welcome. I've been making it for 15 years and every single time I have dinner guests they say, "Yum! What's in this dressing?!" My husband refuses to eat his salad with anything else. Please note that the better the quality of the olive oil and balsamic vinegar, the better the dressing will taste. This is particularly true of the balsamic vinegar, so I spend the extra couple of bucks and splurge for the kind that's been aged 10 years.

Blend the garlic, basil, mustard, and honey into a paste. Add the rice vinegar and balsamic vinegar, mixing thoroughly. Then add the olive oil, slowly blending in a little at a time. Once you've finished adding the olive oil and everything is thoroughly blended, decant.

MAKES ABOUT 3/4 CUP

1 small clove garlic, minced very fine

10 fresh basil leaves, chopped or torn

2 tsp. Dijon mustard

1 Tbsp. honey

2 Tbsp. unseasoned rice vinegar

2 Tbsp. balsamic vinegar

1/2 cup olive oil

Variations

- For **Dill Dressing**: Substitute 2 Tbsp. chopped dill for the basil.
- For **Oregano Dressing**: Substitute 1/2 tsp. dried oregano for the basil.
- For **Parsley Dressing**: Substitute 2 Tbsp. chopped parsley for the basil.
- For **Shallot Dressing**: Substitute 1/2 small shallot, minced, for the garlic and omit basil.

BASIL

Greek Salad Dressing

*I created this dressing one summer on Cape Cod while trying to think
up uses for the overabundance of mint that had sprouted up around our garden
hose. Back then I used feta cheese, but this version works just as nicely.
Try it over thinly sliced cucumbers or the Greek Salad (p. 52).*

1 small clove garlic, finely minced

1/4 cup chopped mint

1/2 tsp. oregano

1 tsp. honey

2 Tbsp. red wine vinegar

juice of 1 lemon

1/2 cup extra virgin olive oil

salt and pepper to taste

Blend garlic, mint, oregano, and honey. Then add vinegar and lemon juice. Once mixed, begin to add extra virgin olive oil, a little bit at a time. Season with salt and pepper to taste.

MAKES ABOUT 1 CUP

Creamy Avocado Dressing

*This is my substitute for creamy dressings. It's great in place of mayo-based
dressings and has NO cholesterol. Experiment with it in salads and on
sandwiches, as well as over steamed veggies or chicken.*

1 clove garlic

2 tsp. honey

2 Tbsp. chopped cilantro or fresh basil

1 ripe avocado (for less fat and calories, use
    a slimcado—they're the really big ones
    with the smooth emerald green skin)

3/4 cup enriched rice milk

3 Tbsp. lime juice

2 Tbsp. cider vinegar

1/4 tsp. salt

pepper to taste

In food processor, blend garlic, honey, and cilantro or basil. Add avocado and puree. Add rice milk, lime juice, and vinegar. Then add salt and pepper. Thin with a little more rice milk if you want it more liquid. I prefer it nice and creamy myself.

MAKES ABOUT 1 1/2 CUPS

Carrot Ginger Dressing

This tangy bright orange dressing tastes fresh and Asian, even without the soy sauce. Back in the days when I could still eat sushi, I'd have sushi and a crispy salad topped with this dressing about three times a week. Well, I can't eat sushi anymore, but I can still eat vegetable rolls. If you've been sworn off soy, fish, and shellfish, you might try ordering avocado cucumber rolls, or yam asparagus rolls—they satisfy the craving (but stay away from the shiitake mushroom rolls; I learned the hard way that the shiitakes are marinated in soy sauce). Pair up this dressing with the Crispy Asian Salad (p. 51), or over fresh baby spinach.

Puree carrot, ginger, and shallot in a food processor. Add the rice vinegar, honey, and salt. Blend very well. Add canola oil in two batches. Blend. Store in refrigerator.

MAKES ABOUT 1 CUP

1 large carrot

1-inch piece fresh peeled ginger (about 1 tsp.)

1 very small shallot, or half a regular-sized one

4 Tbsp. unseasoned rice vinegar

1 Tbsp. honey

1/2 tsp. salt

1/2 cup canola oil

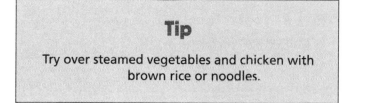

Tip

Try over steamed vegetables and chicken with brown rice or noodles.

Avocado Mayonnaise

Use anywhere you would use regular mayonnaise.

Mash the avocado and stir in other ingredients until well blended—or just throw it all in the food processor or mini chop. Use within one or two days.

MAKES ABOUT 1/2 CUP

1 ripe avocado

1 Tbsp. rice milk or oat milk

1 Tbsp. lemon juice

1 tsp. Dijon mustard

pinch of paprika

salt to taste

dash of hot sauce (optional)

Red Wine Vinaigrette

This simple dressing is one my mother, Susanna, always makes and usually serves over lettuce. She learned to make it growing up in Italy. She likes it very tart, but if you prefer a milder taste, just add a little more olive oil. Again, the better the quality of your oil and vinegar, the better the dressing will taste. Cheap vinegars often are extremely bitter. The higher quality vinegars are smoother, so I think they're worth the extra cost.

1 small clove garlic, finely minced
1/2 tsp. oregano
1/4 tsp. sea salt
1/4 cup red wine vinegar
1/2 cup olive oil

Combine garlic, oregano, and sea salt. Stir in red wine vinegar. Slowly add olive oil a little at a time, stirring to blend as you pour. Taste and adjust salt.

MAKES ABOUT 3/4 CUP

Lemon Tahini Dressing

I've always loved tahini. I spread it on toast in place of butter, and eat it with jam or honey. It's great in hummus, baba ghanoush, and, of course, as a dressing.

1 clove garlic
1/2 cup sesame tahini
3 Tbsp. lemon juice (about 1 lemon)
3/4 cup water
1/4 tsp. salt
1/4 tsp. cumin
cayenne or black pepper to taste

Puree garlic in food processor. Add lemon juice and tahini. Blend. While still blending, begin pouring in water a little at a time. You may wish to add more or less to reach your desired consistency. Add salt and cumin. When completely blended, adjust salt and pepper to taste. Store refrigerated in an airtight container. It keeps for a couple of weeks. Serve over salads, steamed or grilled vegetables, chicken, rice, Falafel (p. 133), or buckwheat noodles. This sauce is endlessly versatile.

MAKES ABOUT 1¼ CUPS

Sesame Seeds

Sesame seeds are considered one of the nine most common food allergens by the Canadian Food Inspection Agency, so please check with your allergist or doctor before consuming any sesame products.

Garden Salad

*This salad is a staple at my table. We eat it night after night,
and it seems to go well with just about everything.*

Combine greens,
carrots, and tomatoes
in large salad bowl.
Drizzle outer perimeter
of salad with dressing.
Toss gently. Taste and adjust dressing as necessary.

SERVES 2–4

8 cups mixed baby greens

2 carrots, peeled and chopped

8 ripe cherry tomatoes, halved

My Favorite Dressing (p. 45) to taste

Renaissance Salad

*This salad is teeming with color and creativity. Its many flavors blend
superbly, pleasing the palette with a little bit of everything.*

Put lettuce in a large salad bowl. Put corn, olives, and
hearts of palm in center. Around the edges, intersperse
endive leaves with tomato wedges and avocado wedges.
Drizzle everything with Creamy Avocado Dressing.

SERVES 4

6 cups romaine lettuce, chopped

1/4 cup fresh corn kernels (or canned
corn, well drained)

4 black or kalamata olives

4 green olives

3 hearts of palm, cut into 1/4-inch rounds

1 medium endive, leaves separated and
left whole

1 ripe tomato, cut into wedges

1 avocado, cut into wedges

Creamy Avocado Dressing (p. 46) to taste

Common Ground Salad

This salad is a tribute to my favorite salad as a teenager. It comes from a communal hippy restaurant in Brattleboro, Vermont, called, fittingly, The Common Ground.

4 cups green leaf lettuce, chopped or torn, or 4 cups mixed baby greens

2 carrots, peeled and shredded

1/2 cucumber, peeled, halved, and sliced into half-moons

1 cup shredded or finely chopped red cabbage

alfalfa sprouts to taste

2 Tbsp. toasted sunflower seeds (to toast, put on a baking tray in oven at 375 degrees for a couple of minutes, shaking tray occasionally)

Lemon Tahini Dressing (p. 48) to taste

Combine lettuce, carrots, cucumber, and cabbage in large salad bowl. Top with sprouts and toss in sunflower seeds. Drizzle outer perimeter of salad with dressing. Toss gently. Taste to adjust dressing as necessary.

SERVES 2–4

Endive, Radicchio, and Arugula Salad

Endive, radicchio, and arugula are a simple but perfect combination of salad greens. If you wish, you may sprinkle a little sea salt on it at the end, but I like it just as is, in all its tricolor glory.

1 large endive or 2 small, cut horizontally into 1/4-inch pieces

1 cup radicchio, torn into small pieces

4 cups well-washed and dried arugula, cut up or torn

My Favorite Dressing (p. 45) to taste

sea salt (optional)

Combine endive, radicchio, and arugula in large bowl or on a plate. Drizzle with dressing and toss.

SERVES 2–4

Baby Spinach with Roasted Portobello Mushrooms and Red Bell Pepper

Roasted portobello mushrooms are a revelation. They caramelize and crisp up beautifully, and are wonderful paired with spinach. The red bell pepper adds a lovely bit of color and vitamin C to this salad, but you could just as easily add tomatoes.

Preheat oven to 500 degrees. Line a cookie sheet with aluminum foil and pour olive oil on it. Tilt the cookie sheet to coat with oil evenly. Slice mushrooms in half and then cut into 1/2-inch-wide strips. Toss mushrooms in olive oil on cookie tray, coating both sides. Cook about 20 minutes, turning them after 10. Remove from oven and let cool. Combine baby spinach, bell pepper, and portobello mushrooms in salad bowl. Drizzle outer perimeter of salad with dressing. Toss gently. Taste to adjust dressing as necessary.

SERVES 2–4

4 Tbsp. olive oil
2 large portobello mushrooms
6 cups baby spinach
1/2 red bell pepper (or yellow, or orange), diced or sliced however you like it
1/4 cup My Favorite Dressing (p. 45)

Crispy Asian Salad

So much of the appeal of salad is about texture. And I love a big juicy salad that's full of crispy crunch. So I created the following salad with crispy romaine and iceberg lettuce, crunchy cucumbers and carrots, and soothing avocado and tomato for a little contrast. If you want to make a complete meal out of this, just add some julienned turkey breast or ham.

Combine lettuces, carrot, tomato, cucumber, and avocado in large salad bowl. Drizzle outer perimeter of salad with dressing. Toss gently. Taste and adjust dressing as necessary.

SERVES 2–4

3 cups chopped romaine lettuce
3 cups chopped iceberg lettuce
1 carrot, peeled and shredded
1 ripe tomato, cut into wedges
1/2 cucumber, peeled, halved, and sliced into half-moons
1/2 avocado, chopped up (optional)
Carrot Ginger Dressing (p. 47) to taste

Greek Salad

Greek salad is a great lunch or light supper in summer. It also pairs up well with Hummus
(p. 62) and Eggplant Spread (p. 61) for an appetizer platter, which is great to serve at parties.

5 cups romaine lettuce, cut into
    1/4-inch strips
1/2 cucumber, peeled, halved, and
    cut into 1/4-inch pieces
1 ripe tomato, sliced into wedges
1/4 red onion, cut into thin rounds
8 kalamata olives
4 stuffed grape leaves (optional)
oregano
Greek Salad Dressing (p. 46) to taste

Combine lettuce, cucumber, tomato, onion, olives, and
grape leaves in large salad bowl. Sprinkle with oregano.
Drizzle outer perimeter of salad with dressing. Toss gently.
Taste and adjust dressing as necessary.

SERVES 2–4

Cuban Salad with Oranges and Red Onion

I adore this tangy salad alongside Raf's Cuban Rice and Beans (p. 127), but it's also great with
just about any hearty Caribbean, Latin American, or Mediterranean type of food.

6 cups red leaf or green leaf lettuce
1 navel orange, peeled, sliced into slender
    rounds horizontally, and then cut into
    halves
1/4 red onion, cut into slender rounds and
    separated into rings
Red Wine Vinaigrette (p. 48) to taste

Lay out lettuce on a large plate or platter. Spread oranges
and onions on top of lettuce. Then drizzle with dressing and
toss gently.

SERVES 2–4

Frisee with Figs, Pear, and Crispy Bacon

The sweetness of the figs and pear against the salty crispiness of the bacon is the perfect complement to the slight bitterness of the frisee. This salad is a great accompaniment to a light soup such as Cauliflower Soup (p. 34), or as a starter at dinner.

Cook bacon until crispy. Crumble or dice. Combine frisee lettuce, figs, and pear on a large plate. Sprinkle bacon on top, drizzle with dressing, and toss gently.

SERVES 2–4

6 cups frisee lettuce, torn into bite-sized pieces

6 dried figs, cut into small pieces

1 ripe pear, cut into small pieces

1/4 cup (about 2 oz.) crispy fried organic nitrite-free bacon (regular or turkey bacon, or thick bacon, or pancetta, or lardon), crumbled or diced

1/4 cup Shallot Dressing (a variation of My Favorite Dressing, p. 45) to taste

Bib Lettuce with Fennel, Apple, and Roasted Beets

The delicate flavor of the bib lettuce makes the perfect backdrop for the earthy sweetness of the fennel, apples, and beets.

To roast the beets, preheat oven to 425 degrees. Wrap each beet in aluminum foil and roast about 1 hour and 15 minutes. Let cool. Peel and dice. If you don't want to bother with all this, you may use canned or jarred beets, but be sure they're not pickled.

Combine lettuce, fennel, and apple in a large bowl or plate. Sprinkle diced beets on top. Drizzle with dressing and toss gently.

SERVES 2–4

2 small beets, diced (about 1/2 cup)

6 cups bib lettuce (or Boston or butter lettuce)

1 cup chopped fennel

1 golden delicious apple, peeled, cored, and cut into bite-sized pieces

Parsley Dressing (a variation of My Favorite Dressing, p. 45) to taste

Waldorf Salad

The original version of this salad calls for loads of mayonnaise.
I prefer this streamlined low-fat alternative.

6 cups Boston lettuce

1 cup cubed cooked chicken breast

1/2 cup green or red grapes, halved

1 apple, peeled, cored, and cut into
   1/2-inch cubes

1 stalk of celery, chopped into
   1/4-inch pieces

6 sprigs of watercress, separated

1/4 cup My Favorite Dressing (p. 45)

Combine all ingredients except for the lettuce. Lay lettuce out on a large plate. Put chicken salad on top.

SERVES 2–4

Cole Slaw

When I was growing up, my mother never served the thick cole slaw you get at diners and delis,
the kind that's dripping in mayonnaise. Rather, she made a lighter sweet version with apples and
raisins. The following is the dairy-free version of my mother's cole slaw.

1 package shredded traditional cole slaw
   mix (Dole, Hains, etc.)

1/2 cup shredded or grated carrot

1 McIntosh apple, peeled, cored,
   and cut into 1/4-inch pieces

1/2 cup raisins

1 Tbsp. enriched rice milk

3 Tbsp. white vinegar

2 Tbsp. orange juice

1 tsp. honey

1 Tbsp. lemon juice

6 Tbsp. olive oil

In a large bowl, combine the slaw mix, carrot, apple, and raisins. In a small bowl, combine the rice milk, vinegar, orange juice, honey, and lemon juice. Slowly whisk in the olive oil a little at a time. Pour dressing over cole slaw and combine thoroughly. Cover bowl and let chill 1 hour before serving.

SERVES 8–10

Creamy Avocado Chicken Salad

This salad substitutes nicely for tuna salad.

Combine all ingredients, adding salt and pepper to taste. Eat on bread for a sandwich, or rollup, or serve on a bed of Boston lettuce with tomato wedges.

SERVES 2–4

1 cup cooked chicken (baked, grilled, boiled) or canned chunk chicken, drained and broken up with a fork

1 Tbsp. finely minced onion

1 stalk celery, chopped (very fine if for babies)

2 tsp. Dijon mustard

5 Tbsp. Creamy Avocado Dressing (p. 46)

salt and pepper to taste

American Picnic Potato Salad

No picnic or summer party is complete without a good old-fashioned potato salad.
The following recipe is my spin on the traditional.

Peel potatoes and cut into 1½-inch chunks. Put in a pot and cover with water. Bring to a boil and boil about 15 minutes until potatoes are tender when pricked with a fork. Drain and pour potatoes into a bowl. Drizzle with vinegar, olive oil, salt and pepper. Toss. Add onion, celery, cucumber, mustard, gherkin juice, gherkins, and parsley. Cover and refrigerate overnight if possible, or at least a couple of hours. Just before serving, sprinkle top with paprika.

SERVES 4–6

2 lbs. boiling potatoes (red potatoes or Yukon gold work well)

2 Tbsp. white vinegar

1/2 cup olive oil

salt and pepper

1/4 cup onion, finely chopped

2 stalks celery, finely chopped

1 medium cucumber, peeled, quartered, deseeded, and cut into 1/4-inch pieces

3 Tbsp. Dijon mustard

3 Tbsp. sour gherkin juice

8 sour baby gherkins, cut up small

2 Tbsp. chopped parsley

paprika

Dill Potato Salad

Dill is an old-world flavor that deserves more attention in contemporary cooking. I think too often people associate it with bland, overly rich salmon steaks swimming in sauce. But it's a fresh and sprightly herb that is wonderful with, among other things, potatoes. Try this salad at room temperature, or warmed alongside chicken or steak.

1½ lbs. new potatoes (about 25 1-inch potatoes)

1/2 cup Dill Dressing (a variation of My Favorite Dressing, p. 45)

1/2 English cucumber, diced small

1 Tbsp. finely minced shallot

2 Tbsp. finely minced red onion

1/2 tsp. salt

fresh ground pepper

Wash new potatoes and cut in half unless already very small. Put in a pot and cover with water. Bring to a boil and boil about 20 minutes until potatoes are tender when pricked with a fork. Drain and pour potatoes into a bowl. Pour dressing over them and toss. Mix in cucumber, shallot, onion, salt, and pepper. Let cool. Cover and refrigerate overnight if possible, or at least a couple of hours. You may also serve this warmed.

SERVES 4

Quinoa Tabouli

Tabouli is usually made with bulgur, a form of wheat. I devised this adaptation using quinoa. It's just as delicious, and has the extra benefit of additional protein, since quinoa is a high-protein grain.

4 cups cooked quinoa

1/2 unpeeled English cucumber, diced small, or one small cucumber, peeled and deseeded

1/2 cup ripe tomato, diced small

2 scallions, minced (green and white parts)

1/4 cup lemon juice

1/4 cup olive oil

1/2 cup chopped parsley

1/4 cup chopped mint

2 cloves garlic, minced fine

salt and pepper

Combine all ingredients in a bowl, cover, and refrigerate. This gets better after the flavors have melded a bit, so give it at least a couple hours if you've got the time.

SERVES 6–8

Rice Salad

Rice salad is a great way to use up leftover rice. This recipe makes a lovely confetti-like salad, bursting with color and crunch. Add a little chicken or turkey alongside and you've got a complete meal.

Combine all ingredients in a bowl, cover and refrigerate. This salad gets better after the flavors have melded a bit, so give it at least a couple hours if you've got it. Otherwise, dig in—it still tastes great.

SERVES 6–8

4 cups cooked rice of any kind (I usually use brown basmati)

1 green bell pepper, washed, deseeded, and diced small

1 red bell pepper, washed, deseeded, and diced small

4 scallions, minced (white and green parts)

8 radishes, quartered, and then chopped small

1/4 cup minced red onion

1/4 cup red wine vinegar

1/2 cup olive oil

1/2 cup finely chopped herbs (basil, parsley, cilantro, chervil, etc.)

1 tsp. honey

salt and lots of fresh ground black pepper

ground chili pepper to taste (I like cayenne or chipotle) (optional)

1 cup chick peas (optional)

Grilled Vegetables

These succulent and smoky grilled vegetables are endlessly versatile. Serve them as an after-school snack, as appetizers at a party, over grains, or mixed with pasta. If you want to exchange other vegetables for the ones I've listed, go right ahead. The following are merely suggestions.

1 medium eggplant

1 medium zucchini

1/2 red onion

1 red bell pepper

8 artichoke hearts, or 4 baby artichokes
   halved (stem and top third cut off, then
   boiled 5 minutes in water to cover)

olive oil

salt and pepper

balsamic vinegar

1 Tbsp. chopped parsley

Slice the eggplant into 1/4-inch rounds. Slice the zucchini into about 6 strips vertically. Cut the onion into 4 wedges. Cut the red pepper into 1/2-inch-thick strips. Add the artichoke hearts or baby artichokes. Toss with olive oil to coat. Sprinkle with salt and pepper. You can cook this on the grill, or under the broiler. You should flip the vegetables once. When cooked, but not falling apart, remove from heat, drizzle with balsamic vinegar and parsley. You may wish to add more salt and pepper. If you're making these to add to pasta, skip adding the vinegar and parsley.

SERVES 4

Thanya's Corn Salad

My sister-in-law, Thanya Suwansawad, taught my family how to make this famous corn salad one summer when sweet corn had just come into season in Western Massachusetts. I often add jalapeno pepper to it because I love the heat, but Thanya keeps it simple. I've also been known to substitute basil for cilantro when I don't have any of the latter, and that tastes great too.

4 ears corn

1 green bell pepper, diced

1 red bell pepper, diced

1 red onion, diced

2–4 Tbsp. chopped cilantro

1/4 cup fresh-squeezed lime juice with pulp

2–4 Tbsp. olive oil

salt and pepper to taste

1 small jalapeno pepper, deseeded and
   minced very fine (optional)

Steam or boil corn about 7 minutes. Cut off kernels with a very sharp knife. Combine all ingredients and adjust salt and pepper to taste.

SERVES 4–6

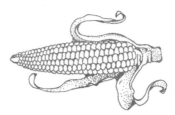

Pasta Salad

Pasta salad is a great way to make lunch for the family the night before.
Just whip this up and stick it in the fridge for the following day.

Cook pasta according to instructions on packet. Drain, and toss with all the other ingredients. Cool to room temperature, cover, and refrigerate.

SERVES 6–8

1 lb. short pasta (penne, rigatoni, ziti, spirals, fusilli, shells, etc.—made from whatever type of flour you're allowed)

1/2 cup olive oil

20 sun-dried tomatoes, cut into small pieces

20 small black olives, cut up

1 cup chopped fresh basil

1 can artichoke hearts in water, drained and cut into small wedges

10 cherry tomatoes, quartered

2 cups grilled chicken, cut into bite-sized pieces (optional)

salt and pepper to taste

Guacamole

Avocados are one of my favorite foods, and my son Lennon seems to have inherited the love. When all else fails, I feed him guacamole. It's great as a dip or on a sandwich.

2 medium-sized ripe avocados

1/4 cup finely minced onion

2 tsp. minced jalapeno pepper (about half a small pepper)

2 Tbsp. lime juice (about 1 lime)

1/8 tsp. salt

4 tsp. chopped cilantro (or parsley)

Halve the avocados. Remove pits. Carefully cut avocado into strips lengthwise, then crosswise, making a checkerboard pattern. Scoop out avocado into a bowl. Add minced onion, jalapeno pepper, lime juice, salt, and cilantro. Combine, gently mashing the avocado, but not too much—it's good a little chunky. Taste. Add more salt if necessary. Serve on a sandwich, with Mexican food, with tortilla chips, over grilled chicken, etc. If not using it right away, gently press pits into guacamole to stop it from browning, and refrigerate tightly covered until ready to serve.

MAKES ABOUT 1 CUP

Artichoke Spread

This spread is good as a dip, on crackers, or in a sandwich. I like it on a toasted pumpernickel bagel with sliced ripe tomato and coarse cracked pepper. It's also very good on pasta, used like a pesto—in which case, you'll want to thin it with a little bit of olive oil.

1 13.75-oz. can artichoke hearts, drained

1/2 cup wheat-free bread crumbs

2 tsp. capers and their juice

1/4 cup green olives

1 tsp. honey

1 Tbsp. lemon juice

1 Tbsp. chopped parsley

1/2 cup olive oil

fresh ground pepper

Puree all the ingredients in a food processor until smooth.

MAKES ABOUT $1\frac{1}{2}$ CUPS

Eggplant Spread

This dish is light, lemony, and gorgeous.
It's great on a sandwich or served with crackers.

Preheat oven to 375 degrees. Grease a cookie sheet with olive oil. Cut eggplant in half and place cut side down on sheet. Cook about 45 minutes until skin has started to wrinkle and eggplant is soft. Meanwhile, sauté enough onion to make 2 Tbsp. cooked (start with about 1/4 cup). When eggplant is done, remove from oven and let cool. In food processor, mince garlic. Add onion and blend. Once eggplant has cooled to where you can handle it, scoop out the eggplant from the skin into food processor. Puree. Add lemon juice, salt, and a little fresh pepper. Combine. Slowly drizzle in 1/4 cup olive oil, blending. Add parsley at very end, mixing until just combined. Spoon onto plate or bowl, hollow out a little well in the center, drizzle in olive oil, and sprinkle with pomegranate seeds. Serve with crackers, tortilla chips, or on a sandwich.

MAKES ABOUT 1 ½ CUPS

1/2 large eggplant or 1 small (1 cup when cooked)

2 Tbsp. sautéed onion

1 small clove garlic

2 Tbsp. lemon juice

1/4 tsp. salt

pepper

1/4 cup olive oil plus a little more to drizzle on at end

2 Tbsp. chopped parsley

1 Tbsp. pomegranate seeds (optional)

White Bean Spread

This white bean spread is rich, slightly spicy, and has a nice amount of protein.

Mash beans with a fork or blend just slightly in processor. Add all other ingredients. Taste for salt and pepper. If you use a food processor, don't blend too much—you don't want a paste, it's better with a little texture.

MAKES ABOUT 1 CUP

1 15-oz. can cannellini or other white beans, drained (about 1½ cups)

1 clove garlic, minced fine

2–3 Tbsp. olive oil

1 tsp. dried rosemary, crumbled or 1/2 tsp. chopped fresh rosemary

2 tsp. lemon juice

1/4–1/2 tsp. sea salt

fresh ground black pepper

1/8 tsp. cayenne pepper

Tip

To use this book while doing an elimination or rotation diet, reference *Prescription for Nutritional Healing* by James F. and Phyllis A. Balch (see Resources, p. 200).

Hummus

I like to make my own hummus because often the store-bought kind has soy oil in it. This hummus is very tasty and good alone as a dip, or as a spread on bread for a sandwich. For kids who've been forbidden legumes, try the yummy Eggplant Spread (p. 61). All others, enjoy!

1 clove garlic

1 15.5-oz. can chick peas

3 Tbsp. lemon juice

3 Tbsp. olive oil, plus a little more to drizzle at end

2 Tbsp. sesame tahini (see inset on page 48 about sesame allergies and omit tahini if necessary)

3 Tbsp. water

1/4 tsp. cumin

salt and pepper to taste

sumac to sprinkle at end (optional, but it adds a nice little zip—order from Penzeys Spices, see Resources, p. 197)

In food processor, mince the garlic, then add chick peas, lemon juice, 3 Tbsp. olive oil, tahini, water, cumin, salt and pepper to taste. Puree. Spoon out into bowl or onto plate. Using the back of a spoon, make a little shallow well in the center of the hummus. Drizzle in a little more olive oil. Sprinkle sumac around perimeter of hummus and serve with crackers, bread, baby carrots, or other raw vegetables.

MAKES ABOUT 1½ CUPS

Chopped Liver

I love chopped liver. Call me crazy, but I think it's a real treat spread on a warm piece
of toasted rye bread. My recipe is much lower in cholesterol than normal chopped liver,
as I've substituted olive oil for the traditional rendered chicken fat, and it has no egg.
Make this up for a party and serve on appetizer-sized pieces of dark or light rye or on crackers.
If you wish, you might top with a little minced onion or parsley, or sautéed onions,
or sautéed chopped mushrooms. If you're not making it for a party, you may wish
to halve this recipe. Remove from fridge half an hour before eating.

Wash the chicken livers well. Boil a pot of water. Once boiling, add chicken livers, reduce heat to medium, and cook at a simmer about 10 minutes. Drain and set aside. Sauté onions in olive oil over low heat about 20 minutes, stirring frequently, until soft and lightly golden brown. Do not crisp them. Remove from heat. Break up chicken livers into small pieces in food processor. Add onions, salt, and pepper. Mix on pulse, blending until pretty smooth, but not completely. You want a little texture, and don't want to completely pulverize the onions. Taste for seasonings. Transfer to a container and refrigerate until ready to serve.

MAKES ABOUT 2½ CUPS

1½ lbs. chicken livers (Murray's has organic ones that are hormone-free)
2 large onions, coarsely chopped
6 Tbsp. olive oil
1/2 tsp. salt
fresh ground black pepper

Sandwich Ideas

- Organic nitrite-free turkey bacon (or regular bacon), green leaf lettuce, and tomato with Creamy Avocado Dressing (p. 46), rolled in a corn tortilla.

- Sliced Baked Ham (pp. 110–111) with mustard and Boston lettuce on Ener-G Tapioca Thin-Sliced bread.

- Creamy Avocado Chicken Salad (p. 55) on Ener-G Seattle Brown Hamburger or Hot Dog Bun.

- Grilled Vegetables (p. 58) rolled in a corn or brown rice tortilla .

- Sliced Roast Turkey Breast (p. 99) with Cole Slaw (p. 54) on light or dark rye, or black rice bread.

- Sliced Roast Turkey Breast (p. 99) with Avocado Mayo (p. 47), lettuce, and tomatoes on Ener-G Seattle Brown Bread.

- Thanksgiving on a Roll: Sliced Roast Turkey Breast (p. 99) with crumbled Sausage, Dried Fruit, and Apple Stuffing (p. 150), and Dora's Cranberry Sauce (p. 151) on an Ener-G Tapioca Dinner Roll.

- Lamb Kebabs (p. 116) with Lemon Tahini Dressing (p. 48) in a brown rice tortilla.

- Marinated Chicken Skewers (p. 92) with sliced cucumber, tomato, and Creamy Avocado Dressing (p. 46) or Avocado Raita (p. 154) in a brown rice tortilla.

- Breaded Chicken Cutlets with Roasted Red Peppers (p. 86) and romaine lettuce on light rye.

- Lime Skirt Steak with Pineapple Salsa (p. 103) with chopped iceberg lettuce in a corn tortilla or taco shell.

- Chopped Liver (p. 63) on toasted pumpernickel with mustard.

- Hummus (p. 62) with cucumbers, mixed baby greens, tomato, shredded carrot, and avocado on any type of bread.

- White Bean Spread (p. 61) with sliced red bell pepper and red leaf lettuce on light rye.

- Artichoke Spread (p. 60) with romaine lettuce and tomato on Ener-G White Rice Flax Bread.

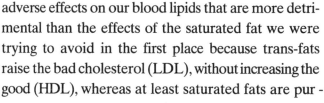

ABOUT COOKING OILS

These days, it seems that you see the terms *trans-fat*, *hydrogenated*, *saturated*, *unsaturated*, *polyunsaturated*, and *monounsaturated* just about everywhere you look. But what do all these terms mean to those of us who want to cook with the healthiest oils we can find? Let me try to demystify this for you the best I can. Animal fats are controversial. Some research indicates they are bad for you (i.e., butter, lard, etc.) because they are high in *saturated* fat, which may have adverse effects on our blood lipids. Other research indicates that saturated fats are necessary in our diets. I do consume saturated fats when cooking meat and in coconut oil, but I generally avoid cooking with animal fats.

Because of the negative press saturated fats have gotten, many people turned to cooking with vegetable fats, which were initially thought to be better for us because of their *unsaturated* fat content. Unfortunately, this isn't always true. Unsaturated vegetable oils aren't necessarily better for you, because often they are *hydrogenated* to improve their stability, rendering them less likely to oxidize when cooking at high temperatures. Unfortunately, the hydrogenation process produces a variety of *trans-fat* acids. The hydrogenation process was originally developed for frying purposes since *polyunsaturated*-rich vegetable oils can readily undergo oxidation when cooked at high temperatures. Trans-fats from hydrogenated vegetable oils, it turns out, have adverse effects on our blood lipids that are more detrimental than the effects of the saturated fat we were trying to avoid in the first place because trans-fats raise the bad cholesterol (LDL), without increasing the good (HDL), whereas at least saturated fats are purported to increase both. So what to do? Avoid hydrogenated vegetable oils and shortening and avoid cooking polyunsaturated oils at high temperatures.

Luckily there are a variety of tasty vegetable oils that are great for cooking at whatever temper-ature you need—medium, high, or medium-high heat. Many polyun-saturated oils that have not been hydrogenated are very good for you as long as you don't heat them too much. When cooking at high temperatures, try to use *monounsaturated* vegetable oils as much as possible. Generally speaking, if you're cooking at a high heat, you want to make sure you're using oil with a high smoke point.

I use mostly olive oil, canola oil, safflower oil, and Spectrum Naturals Organic Shortening (a nonhydrogenated trans-fat-free shortening made from palm oil). The following is a more comprehensive list of healthy cooking oils, if you wish to experiment.

Olive Oil—olive oil is endlessly versatile. It has been used for thousands of years and is an integral part of a healthy diet. Virgin olive oil is high in monounsaturated fats. Heating some olive oils, like Spectrum's Everyday Olive Oil, at a high temperature doesn't change its health benefits, only its flavor. If you're going to fry with it, use a mild olive oil to begin with. Use more flavorful and delicate olive oils for dressings, adding to food at the table, and cooking at lower temperatures. Use organic and cold-pressed olive oil when possible.

Canola Oil—great for cooking at medium-high heat.

Safflower Oil—great for cooking at medium-high heat.

Sunflower Oil—great for cooking at medium-high heat.

Coconut Oil, Refined—great for cooking at medium-high heat and to use as a substitute for shortening in baking. (See note at right.)

Coconut Oil, Unrefined—use for medium-heat cooking and as a substitute for shortening in baking. The unrefined oil has the added benefits of antibacterial properties and antioxidants. (See note at right.)

Sesame Oil, Unrefined—great for cooking at low to medium temperatures.

Avocado Oil—great all-purpose oil that can be used at all temperatures (a little more expensive).

Apricot Kernel Oil—another great all-purpose oil for cooking at all temperatures (also a little more expensive).

Grapeseed Oil—great all-purpose oil for cooking at all temperatures (also a little more expensive).

Vegetable Shortening—a great product for baking. Use an organic, nonhydrogenated brand. Several dairy-free, soy-free brands are on the market. Look for them at your local health food store or Whole Foods Market.

Note: Coconut is an allergen that is on the fence, so ask your doctor if you need to avoid it. Until recently, coconut was not declared an allergen, and was considered a member of the date family, not a tree nut. It is the seed of a drupaceous fruit, and has typically not been restricted in the diets of people with tree nut allergy. However, in October of 2006, the FDA began identifying coconut as a tree nut. According to the Food Allergy and Anaphylaxis Network, "The available medical literature contains documentation of a small number of allergic reactions to coconut; most occurred in people who were not allergic to other tree nuts." It is my understanding that the FDA is considering revising its classification once again to exclude coconut from the tree nut category, but until this is all sorted out, check with your allergist.

DINNER

- Red Sauces
- Pasta
- Risotto
- Meat Entrees
- Vegetable Entrees
- Side Dishes

Dinner is the main meal in my house, and the one I most enjoy. Though this chapter may seem a little heavy on meat and poultry, in a diet without eggs, cheese, soy, seitan, tofu, tempeh, fish, shellfish, or nuts—and further restricted to no legumes or seeds for some—you've got to get your protein somewhere; there is simply no alternative. If we didn't eat poultry and meat in my house, we'd waste away to nothing. If you worry about the health consequences of this, con - sider the fact that having cut out dairy completely, you've probably cut way back on saturated fats. Still, we try to limit our red meat consumption to no more than once a week, if that. The rest of the time, we eat chicken, lean turkey, lean pork, and vegetarian dishes. As always, the proof is in the pudding. My husband and I are leaner than we've been in years, and Lennon and Montgomery are growing like healthy little bean stalks. We must be doing *something* right!

I suggest making up My Favorite Dressing (p. 45) to have available at all times. It comes in very handy and is used in a variety of recipes.

I also suggest that you make up big batches of The Lady from Naples Red Sauce (p. 69) and keep it in your freezer because it is used in quite a few recipes and is so much better than store-bought sauce.

At the end of this dinner section, I've included recipes for side dishes. You can mix and match as you like, but often I'll make a suggestion about what pairs well with what.

Pasta

Pasta has become an American staple—I know we eat it at my house at least once a week. So I've begun this section with my most basic red sauce, which you can use on any shape of pasta at any time. Additionally, with almost all of these pasta dishes, you may prepare the sauce up to several hours ahead of time and then reheat it when you cook your pasta—a time-saver bonus.

Much to most people's surprise, you can thoroughly enjoy pasta and risotto without Parmesan cheese. I'll admit, this was news to me too, having grown up on baked pasta dishes that contained not one, but *three* types of cheese: Ricotta, Mozzarella, and Parmesan. However, I have grown to love the purity of these foods without the salty fat (which is how I've come to view cheese). The pasta and risotto dishes included here were chosen because they all taste great without cheese. Just add a little salt, and a tiny extra bit of olive oil, and "mangia, mangia, mangia"—you'll be going back for thirds.

The Lady from Naples Red Sauce

*In my family, we all have a slightly different version of this sauce. My grandmother
Catherene first learned it from a cook in Naples. Family lore has it that my uncle's
fashion-model girlfriends would come from far and wide on their work-breaks to our house
in Positano to eat my grandmother's pasta, having saved up all their extra calories for her
food, and her food alone. She was a legendary cook. She used anchovies in the base of
her red sauce to give it zip, and a little chopped parsley at the end. I make it without
anchovies, but have added fresh basil. It is probably the first thing I learned to cook.
The sauce is endlessly versatile, and always delicious. Use it on any type of pasta, as sauce
for pizza, over chicken, in turkey meatloaf, with meatballs, sausage, or a rich vegetable like
eggplant or Portobello mushrooms. As none of us ever had a recipe, writing down
proportions was a bit of a trial, but after some experimenting, here goes. If you have some
left over, either freeze it or store it in the fridge for a meal later in the week.
I usually double the following recipe and store it in containers in the freezer
for the next few weeks, so I always have red sauce on hand.*

Add olive oil, onion, and garlic to large heavy pot. Bring
heat up to medium-high. Sauté until onions are soft, being
careful not to burn the garlic. Add oregano and bay leaves.
Cook another minute or two. Add canned tomatoes, red wine,
and honey. Stir. Add a couple grindings of black pepper
(not too much or it will taste bitter). Bring to a simmer.
Reduce heat to low and cover, leaving lid slightly ajar. Stir
occasionally. After 30 minutes, use a potato masher to crush
the whole tomatoes (if you don't have one, chop them before
you add them). Then add chopped olives. Cook another hour,
continuing to stir occasionally. Taste and adjust seasonings
as desired. Remove from heat, stir in basil, and serve with
your pasta of choice.

MAKES ABOUT 6 CUPS

3/4 cup olive oil

1/2 large red onion, diced

2 large cloves garlic, minced or crushed

1½ tsp. oregano

2 bay leaves

1 28-oz. can crushed Italian tomatoes

1 28-oz. can whole Italian tomatoes

1 cup red wine

2 Tbsp. honey

a couple of grindings fresh black pepper

5–10 black Italian olives cut up (optional)

salt to taste (I don't add any because I find
the olives and canned tomatoes are
salty enough)

1/4 to 1/2 cup fresh basil leaves, chopped
or torn

Simple Red Sauce

*As much as I adore The Lady from Naples Red Sauce, sometimes I like
a lighter sauce with a less intense flavor—especially in the summer. The recipe
on the opposite page is a re-creation of a sauce I ate in Rome when I was
a teenager. My best friend Tracy and I were hanging out on the Spanish Steps
one day where we met a jazz musician named Jamo. He invited us for lunch at his friend's
house in the outskirts of Rome. Being very young and foolish, Tracy and I got in a car with
him and a friend who spoke no English. We were taken about half an hour outside
the city to an apartment building in the modern outskirts of Rome. There we met
a Sicilian college student. Tracy and I had no idea what we were in for, and sat with
mounting anxiety as Jamo translated back and forth between us and the other two guys
who moved around in the kitchen. Very little was actually said—but half an hour later,
we were seated at a small round table and served the most wonderful lunch
I'd ever tasted. Spaghetti with the simplest, most delicious red sauce, a lovely
flavorful green leaf lettuce salad dressed only in olive oil and salt, a loaf of crusty
Italian bread, a dry white wine, and finally, slices of watermelon. We ate voraciously,
smacked our lips, wiped our faces, graciously thanked our Sicilian host, and
were driven back to the Spanish Steps, where we were left to ponder the simple
majesty of fresh ripe tomatoes. I went home to America and started trying to recreate that
meal. The following sauce is the closest I can get. This simple fresh red sauce can
be used on its own with thin pasta like spaghetti, spaghettini, or cappellini, or mixed
with any variety of vegetables for a pasta primavera. I usually double pasta
sauce recipes and freeze or refrigerate half for later use.*

The truly orthodox way to make this sauce is to blanch and peel your fresh tomatoes. To do so, boil a pot of water, drop the tomatoes in, bring back up to a boil, and cook for 1–2 minutes. Some of the skins will start to split, telling you they're ready. Drain and let cool. When cool, peel the skins off and chop (or keep whole and mash with a potato masher if you prefer).

In a large sauté pan, add olive oil and chopped garlic. Cook over medium-high heat just until garlic begins to sizzle. Do not try to brown it—you want it soft. Add tomatoes, wine, honey, salt, and a few grindings of fresh pepper. Bring to a medium simmer, reduce heat to medium, and cook uncovered for about 25 minutes. Taste for salt and remove from heat. Put basil leaves in food processor and chop. Add sauce and blend. You will have a lovely smooth sauce that will cling to slender pasta like capellini and spaghettini. If you prefer a chunky sauce, don't bother with the food processor. Tear or chop your basil leaves instead and toss them in when sauce has finished cooking. Serve with any pasta of your choice.

MAKES ABOUT 2 ½ CUPS

4 cups ripe fresh tomatoes (preferably Italian plum)

1/2 cup olive oil

6 cloves garlic, minced fine (don't be alarmed, the poaching sweetens it)

2 Tbsp. dry white wine (optional)

1 Tbsp. honey

1/2 tsp. salt

black pepper

1 large bunch of basil, leaves thoroughly washed and dried (you can add up to 2 cups)

Spaghettini with Spicy Eggplant

*I love fried eggplant. My grandmother Catherene used to batter fry it and serve it hot
with a little sea salt sprinkled on top. It was heaven. This recipe is a slightly more health
savvy version, but it has that same fabulous fried eggplant flavor that I can still recall from
my early childhood. You may prepare the sauce (excluding the parsley) up to a day in advance,
and then reheat it when you cook the pasta, adding the parsley at the very end.*

1 large eggplant

canola oil for frying

1 lb. spaghettini (thin spaghetti made
from rice, quinoa, corn, regular durum
wheat if allowed, etc.)

3 cups The Lady from Naples Red Sauce
(p. 69) or store-bought red sauce

chili pepper flakes

1/4 cup chopped parsley

salt and fresh pepper

Peel and slice eggplant horizontally into 1/4-inch rounds.
Place colander in sink, and add eggplant rounds, being sure
to lay them out in a single layer. Use two colanders if necessary. Salt the eggplant thoroughly. Let sweat about
1 hour. Lay out paper towel on a counter, place eggplant
on paper towel and pat dry with more paper towel. Pour
enough canola oil into a frying pan to come up the sides
1½ inches. Over medium-high heat, when oil is hot, slip in
eggplant. Be careful not to overcrowd, as you don't want
the eggplant overlapping. Cook until golden brown on one
side, flip, and cook on other side. Remove with slotted
spoon to a platter covered in paper towel to drain off excess
oil. Cover with another layer of paper towel. Blot gently.
When cooled enough to handle, slice into strips
with a sharp knife.

Boil water for pasta. While pasta is cooking, heat The
Lady from Naples Red Sauce in a pan, add chili pepper
flakes to taste, and sliced eggplant. When pasta is cooked
to al dente, and sauce is hot, remove from heat, stir in
chopped parsley, toss with pasta in a large bowl, and serve.
You may wish to add a little more salt and some freshly
ground pepper.

MAKES 6–8 SERVINGS

Note: If you wish, you may wait to add the chili pepper
flakes individually to your plates.

Penne with Cauliflower and Olives

This dish makes a light, simple dinner. If you like, you may prepare the sauce several hours in advance, doing everything but adding the parsley. When ready to cook the pasta, gently reheat sauce, remove from heat, and then add parsley.

Cut outer leaves off cauliflower, but leave tender inner ones. Wash and cut in half. Cook in pot of boiling water about half an hour until tender but not falling apart. Drain and set aside. Put water for pasta on to boil and add pasta when boiling. Cook, following instructions on package. Meanwhile, put garlic and olive oil in a sauté pan, and cook over medium heat until garlic begins to sizzle lightly and release its fabulous garlicky scent. Add pulverized olives and continue stirring over medium heat, using the back of a wooden spoon to blend them with garlic and oil. Cook this way about 1 or 2 minutes. Add cauliflower to pan and, using a fork, quickly break it up into tiny pieces, no more than 1/4 inch in size. Use the fork to mash some into a paste. You want the pieces to be small enough that they'll cling to the pasta. At this point, you may want to set a little sauce aside in a bowl for the kids. Add chili pepper and sea salt to taste. Cook a few more minutes. Remove from heat and stir in chopped parsley. Toss with cooked penne.

MAKES 6–8 SERVINGS

1 head cauliflower

1 lb. of penne (rice, quinoa, corn, regular durum wheat if allowed, etc.)

1/2 cup olive oil

3 cloves garlic, minced fine

12 Italian black olives, chopped so fine they're almost paste (i.e., pulverized)

chili pepper flakes to taste (optional)

sea salt

1/4 cup chopped parsley

Pasta Primavera

*Pasta Primavera isn't actually an Italian dish—it was created here in America
at the restaurant La Cirque. However, it really took off, and now almost everyone has
his or her own version. You can make it with three or four ingredients, choosing whatever
looks freshest from the produce section or whatever is in season at the farmer's market.
For this recipe, I've listed vegetables that are readily available every season of
the year. I like to eat it with cappellini, as I think the delicate nature of the pasta picks
up the delicate flavor of the sauce. However, it's also wonderful with spiral pasta,
which is very nice leftover the next day as pasta salad.*

4 cloves garlic, minced fine

1/2 medium red onion, diced

1/3 cup olive oil

2 small zucchini, halved and cut into
half-moon pieces about 1/4 inch thick
(2 cups)

1 cup broccoli florets, cut small

1 Tbsp. white wine (or more broth instead)

2 Tbsp. low-salt chicken broth (or
vegetable broth)

1/2 tsp. salt

1 lb. cappellini or spirals (rice, quinoa, corn)

2 lbs. plum tomatoes, chopped into small
pieces (4 cups); you may choose to
blanch and peel them first (p. 71)

8 black Italian olives, cut up

1/3 cup chopped basil

freshly ground pepper

chili pepper flakes (optional)

Cook garlic, onion, and olive oil in large sauté pan over medium-high heat for about 5 minutes, stirring often. Put water on to boil for pasta. Add zucchini to sauté pan and cook, stirring often, about another 10 minutes, until zucchini has become a bit tender. Add broccoli florets, wine, chicken broth, and 1/4 tsp. salt, and sauté about 2 or 3 more minutes. Put cappellini in to cook following instructions on package. Add chopped tomatoes and olives to sauté pan. Cook about 1 more minute just until tomatoes are warm. Turn off heat and stir in basil, remaining 1/4 tsp. salt, and freshly ground pepper. Drain pasta, pour into a bowl and toss with sauce. Serve with more freshly ground pepper, and chili pepper flakes if you like it more highly seasoned.

SERVES 6–8

Linguine with Mock White Clam Sauce

I've always been a big fan of linguine with clam sauce, so I decided to make up a mock version. It really tastes very much like the original, and is probably better for you too. You can adjust the amount of chili pepper flakes as you wish for children.

Toast bread crumbs in oven or toaster oven until lightly golden, and set aside. Put pasta water on to boil. When it boils, add pasta. Meanwhile, cook olive oil, garlic, chili pepper flakes, and half the parsley in a sauté pan over medium heat, stirring frequently for a couple of minutes. Do not burn the garlic. Add the wine and cook a minute or two more, stirring constantly to reduce the wine a bit. Remove from heat and stir in salt. Drizzle bottom of pasta bowl with a little more olive oil. Drain pasta when cooked, and pour into bowl. Toss with sauce, add other half of parsley and bread crumbs, making sure all pasta is well coated. Serve with sautéed zucchini or a nice green leaf salad with Red Wine Vinaigrette (p. 48) or My Favorite Dressing (p. 45).

SERVES 6–8

1/2 cup brown-rice bread crumbs (or other allowed fine unseasoned bread crumbs)
1 lb. linguine (rice, quinoa, corn, regular durum wheat if allowed, etc.)
6 Tbsp. olive oil
3–4 cloves garlic, minced fine
1/4–1/2 tsp. chili pepper flakes
6 Tbsp. chopped parsley, divided
1/2 cup dry white wine
1/2 tsp. salt (more or less to taste, but this dish really does need salt)

Royal Fusilli with Asparagus, Fresh Peas, and Tomatoes

*I used to make this with pine nuts, fresh Mozzarella, and lots of fresh Parmesan.
I realized that if I just upped the olive oil and salt quota a tiny notch, it would taste
just as fabulous without these allergenic ingredients. This can be eaten hot
or cold. It's great for lunch, dinner, or a snack. I often make it in large
quantities and serve it at outdoor parties. It's **really** easy.*

1 lb. royal fusilli, or regular fusilli, or spirals
(rice, quinoa, corn, regular durum wheat
if allowed, etc.)
2/3 cup olive oil
4 cloves garlic, minced fine
1 bunch asparagus cut into 1/2-inch pieces
(about 2 cups)
1/2 dry pint cherry tomatoes, halved or
quartered, depending on their size
(1½ cups)
1 cup fresh peas
1/2 tsp. chili pepper flakes
1/4 tsp. sea salt
1 large bunch basil, chopped (about
2 cups packed)
fresh ground pepper

Put water on to boil for pasta. While pasta is cooking according to instructions on package, heat olive oil and garlic in large sauté pan over medium heat. Cook about 2 minutes, stirring until just slightly golden. Add asparagus. Bring heat up to medium-high, and cook, stirring frequently, about 4 or 5 minutes. Add tomatoes, peas, chili pepper, and salt. Cook about 2 minutes more. Remove from heat. Stir in basil. Drizzle bottom of pasta bowl with more olive oil. Pour in pasta, top with sauce, and toss gently. Add a few grindings of fresh pepper.

MAKES 6–8 SERVINGS

Note: After cooking the asparagus, you may wish to add the cherry tomatoes, cook 1 minute, and remove some sauce for the kids or grownups who can't eat chili peppers or peas. Add a little basil and salt to theirs separately. Then proceed with the rest of the dish.

Spaghetti with Turkey Meatballs

Whenever my husband is feeling blue and I ask him what he'd especially like for dinner, he inevitably says spaghetti with meatballs. I think it might just be our all-time favorite comfort food. If you wish, you can prepare the meatballs and sauce ahead of time and then just rewarm them when you cook your pasta.

Combine corn flakes and rice/oat milk in a large bowl. Let sit 10 minutes. Add turkey, garlic, onion, oregano, parsley, olive oil, salt, and pepper. Combine, and roll mixture into small balls about 1 inch in diameter. You should have about 35–40 meatballs. Heat the red sauce to a simmer in a large pan, then add the meatballs and cook over low heat, loosely covered, for about 1 hour, stirring very gently once or twice. In last 15 minutes of cooking, put on water to boil and cook your pasta. Put a little olive oil in the bottom of your pasta bowl, pour in cooked pasta, and toss. Pour the meatballs and sauce over the pasta, sprinkle with chopped basil, toss gently, and serve.

SERVES 6–8

1/3 cup crushed corn flakes
1/4 cup rice or oat milk
1⅓ lbs. ground turkey meat
2 cloves garlic, minced fine (or
    1 shallot, minced fine)
1/2 onion, minced
1/2 tsp. oregano
1/4 cup chopped parsley
2 Tbsp. olive oil
1/2 tsp. salt
pepper
3 ½ cups The Lady from Naples Red Sauce
    (p. 69) or store-bought red sauce
1 lb. spaghetti (rice, quinoa, corn, regular
    durum wheat if allowed, etc.)
chopped basil

Rigatoni with Italian Sausage, Peppers, and Onions

This is a fun, colorful, and filling dish, which is equally tasty
as leftovers the next day. You may prepare the sauce several hours
in advance and then rewarm it when ready to cook the pasta.

2 large bell peppers, 1 red and
   1 yellow or orange

1/4 cup olive oil

1 onion, chopped (1 cup)

2 cloves garlic, minced

1/2 tsp. oregano

1 lb. Italian sausage (Murray's
   Chicken Sausage is also great),
   cut into 1/2-inch pieces

salt and pepper

1½ cups crushed or chopped canned tomatoes

1 lb. of rigatoni (rice, quinoa, corn,
   regular durum wheat if allowed, etc.)

1 Tbsp. balsamic vinegar

Wash, core, and deseed the peppers. Cut into 1-inch squares. Put olive oil, onion, and garlic in large pan. Sauté over medium-high heat until soft, stirring often. Add the sausage and oregano, and cook until sausage browns a bit, stirring often, about 5 minutes. Add peppers and cook about 8 minutes, stirring gently once in awhile. Put water on to boil for pasta. Add salt and pepper and tomatoes to sauce. Turn heat to medium and cook at a simmer. Meanwhile put rigatoni in to cook. After sauce has cooked 10 minutes, add balsamic vinegar. Cook another 10 minutes or so. Toss with pasta and serve with fresh ground pepper.

MAKES 6–8 SERVINGS

Spirals with Grilled Vegetables (and Chicken)

*This is a healthy rustic dish that is great hot or cold. Feel free to prepare the sauce
or even the whole dish up to a day in advance of serving it.*

Cut grilled vegetables into bite-sized pieces. Combine with red sauce (and chicken, if using) and heat. Boil pasta. Drain, and toss with sauce and vegetables. Top with chopped parsley or basil.

SERVES 6–8

1 lb. fusilli or spiral pasta (rice, corn, quinoa, regular durum wheat if allowed, etc.)

1 recipe Grilled Vegetables (p. 58) minus the balsamic vinegar and parsley

2 cups The Lady from Naples Red Sauce (p. 69) or store-bought red sauce

chopped parsley or basil

1 cup cubed grilled chicken (optional)

Tagliatelle with Bolognese Ragu

*This sauce is simple, but time-consuming. You may wish to double it and freeze
half to save yourself time on another meal. It freezes very well, and when refrigerated,
is even better the second day. This sauce can be made hours or even a couple
days before using it. I try to avoid beef as much as possible, so I usually make
this dish with ground turkey and ground pork, which are lower in saturated fats.
But if you prefer beef, by all means use that instead.*

1 lb. tagliatelle or ziti (rice, quinoa, corn,
   regular durum wheat if allowed, etc.)

olive oil for tossing with cooked pasta

Bolognese Ragu:

2 carrots, peeled and chopped

2 stalks celery, chopped

1 medium onion, minced fine (1 cup)

2 oz. pancetta, diced small (or nitrite-
   free bacon)

6 Tbsp. olive oil

1 lb. ground turkey

1/2 lb. ground pork

salt and pepper

1 cup rice milk

1/8 tsp. ground nutmeg

1/8 tsp. cinnamon

1 cup dry white wine

1 28-oz. can crushed tomatoes

Sauté carrots, celery, onion, and pancetta with olive oil in large heavy pot over medium heat about 5 minutes, until onions are soft and pancetta has released its fat a bit. Add turkey and pork, an ample sprinkling of salt, and a few grindings of fresh pepper. Cook until meat has lost its pink color, breaking it up with the back of a spoon. Add the rice milk and simmer until it has mostly evaporated. Add the nutmeg and cinnamon. Then add the wine and also let it evaporate. Add the tomatoes. Bring to a simmer and cook over lowest possible heat for 3 hours, uncovered. Stir about every 20 minutes. Add a little water as necessary because it may begin to dry out. You want this sauce quite thick so only add a little water at a time. If you can't cook it for 3 hours at once, you may turn it off and finish cooking when convenient. However, it must cook the full 3 hours to have the right flavor. When ready to serve, put water on to boil for pasta. Cook pasta according to instructions on package, drain, and toss with a little olive oil to coat. Serve individual portions topped with sauce.

SERVES 6–8

Polenta Radiatore with Prosciutto, Shiitake Mushrooms, and Spinach

The smokiness of the prosciutto in this recipe blends wonderfully with the shiitake mushrooms and spinach. I like to use multi-colored pasta made with spinach, beets, and tomatoes as it makes a lovely colorful bowl when combined with the other ingredients. Polenta pasta (or corn pasta) is never going to be al dente, but you should still avoid overcooking it, as it has a tendency to fall apart, making mush—appreciated by the one-year-old, but not by the grown-ups at the table. If you don't feel like taking the trouble to make your red sauce from scratch, you can use a very basic store-bought red sauce, but read the ingredients carefully. It should have little more than tomatoes, garlic, olive oil, and some herbs. Polenta and corn pasta usually come as radiatore, but this dish can also be made with any other type of short pasta. I love to make a one-dish dinner if I can get away with it, and this dish covers all the bases.

Put a large pot of water on to boil. Dice up prosciutto. Add the olive oil to a pan over medium-high heat. Add prosciutto and sauté until slightly crisped. Add shiitake mushrooms. Sauté until just cooked, but not browned. Add tomato sauce. Warm. Add spinach. Stir gently, cooking down the spinach until wilted. Cover and remove from heat. The water should be boiling by now. Add polenta pasta. Stir occasionally to keep from sticking. When pasta is cooked, drain. Put a little olive oil in the bottom of the pasta bowl, add the pasta, toss with the sauce and serve.

MAKES 6 SERVINGS

12 oz. polenta pasta or corn pasta

2 large slices nitrite-free prosciutto

1 Tbsp. olive oil

2 cups sliced shiitake mushrooms

2 1/2 cups Simple Red Sauce (p. 70)
   or store-bought red sauce

4 heaping cups fresh baby spinach, washed
   and dried

olive oil for the pasta bowl

Lasagna with Eggplant, Portobello Mushrooms, and Fresh Tomatoes

I refuse to forsake baked pasta dishes just because I can't have dairy. I created this lovely lasagna to use up fresh tomatoes from my neighbor, and was thrilled to discover that I liked it just as much as the high-fat version from the old days. You may substitute other vegetables if you wish, but I find that meatier vegetables such as eggplant and Portobello mushrooms add depth to the dish, which is more necessary when cooking without cheese. Ideally, you should make this the night before to really let it set.

1 medium eggplant, peeled and sliced into
    1/4-inch rounds

8 oz. rice lasagna (or corn, quinoa,
    or regular durum wheat if allowed)

2 cups enriched rice or oat milk, hot

1/4 cup olive oil

1/4 cup + 2 Tbsp. oat or rice flour

pinch of ground nutmeg

bay leaf

fresh ground pepper

2 large Portobello mushrooms, sliced
    into 1/4-inch strips

12 shiitake or white mushrooms, sliced

3 ripe medium tomatoes, deseeded and
    sliced into thin rounds (really important
    to drain as much as possible)

4 cups red sauce, either The Lady from
    Naples Red Sauce (p. 69) or store-
    bought red sauce

20 basil leaves

brown-rice bread crumbs or corn-flake
    crumbs (or other allowed bread crumbs)

3 or 4 more Tbsp. olive oil

salt

Preheat oven to 350 degrees. Cook sliced eggplant in microwave about 2 minutes, until just tender. Set aside. Cook lasagna according to directions on box. While pasta is cooking, make a cream sauce. Start by warming your rice/oat milk. Then heat the olive oil in a saucepan over medium heat, stir in oat flour, and cook 2 minutes, stirring continuously. Don't burn. Add heated rice/oat milk slowly while stirring. Add pinch of nutmeg and bay leaf. Bring to simmer, then reduce heat to low and thicken, still stirring (10 minutes or so). When cream sauce has thickened, re - move from heat, and grind in a few turns of fresh pepper. Put about 1 Tbsp. olive oil in bottom of lasagna pan. Cover bottom of pan with half the eggplant. Cover eggplant with mushrooms, then sliced tomatoes. Cover vegetables with 1½ cups red sauce. Spread out 10 of the basil leaves. Drizzle with half of cream sauce. Cover with a layer of lasagna noo- dles. Sprinkle about 1 Tbsp. olive oil over noodles. Layer the vegetables, another 1½ cups red sauce, basil, and cream sauce again. Top with lasagna noodles. Drizzle final cup of red sauce, sprinkle with bread crumbs, and drizzle with a lit- tle more olive oil. Bake uncovered about 1 hour. Remove from oven and let cool completely before serving, ideally overnight; otherwise, just let it come to room temperature to set, or you'll have a soupy mess. Cut into portions with sharp serrated knife.

MAKES ABOUT 8 SERVINGS

Porcini Mushroom Risotto

Risotto gets a bad rap. It's really not as daunting as it seems. In fact, it's quite simple—it just takes time, usually about 40 minutes. But look at it this way: It's a good arm workout, and the end results are worth every stir. This recipe is packed full of rich flavor, so much so you won't even notice the lack of Parmesan cheese. Our son Lennon loves this dish, and gets a good chuckle out of the grandparents for his sophisticated little palette.

Soak the mushrooms in the water at least 30 minutes. Lift mushrooms out by hand, squeezing as much water as possible out of them, letting the water flow back into the bowl to be saved for cooking later. Rinse the mushrooms in a strainer, making sure to wash away any soil. Pat dry in paper towels and chop. Strain the mushroom-soaking water and set aside to use later. Bring the chicken broth to a slow steady simmer. In a nice sturdy pot, add the olive oil and chopped onion and heat on medium-high. Cook, stirring the onion until it becomes translucent, then add rice. Stir quickly until all the grains are well coated and glossy. Add 1/2 cup (I use a ladle) of the simmering chicken broth and cook, stirring constantly with a long wooden spoon until all broth has been absorbed. Don't stop stirring. When there's no more liquid in the pot, add another 1/2 cup of broth and repeat, stirring constantly. Continue this process for 10 minutes. After 10 minutes, add the reconstituted mushrooms and half their soaking water. Continue stirring and when the water has been absorbed, add the other half of the soaking water. Once this has evaporated, add 1/2 cup of wine and, stirring constantly, let this evaporate. Finish cooking rice by alternately adding 1/2 cups of wine and chicken broth. Cook the rice until it's tender, but still firm (not mushy) and all the liquid has been absorbed. You may wind up with leftover wine and broth, or you may run out and have to start adding water. It depends on the brand of rice. Once the rice is cooked, take the pot off the heat and add a few grindings of fresh pepper. Salt to taste. Stir in the chopped parsley and serve. Top individual portions with a little extra virgin olive oil.

MAKES 6 SERVINGS

1 oz. dried Porcini mushrooms (about 1 cup)
2 cups barely warm water for reconstituting mushrooms
4 cups chicken broth
1/4 cup olive oil
1 small yellow onion, finely chopped
2 cups Arborio or other imported risotto rice
2 cups white wine (or more broth instead)
sea salt and fresh pepper to taste
4 Tbsp. chopped fresh parsley
good quality extra virgin olive oil to drizzle at end (optional)

Asparagus Leek Risotto

This lovely green-hued risotto is light, fresh, and summery.

6 cups chicken broth

3 shallots, minced fine

1/4 cup olive oil

5 leeks, chopped (wash well and
    cut off tops and bottoms)

2 cups Arborio or other imported
    risotto rice

1/2 cup white wine

2 cups asparagus, chopped into
    1/4-inch pieces

1 cup fresh basil, chopped or torn,
    with a few whole leaves reserved
    for decoration

sea salt and fresh pepper to taste

good quality extra virgin olive oil to drizzle
    at end (optional)

Put chicken broth in a pan and heat to a very slow simmer. Put shallots and olive oil in a large heavy pot and cook over medium-high heat about 2 minutes, stirring. Add chopped leeks and stir, cooking until leeks wilt and become somewhat translucent. Add rice and stir quickly until all the grains are well coated and glossy. Add white wine and stir until absorbed. When absorbed, add a ladle full of chicken broth. Stir continuously until absorbed. Add another ladle full. Repeat process, stirring constantly for about 20 minutes. Then add chopped asparagus and two ladles full of broth. Stir until liquid is absorbed. Add another ladle full of broth. Repeat this process until you've used up all the broth, about another 10 minutes. Test to see if done. Rice should be tender but still firm. When cooked, remove from heat; stir in chopped basil, salt (don't scrimp on salt, this dish needs it, especially without the saltiness of cheese), and a few grindings of fresh pepper. Spoon into bowls or plates, drizzle with a little bit of extra virgin olive oil, and top with a basil leaf or two.

MAKES 6 SERVINGS

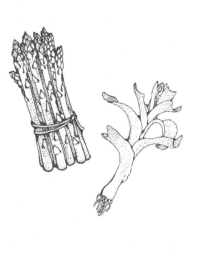

THE BENEFITS OF ORGANIC, FREE-RANGE, AND WILD MEATS

Whenever possible, buy organic, free-range, and wild meats. This shouldn't be too difficult, since virtually any meat product imaginable is now available as certified organic. Supermarkets and health food stores carry organic poultry, beef, pork, lamb, sausages, and deli meats. Why buy organic? Because cer-tified organic poultry and meat products are premium quality meats that combine the benefits of great taste with the safety assurance that they've been raised and processed according to strict USDA Organic guidelines.

Unlike conventional meat producers, organic farmers use sustainable practices. Organic and free-range meats come from livestock that have been raised without antibiotic-laced feed, without feed containing animal by-products (which has been linked to Mad Cow Disease in beef), and without synthetic hormones. They are fed only 100 percent certified organic feed or grass grown without the pesticides and fertilizers that are so harmful to our environment and us. Cer-tified organic meat is meat that has *not* been processed with chemical additives and preservatives like phosphates and sodium nitrites.

All certified organic meat also comes from livestock that have been raised humanely. They are raised in uncrowded living conditions with access to the outdoors. Wild meat has all the same benefits of farm-raised organic and free-range meat, with the add-itional benefit of generally being leaner and thus lower in fat.

Game

Wild or farm-raised game is a festive alternative to the everyday staples of chicken, beef, and pork. Game is generally leaner than the meats most Americans are used to and often has a richer flavor. All of the recipes for game are full flavored but, I promise you, none of them are *gamey*. I am not a fan of gamey meat, and wouldn't put it off on anyone else. These recipes are for succulent, robust, yet delicate game.

Breaded Chicken Cutlets with Roasted Red Peppers

This dish is the first meal my husband ever made for me. We'd only just started dating, when he invited me over to his apartment for dinner one night. I didn't expect him to really cook, but lo and behold, I arrived to the sight of him removing the skins from freshly roasted peppers. He went all out, doing the whole darn thing from scratch. It was a truly delicious meal, and cooking it for me was just one of the many ways in which he won my heart. Now, if you're short on time, and aren't trying to woo somebody, you can just buy preroasted peppers from any Italian deli or the supermarket, and doctor them up a bit following the recipe below. Or, you can make them up to several days in advance and refrigerate them tightly covered. If you do this, bring them to room temperature before serving.

Peppers:
3 red bell peppers
olive oil to coat them
1 Tbsp. olive oil
1 tsp. balsamic vinegar

Chicken:
1½ cups corn-flake crumbs (made from 3 cups corn flakes pulsed into crumbs in the food processor or blender—don't use the premade ones, they're too soggy)
2 tsp. oregano
1/2 tsp. cayenne pepper (or less if for young children)
1/2 tsp. salt
1/2 tsp. poultry seasoning (or 1/4 tsp. dried thyme and 1/4 tsp. dried sage)
fresh ground black pepper
3 Tbsp. oat milk mixed with 6 Tbsp. olive oil (blend well with a whisk or fork)
1/2 cup oat flour
1½ lbs. chicken breast cutlets, pounded thin
3 Tbsp. olive oil for baking

Rub peppers with olive oil and put in broiling pan under broiler, until charred. Turn them about every 5 minutes. Once they've cooked about 20 minutes and are nicely charred, remove from under the broiler and put into a paper bag folded over at the top to steam. After they've steamed about 10 or 15 minutes, remove them from the bag, deseed and skin them, then slice into strips about 1/4 inch thick. Combine in a bowl with the olive oil and balsamic vinegar. Set aside.

Preheat oven to 425 degrees. Line a baking sheet with aluminum foil and preheat in oven. Combine corn-flake crumbs with seasoning in a large shallow bowl. Combine oat milk and olive oil, blending well in a shallow bowl or plate. Put oat flour in a zip-top plastic bag. Add chicken cutlets to the bag and shake to coat. Remove one at a time, shaking off extra flour. Turn cutlet in olive oil/oat milk mixture, then roll in corn-flake crumbs, using your fingers to press the crumbs in. Put on a plate. Once you've breaded all the cutlets, remove preheated baking sheet from oven, add 3 Tbsp. olive oil on top of foil, and tilt to coat completely. Place cutlets on baking sheet. Cook for 10 minutes, flip and cook 10 minutes more. Serve topped with roasted peppers. Eat with New Potatoes with Parsley (p. 141) or Brown Rice with Celery and Mushrooms (p. 147) and Endive, Radicchio, and Arugula Salad (p. 50).

SERVES 4–6

Grilled Chicken Breasts with Mango Salsa

*I first learned about combining fruit and chili peppers from an amazing Caribbean chef
who must remain anonymous due to his status as an illegal alien. Sadly for the culinary
community, this fantastic chef gets deported every couple of years. I am also not at liberty
to name the restaurant where we worked, but I will say, this chef was making dynamite
salsas before salsa ever became popular. He was truly an innovative chef, in the vein of
Nobu Matsuhisa, making divine combinations like New Zealand Green-Lipped Mussels
steamed in Bass Ale with shallots, lemon grass, and scotch bonnet chili peppers.
(I'll save that recipe for another book if I ever eat shellfish again.) The following recipe
is inspired by the cooking of my notoriously criminal friend. It is simple, quick, low calorie,
and packed full of flavor. You can prepare the Mango Salsa a day in advance if you like.
If you do this, bring the salsa to room temperature before serving. Please note that you may
also broil the chicken if you don't have a grill handy.*

Put minced onion in a bowl and microwave 1 minute to
cook slightly. If you don't have a microwave, do it on the
stove in a small pan with a little bit of olive oil over a
medium heat until just slightly cooked. Combine onion,
mango, cherry tomatoes, olive oil, lime juice, and cilantro.
Mix. At this point you may wish to set a little bit of salsa
aside for the kids, before adding the chili pepper. Add chili
pepper. Set aside covered. Pound chicken breasts to desired
thinness, drizzle with olive oil, sprinkle with salt and pepper,
and then squeeze half a lime over them. Make sure they're
all well coated. Grill about 10 minutes total (a little more
if on the thick side). You may also broil the chicken. If using
a broiler, place breasts in broiling pan and cook under
broiler on high. When done, remove from heat,
plate, and spoon room-temperature salsa over each breast.
Serve with Potato Chips (p. 140) or Saffron Jasmine Rice
(p. 145) and a salad.

SERVES 4–6

Chicken:
2 lbs. chicken breasts, pounded thin
olive oil
salt
fresh pepper
juice of 1/2 lime

Mango Salsa:
1/2 red onion, minced
2 cups diced fresh mango (1 or 2 mangos,
   depending on size of fruit)
1/2 cup cherry tomatoes, cut into quarters
2 Tbsp. olive oil
juice of 1 lime
1/4 cup chopped fresh cilantro
1 chili pepper (jalapeno, habañero, scotch
   bonnet, etc.), chopped fine, or 1/4 red
   bell pepper

Chicken Marsala

Double if you want leftovers or have a bunch of hearty eaters.

1/3 cup oat flour
salt and pepper
1/3 cup olive oil
1 lb. thin chicken breast cutlets
1/4 cup diced nitrite-free prosciutto
8 oz. sliced mushrooms
1 cup sweet Marsala

Preheat oven to 250 degrees. Put oat flour on plate and season with salt and pepper. Heat olive oil over medium-high heat in large sauté pan until really hot, almost smoking and starting to ripple. Meanwhile, dredge chicken in flour, shaking off any extra. Put in pan once really hot (but not burning), and cook until golden, a couple of minutes per side. Don't overcrowd the pan; you will probably have to cook in two batches. Transfer to a baking dish and keep warm in oven. Add mushrooms and prosciutto to pan. Reduce heat to medium and cook until mushrooms are softened and prosciutto has crisped up a bit. Add Marsala to pan and deglaze by using a spatula to scrape up any bits that have stuck to the side, stirring to reconstitute them. Reduce liquid at a steady simmer, stirring frequently about 7 minutes until sauce has thickened. Add chicken back to pan and turn in sauce.

SERVES 2–4

Greek-style Chicken with Lemon and Oregano

This dish is about as simple as it gets. It's fantastic any season, and can be eaten hot or cold.
And it's perfect comfort food when you're feeling under the weather.

Preheat oven to 350 degrees. Combine everything but chicken and lemon slices. Put chicken in baking dish or roasting pan, skin side down. Pour sauce over it. Cook 30 minutes, basting once. Flip and cook 30–40 minutes more, basting a couple of times. Place under broiler for 2 minutes at the end to crisp up skin if necessary. Garnish with lemon slices. Serve with brown rice or Potato Chips (p. 140) and a Greek Salad (p. 52) or steamed green vegetable.

SERVES 4

3-lb. chicken, quartered
1/2 cup olive oil
juice of 2 lemons
3 large garlic cloves, minced
2 tsp. oregano
1/2 tsp. salt
1/2 tsp. pepper
lemon slices

Beer-Battered Chicken Nuggets

*This dish is extremely tasty, and incredibly easy to make. It's great for kids and grownups
alike. I make up a batch and freeze half, reheating a few at a time as lunch for Lennon.
The alcohol cooks out, so don't worry about getting your little ones drunk. This batter tastes
like the fish-and-chips batter I've eaten in England. You can coat basically anything
you like with it, but I think it's best with chicken.*

1½ lbs. chicken breast

1 12-oz. bottle wheat-free beer

1⅓ cup oat flour

2/3 cup barley flour

1 tsp. double-acting baking powder

2 cups canola oil for frying (most gets
poured off at the end)

sea salt and pepper

Open beer and pour into a glass. Let go flat a bit (about
1 hour). Cut chicken into 1½-inch cubes. Combine beer,
oat flour, barley flour, and baking powder. Add chicken
to batter. Heat canola oil in large pan (it should come
up sides about 1 inch) over medium-high heat. Once oil
is *really* hot (the oil looks like it's separating and moving),
add some of the chicken. You will have to cook in batches.
Cook until crispy on bottom and flip, using tongs. Once
cooked, gently lay out on a paper bag or paper towels
to drain off the excess oil. Sprinkle with sea salt and a
few grindings of pepper (pepper optional). Serve with
Grandmother Catherene's Cornbread (p. 21) or Mashed
Potatoes (p. 141) and baby spinach with Carrot Ginger
Dressing (p. 47).

SERVES 6

Tip

There are several good wheat-free,
gluten-free beers on the market. Bard's
and Redbridge are both easy to find.

Chicken Pot Pie with Biscuit Crust

*Almost nothing pleases me more than a one-pot meal, and Chicken Pot Pie is just
the kind of casserole I'm talking about. Eat this dish on a cold winter's night
and your whole family will feel snuggly warm, happy, and full.*

Preheat oven to 450 degrees. If you don't have leftover cooked chicken and potatoes, poach whole boneless chicken breasts along with cubed potato in enough water to fully cover, and boil until cooked, about 15 minutes. Drain and cut up chicken. Set aside. In large sauté pan, lightly sauté onion, carrots, and celery in olive oil until just tender. Set aside. In large oven-safe casserole, make the roux by heating 1/4 cup olive oil over medium-high heat. Add flour and cook, stirring, about 2 minutes. Add the chicken broth and rice milk and cook, stirring, until it thickens into a nice rich cream sauce. Once it's done this, turn off heat, add salt and pepper to taste and a little bit of lemon juice. In a large casserole, combine the roux, the cooked chicken and potatoes, the sautéed onion, carrots, and celery, the corn and the parsley. Season with salt and pepper and add 1 Tbsp. lemon juice. Let cool a bit. While it's cooling, make the Basic Biscuits and cut into 2-inch rounds. Use biscuits to cover the top of the casserole, overlapping biscuits a bit if necessary. If you have extra, cook them on a lightly greased cookie sheet along with the pot pie. Bake about 30 minutes until biscuits are nice and golden and pot pie is really bubbling up.

SERVES 6

1 recipe Basic Biscuits (p. 20)
1½ lbs. cooked chicken, cut into
    bite-sized pieces (about 3 cups)
1 medium potato, cut into 1/2-inch cubes
    and cooked (about 1½ cups)
1 medium onion, diced (about 1½ cups)
2 carrots, chopped
2 stalks celery, chopped
2 Tbsp. olive oil
1/2 cup corn (frozen, canned, or fresh)
1/3 cup chopped parsley
1 Tbsp. lemon juice
salt and pepper

Roux:
1/4 cup olive oil
1/4 cup oat flour (or other flour of choice)
1 cup rice milk
1 cup chicken broth
salt and pepper
squeeze of lemon juice

Variation

If you don't feel like making biscuits, top pie with mashed potatoes from Shepherd's Pie recipe (p. 98).

Marinated Chicken Skewers with Pineapple and Onion

My best friend, Tracy, made this aromatic and lovely dish for me one night when she kindly attempted to cook a hypoallergenic meal (her first one ever). I've upped the spices a bit because I like a lot of flavor in my marinades, but you may adapt it as you prefer.

Marinade:
1 cup tightly packed cilantro
1 cup olive oil
1/2 cup raisins
juice of a lemon
2 tsp. garam masala
5 cloves garlic
salt and pepper

Skewers:
2 lbs. chicken breast, cut into
   1¹/₂-inch cubes
2 Vidalia onions (or yellow onions),
   cut into chunks
6 cups pineapple chunks, fresh or canned

Blend all marinade ingredients in a food processor. Place chicken in bowl, combine with marinade and refrigerate, overnight if possible, but doing it in the morning is okay too. When ready to cook, start by putting a piece of onion on the skewer, followed by chicken, then pineapple, then onion, then chicken, and so on. Once you've completed the skewers, place in broiling pan, brush skewers with remaining marinade to coat the pineapple and onion, and broil on high. Turn every 5 minutes or so until crispy on all sides. Ovens vary in heat, so you'll need to keep a close watch. After about 10 minutes, check for doneness by cutting into a piece of chicken. It should not be pink. When cooked, remove and serve with Coconut Rice (p. 146), Curried Rice with Raisins (p. 147), or Rice Pilaf (p. 148), spooning sauce over the top. This is wonderful with a green-leaf salad with My Favorite Dressing (p. 45).

SERVES 6

Note: If you are using wooden skewers, soak them in warm water for at least 30 minutes before using to prevent them from burning.

Roast Chicken with Root Vegetables

This whole roast chicken is an attractive and hearty dinner for a weekend night. It's great in the colder months, but can also be eaten at room temperature during spring and summer.

Preheat oven to 375 degrees. Wash and dry chicken. Sprinkle cavity with salt. Combine garlic, thyme, olive oil, lemon zest, salt, and pepper. Loosen chicken skin with fingers and use two Tbsp. of the marinade to season chicken under the skin, working it in as much as possible. Place chicken on a rack in a roasting pan. Toss yam, carrots, turnips, rutabaga, and onion in remaining marinade, coating well. Put vegetables in oven in a separate baking dish, one layer deep. Cook chicken and vegetables 30 minutes at 375 degrees. Then turn down heat to 325 degrees. After the first 30 minutes, begin basting the chicken and tossing the vegetables every 20 minutes, and cook about 1 hour more, for a total cooking time of 1½ hours. Test for doneness by pricking thigh; if juices run clear and the joints are loose when you twist, your chicken is generally done. If you prefer to use a meat thermometer to check poultry for doneness, it should read 185 degrees for well done. Remove chicken from oven and let rest about 10–15 minutes loosely covered with tented aluminum foil before carving. Meanwhile, toss vegetables with olive oil, balsamic vinegar, and chopped parsley. Serve with carved chicken, spooning pan juices over chicken and vegetables. Eat with a light green salad or other green vegetable.

SERVES 4–6

4 lb. chicken

2 large cloves garlic, minced fine

3 tsp. fresh minced thyme, or
    1½ tsp. dried

1/3 cup olive oil

grated zest of one lemon (about 2 tsp.)

1/4 tsp. salt

1/4 tsp. pepper

1 large yam, peeled and cut into
    1/2-inch pieces

2 carrots, peeled and cut into
    3/4-inch pieces

2 turnips, peeled and cut into 8 wedges
    each

1/2 medium rutabaga, peeled and cut into
    1-inch cubes

1 red onion, cut into 12 wedges

1 Tbsp. olive oil for tossing at end

1 Tbsp. balsamic vinegar for tossing at end

2 Tbsp. chopped parsley for tossing at end

Chicken Cacciatore

*This is an easy no-brainer meal. You can throw it in the oven and
do homework with the kids or, better yet, go take a bath!*

3½ –4½ lbs. chicken pieces

1 Tbsp. olive oil (more as necessary)

1 tsp. poultry seasoning (or 1/2 tsp. sage
and 1/2 tsp. thyme)

1/2 cup white wine

4 carrots, peeled and cut into 1/2-inch
pieces

1 onion, cut into about 10 wedges

12 mushrooms, cut into halves

8 black olives

2 cups The Lady from Naples Red Sauce (p.
69) or store-bought red sauce

2 cups chopped canned tomatoes

salt and pepper

Preheat oven to 350 degrees. Wash and pat dry chicken pieces. Sprinkle with salt and pepper. Heat olive oil over medium-high heat in oven-safe casserole. Brown chicken pieces skin side down, about 4 or 5 minutes. Sprinkle with 1/2 tsp. poultry seasoning, reserving the rest for later. Flip chicken and cook other side until slightly browned. Remove from pan. You may have to cook the chicken in several batches. Add more olive oil as necessary. When all chicken pieces have been browned and removed from casserole, remove pan from heat and drain off all but 1 Tbsp. oil. Pour in white wine. Using a wooden spoon, scrape up browned bits that have stuck. Put the carrots, onion, mushrooms, and olives in the bottom of the casserole. Cover with the chicken pieces. Combine The Lady from Naples Red Sauce with the chopped tomatoes. Spoon over the top of the chicken. Sprinkle with salt and pepper and cover casserole. Cook covered about 1½ hours. Serve with Polenta (p. 149) or plain pasta or brown rice and a green vegetable.

SERVES 4–6

Crispy Turkey Cutlets with Chopped Arugula and Tomato Salad

This dish is light, fresh tasting, and pretty to look at. It's great for dinner and is very good the next day made into a sandwich for lunch.

Preheat oven to 425 degrees. Combine tomatoes, onion, and My Favorite Dressing. Set aside. Line a baking sheet with aluminum foil and preheat in oven. Combine corn-flake crumbs with seasoning in a large shallow bowl. Combine oat milk and olive oil, blending well in a shallow bowl or plate. Put flour in a zip-top plastic bag. Put turkey cutlets in bag with flour, and shake to coat. Remove one at a time from bag, shaking off extra flour. Turn cutlet in olive oil/oat milk mixture, then roll in corn-flake crumbs, using your fingers to press the crumbs in. Put on a plate. Once you've breaded all the cutlets, remove preheated baking sheet from oven, add the 3 Tbsp. olive oil, and tilt to coat completely. Place cutlets on baking sheet. Cook for 15 minutes, flip and cook 10 minutes more. Mix arugula with tomatoes and onions. Sprinkle with salt. Put cutlets on plates, top with salad and a few grindings of fresh pepper. Serve with Herbed Jerusalem Artichokes (p. 144) or New Potatoes with Parsley (p. 141) or brown rice. Definitely double if you want leftovers.

SERVES 2–4

Cutlets:

3/4 cup corn-flake crumbs (made from 1½ cups corn flakes crushed in the blender or food processor)

1 tsp. oregano

1/4 tsp. pepper

salt to taste

2 Tbsp. oat milk mixed with 1/4 cup olive oil

1/2 cup oat flour

4 turkey cutlets, about 4 ounces each (pounded if not thin enough)

3 Tbsp. olive oil for baking

Salad:

2 medium ripe tomatoes, chopped

1/4 red onion, minced

1/3 cup My Favorite Dressing (p. 45)

4 cups chopped arugula

salt

few grindings of fresh pepper

Turkey Meatloaf

*Meatloaf has been an American staple for decades. You can eat it for lunch or dinner.
I first tried making this dish with rice bread crumbs, but it just didn't taste right. Then
I saw Aretha Franklin on TV making some sort of chopped meat dish using Weetabix or
Wheaties, or some such thing, and a light bulb went off in my head. "Corn flakes!" I thought
to myself. Now, maybe this is an old standard in some kitchens, but I'd never cooked
with corn flakes before. But after making this, I'm absolutely sold!*

2 lbs. ground turkey

1/2 cup minced yellow or red onion

1 cup crumbled unsweetened corn flakes
(or rice flakes or oat flakes)

1¼ cups red sauce, such as The Lady from
Naples Red Sauce (p. 69), Simple Red
Sauce (p. 70), store-bought red sauce,
or chopped fresh or canned tomatoes

1½ tsp. Ener-G Egg Replacer mixed
with 2 Tbsp. water

1 tsp. salt

1/4 cup chopped parsley

black pepper to taste

ketchup, mustard, hot sauce, or
mushroom sauce

Preheat oven to 350 degrees. Mix all the ingredients in a large bowl. Pat into a greased or no-stick loaf pan, or mound into a loaf on a greased shallow baking pan. Bake for 1 hour (top should be browned, sides should just be pulling away from pan a bit, and loaf should feel firm to the touch in the center). When done, remove from oven and let stand at least 15 minutes before cutting. Serve hot with ketchup, mustard, hot sauce, or mushroom sauce, and Oven-Baked Sweet Potato Fries (p. 139) or Mashed Potatoes (p. 141). And serve leftovers cold the next day as a sandwich.

SERVES 6–8

Turkey Burgers with Caramelized Onions

Turkey Burgers are essentially the same as Turkey Meatloaf, with fewer ingredients, and they cook a lot faster. I make them when I'm feeling really lazy. The caramelized onions are simple, but they take awhile, so feel free to make them up to a couple of days in advance and keep them in the refrigerator, rewarming them just before serving. Or, if you're feeling really low-energy, you can just skip them altogether.

Cook onion in olive oil in sauté pan over lowest possible heat for 50–55 minutes, stirring every once in awhile until onions have sweated out and are soft. You will be tempted to turn up the heat, but don't. Once they are soft, turn the heat to medium and cook, stirring constantly, until onions have browned/caramelized, about 15–20 minutes. Add water or white wine and scrape off whatever residue has stuck to the sides of the pan, reconstituting it into the onions. Remove from heat and season with salt and fresh pepper.

Combine all ingredients for burger in a large bowl, mixing thoroughly, and divide into four parts. Pat into four balls. Flatten into burgers and cook by whatever method you prefer: grilled, pan-fried, or broiled. When cooked (no longer pink in the middle), top with caramelized onions, and serve with ketchup, mustard, and whatever other condiments you like. You may also wish to heat up some rolls and use them as buns. Eat with Oven-Baked Sweet Potato Fries (p. 139) or Potato Chips (p. 140) and a Common Ground Salad (p. 50).

SERVES 4

Caramelized Onions:
1 large onion, sliced thin, in rounds
   or pieces, as you prefer
2 Tbsp. olive oil
1 tsp. water or white wine
1/4 tsp. salt
freshly ground pepper

Burgers:
1¹⁄₃ lbs. ground turkey
2 Tbsp. chopped parsley
2 Tbsp. minced shallot or onion
1 tsp. Pickapepper or other hot sauce
   (optional)
salt and pepper to taste

Shepherd's Pie

Shepherd's Pie was a childhood favorite of mine and remains so to this day.
I love just about any home-style meal that tastes like it should be eaten in a pub.
My mom made this dish with ground lamb or beef, but I use ground turkey.
You may substitute as you see fit. It's so simple, and it tastes great.

Mashed Potatoes:
3 large baking potatoes (Idahos, etc.),
   peeled and cubed
3/4 cup enriched rice milk
3 Tbsp. olive oil
1/2 tsp. salt

Filling:
1 medium onion, diced
1 Tbsp. olive oil
3 carrots, chopped
4 stalks celery, chopped
1⅓ lbs. ground turkey
1 cup hot water
1/2 tsp. salt
1 bay leaf
3 whole cloves
1 Tbsp. Pickapepper or other hot sauce
   (optional)
2 Tbsp. ketchup
1 Tbsp. red wine

Preheat oven to 375 degrees. Cook potatoes in water to cover thoroughly. Make sure they're really soft. Drain, and use an electric mixer to combine with milk, olive oil, and salt. Beat until fluffy. Brown onion in 1 Tbsp. olive oil, add carrots and celery, cook briefly, then remove from pan. Add turkey and brown. When browned, add onion, carrots, and celery back in, add all other ingredients, and cover with a thick layer of mashed potatoes. Cook about 1 hour until potatoes are browned a bit on top. Serve with ketchup on the side.

SERVES 6

Tip

Try Annie's Naturals Organic Ketchup.

Roast Turkey Breast

This is an incredibly easy dinner roast, which is also great
for slicing into sandwich meat the next day.

Preheat oven to 350 degrees. Wash and pat dry turkey breast. Rub with olive oil; sprinkle all over with paprika and thyme, salt and pepper. Roast in a roasting pan on a rack, breast side up, for about 20–25 minutes per pound. I find that a 3-lb. breast takes about 1¼ hours, but all ovens run a little differently. You should baste with pan juices about every 15 minutes. When turkey is cooked to a nice crispy golden brown on top and juices run clear when pricked, remove from oven. Tent loosely with aluminum foil, and let sit about 15 minutes before carving. Serve with Caramelized Onion Gravy (p. 153); Grandmother Catherene's Cornbread (p. 21); Holiday Orange Sweet Potato Bake (p. 142); Cornbread and Wild Mushroom Stuffing (p. 152); or Sausage, Dried Fruit, and Apple Stuffing (p. 150); any kind of greens; and Dora's Cranberry Sauce (p. 151).

SERVES 4–6

3–4 lb. split breast of turkey (I prefer on-the-bone as I think it stays moist and is more tender)
3 Tbsp. olive oil
paprika
thyme
salt and pepper

Ancho Turkey Chili

*So often in life the best things are happy accidents. I usually make my chili with red wine,
but one day I didn't have any, so I threw in a beer instead. It was better than ever, and
I've never looked back. This recipe makes a nice big pot of chili so you can have some left
over. Either freeze it, or stick it in the fridge for later in the week. In fact, you can make this
a day ahead if you like. If you want it less spicy, cut back on the chili powder.*

1 large yellow onion, diced

3 cloves garlic, minced

3 Tbsp. olive oil

3 heaping tsp. ancho chili powder

1 heaping tsp. chipotle chili powder (if you
    can't find ancho and chipotle, substitute
    4 tsp. regular chili powder)

2 heaping tsp. oregano (Mexican if you can
    find it)

2 tsp. ground cumin

1½ lbs. ground turkey

kernels from 3 ears fresh corn, or
    1 15.25-oz. can

1 28-oz. can crushed tomatoes

2 15-oz. cans kidney beans (about 3 cups)

1 15-oz. can refried beans (pinto)

1 12-oz. bottle wheat-free beer
    (see p. 90 for tip on wheat-free,
    gluten-free brands)

2 diced carrots

2 Tbsp. honey

2 Tbsp. cider vinegar or red wine vinegar

1 lb. ripe chopped tomatoes

1/4–1/2 cup chopped cilantro or parsley

1/2 tsp. salt (or to taste)

Sauté diced onion and garlic in olive oil in large heavy pot over medium-high heat. Stir in chili powders, oregano, and cumin. Cook until the onions are soft and coated in the seasonings. Add the ground turkey and cook, stirring, until no longer pink. Add corn, crushed tomatoes, kidney beans, refried beans, beer, diced carrot, honey, vinegar, and salt to taste. Turn down heat and cook at a low simmer partially covered for about 1 hour, stirring frequently. Add 1 lb. chopped fresh tomatoes and cook until soft. Adjust seasonings as necessary. Add chopped cilantro/parsley and serve with Grandmother Catherene's Cornbread (p. 21) and a salad.

SERVES 8–10

Braised Beef Short Ribs with Rosemary and Fennel

Beef short ribs are a delicious alternative to pork ribs. They are much thicker, and make a satisfying meal. Braising is a worry-free cooking technique that allows you to put the meal in the oven and go off to do other things for a couple of hours. You can also make this dish up to three days in advance, reheating it when ready to eat. If you can't find beef short ribs, you can make this with beef shank instead, but nothing really compares to the wonderful heartiness of the short ribs; this rich striated meat creates a lovely full flavor.

Preheat oven to 350 degrees. Tie the rosemary, bay leaves, and small bunch of parsley together with kitchen twine, making a bouquet garni. Puree garlic and onion in food processor. Next, brown the short ribs. You will probably have to do them in several batches. Heat olive oil in a very large ovenproof casserole over high heat until really hot, then add short ribs. Brown on all sides, cooking 1–2 minutes per side. Transfer to a platter. When you've finished browning all the short ribs, pour off excess fat, then add the fennel and bacon to the pan. Turn heat down to medium-high. Cook until the bacon crisps up, stirring often. Transfer to platter. Add the onion and garlic puree to the pan and cook about 5 minutes. Add the red wine and, using a wooden spoon, deglaze the pan by scraping up any brown bits that have stuck to the bottom and sides. Add the port, the chicken broth, tomatoes, bouquet garni, allspice, salt, and pepper. Bring to a simmer. Add the ribs, fennel, and bacon. Cover the pot and put in the oven. Cook 2 1/2–3 hours until meat is falling off the bones and is very tender. Put ribs on serving platter, pour sauce over top, and sprinkle with chopped parsley. Serve with Polenta (p. 149), Mashed Potatoes (p. 141), or broad noodles, and a green salad.

SERVES 6

6 cloves garlic

1 large onion, cut into chunks (about 2 cups)

4 lbs. meaty beef short ribs (about 6 ribs), cut into sections

2 Tbsp. olive oil

1 large or 2 medium fennel bulbs, cut into 8 wedges (cut in half, then halve again, and then cut wedges; you should have about 3 cups)

1/4 cup finely minced nitrite-free bacon (about 2 strips)

1 cup dry red wine

1 cup port

3 cups low-salt chicken broth

2 1/2 cups canned crushed or diced tomatoes (not puree or it will be too runny)

1/2 tsp. allspice

4 stalks fresh rosemary

3 bay leaves

small bunch parsley

salt and pepper

chopped parsley for garnish

Steak with Thyme

This dish is great when you're short on time, but not on thyme.
My mother taught me to make it with thick steaks, when you want
a meal that seems fancy, but is actually quite simple.

2 lbs. thick steaks (2 inches or more)
2 scant Tbsp. extra virgin olive oil
2 large cloves garlic, minced
1/4 tsp. sea salt
3/4 tsp. dried thyme
1/2 cup red wine
more sea salt

Preheat oven to 375 degrees. Dry steaks thoroughly. Heat olive oil in an oven-safe heavy skillet or pan over high heat until almost smoking. Add steaks and brown, cooking about 2 minutes per side. Remove pan from heat, remove steaks to a plate, add garlic to skillet and cook, stirring, about 30 seconds. Add steaks back to skillet, sprinkle with thyme and salt. Make sure steaks are coated with garlic and seasoning on both sides. Bake in upper third of oven about 15–20 minutes. Check after 15 minutes for medium rare. When cooked to desired temperature, remove from oven and set steaks aside on a hot platter. Add wine to skillet and cook over high heat at a boil. Reduce until the sauce becomes slightly thickened and syrupy. Pour sauce over steaks. Sprinkle with salt. Serve with baked potatoes or New Potatoes with Parsley (p. 141) and mixed baby greens with carrots and cherry tomatoes.

SERVES 4

Lime Skirt Steak with Pineapple Salsa

This recipe is a trouble-free meal that's great any time of year. The fresh salsa paired with grilled steak is a modern turn on roasted meat with chutney. The tangy sweetness of the pineapple is a lovely complement to the lime and cumin flavors in the skirt steak. To save yourself time, you can make the Pineapple Salsa up to a day in advance. Or, if you're really short on energy, just eat the steak as is, or with a little store-bought fruit salsa. However, I highly recommend taking the few minutes to make the condiment yourself, as nothing compares to the wonderful fresh flavor of a homemade salsa. And as a special bonus, it's chock full of vitamin C. You may also make this dish with flank steak or hanger steak, but I prefer skirt steak, because I think it picks up the flavors of the marinade the best.

Combine all ingredients for Pineapple Salsa and let the flavors meld for at least 1 hour. If you make this in advance and refrigerate it, be sure to let it come to room temperature before serving.

Trim skirt steak of silvery membrane (as much as possible). Combine all ingredients, cover, and refrigerate to marinate 1 hour. Don't let it marinate much longer than this, as it will sap the steak of its nice rosy color.

You may broil or grill this dish. If broiling, preheat broiler on high. Remove skirt steak from marinade and lay out on broiling pan. Broil about 3 minutes per side for medium rare (less if the steak is very thin). If grilling, place over hottest part of grill, and cook about 1½–2 minutes per side. Cut the long piece of skirt steak into sections. Serve Pineapple Salsa alongside steak, or spooned on top. Eat with Potato Chips (p. 140) or rice and mixed baby greens with carrots and cherry tomatoes.

SERVES 4–6

Skirt Steak:

2 lbs. skirt steak

3 cloves of garlic, very finely minced

juice of 4 limes

1/4 cup mirin

1/2 tsp. cumin

salt and pepper

Pineapple Salsa:

1 cup fresh or canned finely chopped
   pineapple

1/4 cup finely minced onion

1/2 cup diced ripe tomato

1/4 cup minced bell pepper (any color)

2 Tbsp. minced cilantro

2 Tbsp. mirin

1 Tbsp. unseasoned rice vinegar

2 Tbsp. lime juice (about 1 lime)

1½ tsp. finely minced jalapeno pepper
   (or other hot chili of choice)

1/4 tsp. cumin

1/4 tsp. salt

Swedish Meatballs

My parents were married in a castle in Sweden with two witnesses and half a bottle of champagne. It was a very 1960s wedding—my mother wore an embroidered mini-dress and my father had a Beatles-style haircut and a very slim black suit. I've always had a fascination with Sweden, in part because I have Swedish ancestors, but also because my parents spent that mysterious year living there while my father completed his final year of medical school on exchange. I'm particularly fond of exotic Scandinavian foods like Reindeer Stroganoff (for another book perhaps) and pungent cheeses. And I truly adore Swedish Meatballs, a close cousin of the Jewish dish, "Sweet and Sour Meatballs." Swedish Meatballs can be eaten with or without sauce and are usually served as part of a smorgasbord or with boiled potatoes and vegetables. I like them with wide noodles, myself.

Meatballs:

1/2 cup oat flakes, or corn flakes ground to
    a meal in a food processor or blender

1/2 cup enriched rice or oat milk

1/2 tsp. salt

1/4 tsp. pepper

1/4 tsp. allspice

1/2 cup minced onion

1 Tbsp. canola oil

1 lb. ground beef

3 tsp. Ener-G Egg Replacer mixed with
    2 Tbsp. enriched rice or oat milk

Sauce:

2 Tbsp. canola oil

2 scant Tbsp. brown rice flour (or oat flour,
    or barley flour)

2 cups low-salt beef broth

2 Tbsp. tomato paste

1/4 tsp. allspice

1/8 tsp. nutmeg

1/4 tsp. sweet paprika

1/4 tsp. salt

pepper

1/4 cup enriched rice or oat milk

Combine ground oat/corn flakes, rice/oat milk, salt, pepper, and allspice, and let swell about 10 minutes. Sauté minced onion in canola oil until soft. Add ground beef, egg replacer, and sautéed onion to oat flake mixture and combine thoroughly. Refrigerate about 1–2 hours.

When ready to cook, preheat oven to 400 degrees. Form small meatballs, 1–1½ inches in diameter, either with hands or a meatball maker. If using your hands, wet them with water periodically to help keep the meat from sticking. Place meatballs on a lightly greased baking sheet and cook about 20 minutes until brown. Meanwhile, to make sauce, heat canola oil over medium-high heat. Add flour and cook, stirring, about 2 minutes. You want the flour to sizzle and brown up a bit so that the sauce will become brown. Add the beef broth, mix thoroughly, and then add tomato paste and seasonings. Reduce heat and simmer about 5 minutes to thicken, stirring frequently. Add oat milk. Taste and adjust salt and pepper to your liking. Serve meatballs either with sauce on the side, or place meatballs in sauce and warm thoroughly. Serve with wide noodles, boiled potatoes, or Mashed Potatoes (p. 141), and a green vegetable.

SERVES 4

Louisiana Sloppy Joes

*Earlier in this book, I said my husband's all-time favorite comfort food was
Spaghetti with Turkey Meatballs, but Louisiana Sloppy Joes are a strong runner-up.
We love Sloppy Joes in my house. They are the only food I remember looking forward
to for school lunch in elementary school, and I've never outgrown them.
This recipe is less sloppy than traditional Sloppy Joes, since they are served over
biscuits and eaten with a knife and fork instead of a disintegrating hamburger bun.
This recipe is also incredibly simple. You can easily make it a day in advance and
then warm it up when ready to serve. I've suggested eating it over Basic
Biscuits, but you can use a soft roll of your choice, or even rice.*

Cook onion, garlic, bell pepper, and ground beef in large pan over medium-high heat. Use a wooden spoon to break up the meat. Cook about 5 minutes, until the meat is no longer pink. Add the red wine vinegar and stir a couple of times. Add the rest of the ingredients. Reduce heat to low and simmer, loosely covered, about 30 minutes more, stir - ring occasionally. Meanwhile, make Basic Biscuits. When ready, place 2 or 3 biscuits on a plate, spoon sloppy joe mixture over top so that they are covered completely, and eat. This is great with a very simple green salad.

SERVES 4

1 recipe Basic Biscuits (p. 20)

1 medium onion, diced (1½ cups)

3 cloves garlic, minced

1 medium green bell pepper, diced (1½ cups)

1½ lbs. ground beef

2 Tbsp. red wine vinegar

1 6-oz. can tomato paste

1 cup water

1 Tbsp. honey

2 Tbsp. Dijon mustard

1 Tbsp. chili powder

1 tsp. sweet paprika

1/2 tsp. cumin

1 tsp. oregano

2 bay leaves

1/2 tsp. salt

pepper

Cherry Dijon Pork Chops

*This recipe is simple and elegant. Children and adults
alike love it. I make it all the time.*

1/2 cup cherry fruit-only jam

1/4 cup Dijon mustard

1 Tbsp. olive oil (more if chops are
   extremely lean)

4 pork chops, bone in, about
   8–12 oz. each

salt and pepper

2 tsp. balsamic vinegar

Combine cherry jam and Dijon mustard. Put olive oil in large sauté pan and heat over medium-high heat. Add chops and quickly brown on both sides (about 3 minutes per side). Add salt and pepper. Reduce heat to low, and spoon jam/mustard mixture over the tops of the chops. Cover and cook at a slow simmer about 20 minutes, turning chops every so often. After about 20 minutes remove chops from pan to a warm plate, and cover with tented aluminum foil. Bring heat up to high, add balsamic vinegar, and stir. Cook at a steady fast simmer, stirring continuously, to reduce sauce to a thicker consistency. When it's thickened up to the consistency of nice rich gravy, pour it over the chops and serve. This dish is wonderful with Wild Rice Pilaf with Cherries, Zucchini, and Carrots (p. 146) or Rosemary Garlic Fingerling Potatoes (p. 143) and steamed asparagus or a simple green salad.

SERVES 4

Pork Chops with Tomatoes and Sage

This is a lovely savory Italian recipe for pork chops. It is cooked at a low temperature for a longer time, essentially braising the chops, which makes the meat extremely tender and succulent. Try this with a medium-bodied dry Italian or Argentine red wine. It makes a simple but special meal.

Heat 2 Tbsp. of the olive oil in a large sauté pan over medium-high heat. You need a pan large enough to fit all four chops at once. When the oil is hot, place the chops in the pan with the sage leaves. Cook the chops until browned on both sides, about 2 or 3 minutes per side. Once brown, add salt and pepper, chopped tomatoes, white wine, and remaining 1 Tbsp. of olive oil. Reduce the heat to low and cook at a slow simmer, covered, with the lid slightly ajar. Cook for about 1 hour until the meat is tender and the sauce has been reduced (not runny, slightly thick and chunky). If the sauce has not reduced enough after cooking 1 hour, remove chops to a warm plate, and cover to keep warm. Bring up heat in pan and cook at a boil, stirring frequently for 1–2 minutes. Serve chops topped with sauce. This dish is delicious with Herbed Jerusalem Artichokes (p. 144), Millet with Sage and Red Bell Pepper (p. 149), or plain brown rice, and a salad.

SERVES 4

3 Tbsp. olive oil
4 center cut pork chops, bone in, at least 3/4 inch thick
10–12 fresh sage leaves
salt and fresh pepper
2½ cups fresh or canned Italian plum tomatoes, chopped
2 Tbsp. dry white wine

Tomatoes Stuffed with Italian Pork Sausage and Rice

*This is one of my family's all-time favorite dishes. My mother-in-law requests it
for Thanksgiving (to supplement the turkey, of course). It does take some prep time,
however, so I recommend it as a weekend dish, or one for special occasions. I've devised this
recipe so that you should have some to freeze or refrigerate for another night as well.
Since you've gone to the trouble to make it, you might as well get to eat it twice.
In addition, you should wind up with a little leftover stuffing, which I usually
freeze and then use later to stuff mushrooms or small zucchini.*

12 medium tomatoes

salt and pepper

1½ lbs. sweet Italian sausage (nitrite-
   free if possible)

1 medium onion, minced (1 cup)

4 cloves garlic, minced fine

6 Tbsp. olive oil

1 tsp. paprika

1 Tbsp. honey

2 Tbsp. balsamic vinegar

2 cups cooked long-grain brown rice, basmati, texamati, etc.

1/3 cup chopped parsley

1/4 cup chopped basil

2 tsp. red wine vinegar

freshly ground pepper

1/2 cup brown-rice bread crumbs (or
   other allowed bread crumbs)

Cut the tops off the tomatoes and discard. Scoop out the pulp and seeds into a bowl to use later. Sprinkle the insides of the tomatoes with salt and pepper, and drain upside down on paper towels. Remove sausage from its casing and coarsely chop. Sauté onions and garlic in 4 Tbsp. of the olive oil for 2 or 3 minutes over medium heat. Stir in the paprika. Add sausage and cook for about 5 minutes until no longer pink, using a spoon to break it up as it cooks. Mash the tomato pulp with a potato masher or large fork and add to sausage along with honey and balsamic vinegar. Bring heat up to medium-high and cook until the liquid is absorbed, about 20 minutes. Meanwhile, preheat oven to 375 degrees. When sausage mixture has absorbed almost all the liquid, remove from heat and stir in rice, parsley, basil, red wine vinegar, last 2 Tbsp. of olive oil, freshly ground pepper, and half the bread crumbs. Put the tomatoes in a greased shallow baking pan so that they fit snugly. Spoon sausage mixture into tomatoes, mounding the tops. Sprinkle with remaining half of bread crumbs and bake 30 minutes. Serve hot, room temperature, or cold with a mixed green leaf salad with My Favorite Dressing (p. 45).

SERVES 6

Pork Tenderloin Medallions
with Raisin Sauce

This dish borrows from a recipe my mother used for baked tongue. It's a dish my father especially liked, because he said the sauce was similar to one his Aunt Lottie made. I've substituted pork tenderloin medallions for tongue, as I think it's more suited to the contemporary palette. Pork tenderloin is the leanest cut of pork and is comparable to chicken breast in fat content. Because it is so lean, it needs to be cooked rather quickly or else it dries out. This dish is wonderful in the colder months for a warming, homey, old-fashioned meal.

Make the raisin sauce by combining honey, mustard, and flour in heavy sauce pan at medium heat. Add red wine vinegar, then lemon juice and lemon zest. Stir until dissolved. Add water and raisins. Bring to a boil. Reduce heat and simmer about 15 minutes until thick, stirring often. Remove from heat.

Sprinkle medallions thoroughly on both sides with ground cloves and allspice, salt and pepper. Heat olive oil in large heavy skillet over high heat. Once hot, add medallions, being sure they don't overlap. If you don't have enough room, you'll have to brown them in batches. Cook about 2–3 minutes per side, until browned. Once all the medallions have been browned, cover them with raisin sauce, reduce heat to low, and cook partly covered about 15–20 minutes more until tender. Serve with brown rice or Mashed Potatoes (p. 141) or quinoa and a salad.

SERVES 4

1/2 cup honey
1 tsp. Dijon mustard
1 Tbsp. oat flour
2 Tbsp. red wine vinegar
2 Tbsp. lemon juice
1/4 tsp. lemon zest
1 1/4 cups water
1/3 cup seedless raisins
1 1/2–2 lbs. pork tenderloin, cut into 1-inch-thick medallions
ground cloves
allspice
salt and pepper
2 Tbsp. olive oil

Fennel-Crusted Pork Tenderloin

My original recipe for this appeared in Good Housekeeping Magazine *as part of a special healthy recipes spread. In that version I used fennel seeds. For this book, I've changed the fennel seeds to fresh fennel (for all the nonseed-eating people), which makes the crust taste almost like a pistachio crust. A delicious meal hot or cold in spring, summer, fall, or winter.*

2 lbs. pork tenderloin roast

1 Tbsp. Dijon mustard

1/2 cup fresh fennel

1 clove garlic

1 tsp. chopped fresh thyme, or
   1/2 tsp. dried

1/2 tsp. salt

1/2 tsp. pepper

Preheat oven to 500 degrees. Rinse and pat dry pork tenderloin. Set aside. Put all other ingredients in a food processor or blender and puree into a paste. Coat tenderloin on all sides with the paste. Put in a roasting pan and cook until crust is browned and crispy and pork is cooked to an internal temperature of 150–155 degrees. Cooking time varies depending on thickness of tenderloin, but is generally between 30–45 minutes. Serve with Oven-Baked Sweet Potato Fries (p. 139), Butternut Squash with Maple Syrup (p. 144), Acorn Squash with Cranberries (p. 145), or Wild Rice Pilaf with Cherries, Zucchini, and Carrots (p. 146), and a salad of mixed baby greens with carrots and cherry tomatoes.

SERVES 4–6

Baked Ham with Pineapple

When I was a kid, my mom used to make this dish for a weekend dinner or during the holidays and it always seemed festive. Made with a fresh uncooked ham, it has the wonderful benefit of being nitrite-free, while a precooked ham is shorter on time and much cheaper. You may use either, but note the different cooking times for each in the recipe instructions on the opposite page. I like to make this with a large enough ham to have leftovers for slicing into sandwich meat later in the week.

Preheat oven to 325 degrees. Place ham in a roasting pan. Using a sharp knife, mark fat surface in squares all the way around (if using a fresh ham that is bound with twine, skip this step). Insert about 12–16 whole cloves into the squares. Sprinkle ham with salt and pepper, then ground cloves and allspice. Add 1 cup water to the bottom of the pan and cook about 45 minutes to brown up a bit.

Meanwhile, make the pineapple sauce. Simmer pineapple chunks and their liquid with honey in saucepan over medium heat. Cook about 10 minutes. In a little bowl, slowly add a bit of cold water to the cornstarch, stirring to make a smooth paste. Add cornstarch mixture to pineapple, turn heat to medium-low and cook, stirring often, until the sauce thickens up a bit, about 20 minutes. Remove from heat.

When ham has cooked 45 minutes, remove from oven. With a fresh ham, there may be a lot of liquid in the pan at this point. If so, pour it off. Pour pineapple sauce over and around ham. Turn oven down to 300 degrees. Cook, basting occasionally with the pineapple sauce for about 1–2 hours more, or until done. Add a little water along the way if it seems necessary. Allow a total cooking time of about 30 minutes per pound for a precooked ham, or 40 minutes per pound for a fresh ham. There is a lot of variation on this because hams are cured in so many different ways, so you need to use your judgment to time out your own particular ham. I usually cook a 4-lb. precooked ham a total of 2 hours, and a 4-lb. fresh ham about 2 hours and 45 minutes. A good rule of thumb is to cook it to an internal temperature of at least 140–150 degrees, nice and browned on the outside with the pineapple soft. Personally, I err on the side of more done with pork these days. I like this served with Lemon Quinoa (p. 148) or plain brown rice and a Crispy Asian Salad (p. 51).

SERVES 6–8

3½–4 lb. ham, either precooked or fresh
12–16 whole cloves
salt and pepper
ground cloves
ground allspice
1 cup water

Pineapple Sauce:
2 20-oz. cans pineapple chunks, including their liquid
1/4 cup honey
3 tsp. cornstarch

Rack of Lamb (or Rib Chops) with Garlic, Rosemary, and Mint

Lamb rib chops are tender and succulent. The fresh herb rub on these is aromatic and a perfect complement to the crispy meat.

1½ lb. rack of lamb rib chops, or
   8 rib chops
1/4 cup fresh mint
2 Tbsp. fresh rosemary
2 Tbsp. lemon juice
1 tsp. lemon zest
4 cloves garlic
1 stalk of celery
salt
pepper
3/4 cup olive oil

Combine all ingredients (except lamb) in a food processor. Coat rack of lamb or chops with marinade on all sides. Refrigerate covered for several hours. Cook rack of lamb on the grill, less fatty side first about 7 minutes, then flip and cook about another 7 minutes until it's nice and crispy. Serve medium to medium rare. If cooking chops, cooking time will be slightly shorter. If cooking rack of lamb in oven, cook less fatty side down in a roasting pan at 350 degrees for about 35 minutes, or broil chops under broiler about 5–7 minutes per side. Serve with Rosemary Garlic Fingerling Potatoes (p. 143) or Acorn Squash with Cranberries (p. 145) and a simple salad.

SERVES 4

Lamb Loin Chops with Molasses Tarragon Glaze

These lamb chops are a real treat, and great with
a hearty Zinfandel or a nice Cote du Rhone.

Sprinkle chops with salt and pepper. Combine molasses, Dijon mustard, cider vinegar, garlic, white pepper, and tarragon. Put chops in a large container or bowl, cover with glaze and gently toss to coat them completely. Cover tightly and put in refrigerator to marinate 1 hour, or more if you have the time. You can actually marinate them up to 24 hours. When ready to cook, heat broiler on high. Line broiling pan with tinfoil and put in chops. Spoon some of remaining glaze over them, so they're all nicely covered (reserving a little). Cook about 4 minutes until crispy, remove from oven, turn chops and spoon more glaze over them. Return to oven and broil about 4 or 5 more minutes for medium rare, longer if you like them more well done. Test by cutting a small slit in the center of one of the chops to look for pinkness. Chops keep cooking once removed from oven, so it's better they be a hair underdone than over. Serve with salad, Tarragon Roast Potatoes (p. 140), or Wild Rice Pilaf with Cherries, Zucchini, and Carrots (p. 146), and a light dessert.

SERVES 4

8 lamb loin chops, 1 inch thick
salt and pepper
1 cup molasses
5 Tbsp. Dijon mustard
2 Tbsp. cider vinegar
4 cloves garlic, minced
2 tsp. white pepper
1 Tbsp. chopped fresh tarragon,
  or 1 tsp. dried

Variation

For a spicier chop, omit tarragon and white pepper and add 1 tsp. ground chili pepper (chipotle, ancho, cayenne, etc.).

Lamb Stew

This wonderful hotpot is a hybrid between Irish and Greek lamb stew.
I prefer it to the traditional form of either as I've taken the best from both
and combined them into one fabulous comfort meal. You may make
it a day in advance and then reheat when ready to serve.

3 lbs. cubed lamb (shoulder, leg, etc.)

1/4 cup olive oil

4 cups low-salt chicken broth

1½ cups dry white wine

1/2 cup ketchup

1 large or 2 small onions, chopped (2 cups)

3 cloves garlic, minced

3 whole allspice berries

bouquet garni made from the following
   tied together:
      1 bay leaf
      3 stalks rosemary
      10 stalks thyme
      small bunch of parsley

freshly ground pepper

4 large potatoes (Idahos work well)

2 stalks celery, cut into 1/2-inch pieces

2 cups carrots, cut into 3/4-inch pieces
   (about 5 carrots)

1 tsp. salt

1/4 cup oat flour (or other allowed flour)

In large heavy pot, brown lamb in two or three batches in olive oil over medium-high heat. Transfer to a bowl. Add chicken broth and deglaze pan by scraping up brown bits with a wooden spoon. Once all the bits have reconstituted, add back the meat, the wine, ketchup, onions, garlic, all-spice, bouquet garni, and a few turns of pepper. Bring to a simmer and cook over very low heat, covered, for 1 hour. Meanwhile peel the potatoes. Cut one of them into 1/2-inch cubes and set aside. For the other three, halve and then quarter them. Then divide the quarters, so that you get 8 pieces from each potato. After lamb has cooked 1 hour, add in the cubed potato (just the one) and the celery. Continue to cook at a simmer, covered, over low heat. After 45 minutes, use the back of a wooden spoon to mash the potato pieces against the side of the pot. Cover and cook another 15 minutes. Add the rest of the potatoes, carrots, and salt. Cook covered another 50 minutes, stirring occasionally. Put the flour in a bowl. Ladle out some of the cooking broth, mixing with the flour until it's no longer a paste. Pour into the pot, stirring well, and cook another 10 minutes until it's thickened up to a nice hearty consistency. Serve piping hot with freshly ground pepper. Eat with a simple green salad or steamed green vegetables.

SERVES 8

Curried Lamb with Apricots over Brown Basmati Rice

Making a curry at home may seem intimidating at first, but it's incredibly easy
if you've got good curry powder. Somebody else already went to the only troublesome
part, which is blending the spices. So I encourage you to try this recipe. Once you've made
it, you'll know what I'm talking about. It melts in your mouth, and is loved by even
curry haters. You may make it a day in advance if you like (just the curry,
not the rice) and then reheat when ready to serve. Enjoy!

Puree onion, garlic, and ginger in a food processor. Combine with spices, lemon juice, apricot fruit-only jam, tomatoes, chicken broth, and salt in a large bowl. Add cubed
lamb. Make sure lamb is well coated with marinade and
refrigerate for about 1 hour (longer if you have the time).
Heat coconut oil in large heavy pot over medium heat.
Remove lamb from marinade with tongs, letting as much of
the marinade as possible run back into the bowl. Brown
lamb, turning frequently. It will not get crispy brown, but
rather the goal should be to get rid of the pink. You may
have to do this in two batches, transferring the first batch
of browned lamb to a plate. When lamb is browned on all
sides, combine lamb with marinade. Bring to a simmer,
reduce heat to low and cook, covered, for about 15 minutes.
Add the apricots and cook, covered, 1½ hours more, stirring
about every 15 minutes. In last hour, combine rice and
water and simmer, covered, over low heat about 45 minutes,
then remove from heat and let sit covered for 10 minutes.
Fluff with a fork. Serve lamb over rice with salad and
Avocado Raita (p. 154).

SERVES 4–6

2¾–3 lbs. cubed lamb (shoulder, leg, etc.)
1 medium onion, quartered
2 cloves garlic
1 Tbsp. minced fresh ginger (about a
    1-inch piece)
2 tsp. garam masala
1 tsp. curry powder
1/2 tsp. cayenne pepper
2 Tbsp. lemon juice
1/2 cup apricot fruit-only jam
1 cup crushed canned tomatoes
1 cup low-salt chicken broth
1 tsp. salt
2 Tbsp. coconut oil (see note on
    p. 66 regarding coconut)
1 cup dried apricots, quartered

Rice:
2 cups brown basmati rice
4 cups water

Lamb Kebabs with Eggplant, Red Onion, and Red Pepper

In addition to being a wonderful family meal, this recipe is also great for dinner parties and barbecues, because you prepare the kebabs in advance, which leaves you time to socialize. They only take about 10 minutes to cook, but be sure to allow plenty of time for them to marinate.

2 lbs. cubed lamb (shoulder, leg, etc.)
the marinade from Marinated Chicken Skewers (p. 92)
1 medium eggplant, quartered lengthwise, then cut into 1/2-inch pieces crosswise
2 red bell peppers, cut into 1½-inch pieces
2 red onions, cut into 8 wedges each

Toss cubed lamb with marinade and refrigerate overnight if possible, or at least 6 hours. When it comes time to make skewers, start with onion, then lamb, then eggplant, pepper, and onion, then lamb, and so on. Place skewers in a roasting pan and pour remaining marinade over them, turning to coat the onion, pepper, and eggplant. Broil on high. Turn every 4 minutes or so until crispy on all sides, being sure not to overcook. I like this dish cooked to medium to ensure tenderness. Ovens vary in heat, so you'll need to keep a close watch. After about 10 minutes, check for doneness by cutting into the center of a piece of lamb.

Unlike the skewered chicken, the meat *should* still be pink in the middle. When cooked, remove and serve with brown rice, Saffron Jasmine Rice (p. 145), or Curried Rice with Raisins (p. 147), and a Greek Salad (p. 52).

SERVES 6

Roman Rabbit

When I was pregnant with my first son, Lennon, my mother and I took a trip to Italy.
We were in Rome and went to have dinner with an old friend of hers at a little trattoria
in an area called Trastevere. It was the kind of place where they have only a few items
on the menu—a real old-fashioned neighborhood restaurant where the locals come to eat
and socialize. I ordered the rabbit cooked in red wine and was transported to heaven. It was
rich, tender, and perfectly seasoned. I have tried to recreate that dish over the past several
years, once failing miserably when I used a wild rabbit that was tough as old shoe leather.
But with trial and error, I finally got it right and as close to that Roman rabbit as I'll ever get.

Place rabbit pieces in a large bowl. Sprinkle salt and honey over them. Add water just to cover. Toss, coating all pieces. Cover bowl and refrigerate for 1 hour. This will tenderize the meat. Drain and pat dry. Preheat oven to 325 degrees. Heat olive oil in large heavy oven-safe casserole over medium-high heat. Put oat flour in a zip lock bag. Add a few pieces of rabbit at a time and shake to cover. Remove from bag and shake off all excess flour. When olive oil is really hot and starting to ripple, add a few pieces of rabbit to the casserole and cook until browned on both sides (about 3 or 4 minutes per side), then remove to a plate. Once you've browned all the rabbit pieces and removed them all from the casserole, reduce heat, add the bacon, and fry until crispy. Add the onion and garlic and cook, stirring until softened. Add the chicken broth and deglaze the pan by scraping up any brown bits that may have stuck to the bottom. Add the wine and tomato paste and bring to a simmer. Add the herbs, reserving half the chopped parsley for later. Add salt and pepper to taste. Add the rabbit to the pot, and spoon some of the onions and broth over the pieces. Cover the casserole and cook 2 hours until tender. Serve over Polenta (p. 149) sprinkled with a little parsley and eat with a light green salad.

SERVES 4

3-lb. rabbit, cut into 10 pieces (ask
   the butcher to do it for you)
3/4 cup kosher salt
3 Tbsp. honey
water
2 Tbsp. olive oil (and more as necessary)
1/2 cup oat flour
1/4 cup diced nitrite-free bacon (about
   2 slices)
1 medium red onion, cut into very thin
   slices vertically
2 large cloves garlic, minced
1/2 cup low-salt chicken broth
1½ cups red wine
1 Tbsp. tomato paste
1/4 cup chopped fresh parsley,
   divided
1 Tbsp. chopped fresh thyme
1½ tsp. dried marjoram
salt and pepper

Venison Osso Buco with Saffron Jasmine Rice

Osso Buco is traditionally a Milanese dish served with a "gremolata" made from parsley, garlic, lemon zest, and often anchovies. I have created this recipe with some of the traditional elements of a veal Osso Buco, but have tailored it to match the richer flavor of venison. Venison is highlighted by gin and juniper berries, and juniper goes well with orange, so here you get all four. This dish serves 4, but if you have particularly hungry eaters, you should double it. If you can't find venison shanks, you could substitute 2 pounds of venison stew meat, for a lovely venison stew, Osso-Buco style.

1 recipe Saffron Jasmine Rice (p. 145)

Osso Buco:

2 bay leaves

small bunch parsley

3 sprigs thyme

1 medium onion

2 cloves garlic

2 carrots

2 celery stalks

6 Tbsp. olive oil

4 meaty venison shanks (also sold as
    Osso Buco), about 8 oz. each

salt and pepper to season

1/4 cup oat flour

2 Tbsp. gin

1 cup veal or chicken stock

1 cup red wine

1 cup crushed tomatoes

8 juniper berries

2 strips orange rind, 1/2 inch thick

1/2 tsp. kosher salt

1/4 tsp. pepper

Gremolata:

2 Tbsp. chopped parsley

1/4 tsp. minced garlic

1/2 tsp. orange zest

2 tsp. orange juice

Make a bouquet garni by tying together the bay leaves, parsley, and thyme. Set aside. Put onion and garlic in food processor. Puree. Add carrots and celery. Puree. Set aside. Preheat oven to 350 degrees. Heat olive oil in heavy-bottomed oven-safe casserole over medium-high heat. Salt and pepper venison shanks, dredge in flour, and brown all over in olive oil. When venison shanks have browned, remove from pan, reduce heat to low, and add vegetable puree. Cook about 5 minutes to soften. Meanwhile, warm gin in a small saucepan. Return venison to pot, pour gin over top. Add stock, wine, tomatoes, bouquet garni, juniper berries, orange rind, kosher salt, and pepper. The liquid should come up at least halfway on the shanks. If it doesn't, add a little more chicken stock or wine. Bring to a simmer. Cover and cook in oven 2 hours, turning and basting the shanks every 30 minutes. In last half hour, make the Saffron Jasmine Rice. Plate by putting an ample serving of rice on the plate, top with a venison shank, and spoon sauce over the top. Sprinkle with combined gremolata ingredients.

SERVES 4

Wild Boar Tenderloin with Green Mole

This dish is wonderful for special occasions. It's not cheap (wild boar tenderloin costs about the same per pound as filet mignon), but is well worth the extra money. The meat is nutty (they eat a lot of acorns), tender, rich, but lean. Green mole is a delicious Mexican sauce, made with green chilies and pumpkin seeds. Different regions of Mexico have their own signature moles. This is my signature green mole, so I suppose you could call it Westchester Mole (though that doesn't have quite the same exotic ring). It pairs extremely well with wild boar, but also goes great with pork and chicken, so if you wish to use this sauce with more easily accessible meats, by all means do so. But I encourage you to be adventurous and try ordering the wild boar tenderloin from D'Artagnan (see Resources, p. 195) at least once. You won't be disappointed.

Heat a heavy skillet over high heat. Add pumpkin seeds and roast, shaking pan until they turn a lovely golden color and puff. They will make a popping sound as you do this. Remove from pan and set aside 1/4 cup of roasted seeds for garnish. Grind the remaining 1 cup in a food mill or food processor until fine. Set aside. In food processor, make a paste of the onion, garlic, and chilies. Then add tomatillos. Puree. Add lettuce, parsley, and cilantro. Puree. Add spices. Heat 2 Tbsp. olive oil in large heavy pot over medium-high heat. Mix 3/4 cup chicken broth with ground pumpkin seeds. Add to pot and cook about 5 minutes, stirring until liquid is absorbed and seeds turn brown. Add green paste, honey, and remaining 1¼ cups chicken broth. Bring to boil, then reduce heat to low and simmer about 30 minutes.

In last 5 minutes, cook wild boar, either by pan-searing in a cast iron skillet over high heat or grilling over high heat (my preference). Cook a total of 3–4 minutes, turning once. Do not overcook. This meat is very tender.

Serve topped with ample mole and a sprinkling of roasted pumpkin seeds along with brown rice or corn tortillas and a green salad with avocados.

SERVES 4–6

2–3 lbs. wild boar tenderloin, cut crosswise into 2-inch strips, then pounded thin to 1/4-inch thickness

Green Mole:

1¼ cups raw pumpkin seeds

1 onion, cut into quarters

3 cloves garlic

3 green chilies, deseeded (serranos or jalapenos)

8 large fresh tomatillos, dehusked and washed

2 cups chopped romaine lettuce

1/4 cup parsley

1/2 cup cilantro

1 tsp. kosher salt (or 1/2 tsp. regular table salt)

1 tsp. cumin

1/2 tsp. cinnamon

1/8 tsp. ground cloves

2 Tbsp. olive oil

2 cups chicken broth

2 Tbsp. honey

Bison Chili

Bison is a lean high-protein alternative to beef. Look for the poblano chili peppers at large grocery stores, such as Super Stop & Shop. If you can't find them, you can substitute green bell pepper.

1/4 cup olive oil

2 medium onions, diced

2 large cloves garlic, minced

2 lbs. ground bison (buffalo)

3 Tbsp. Mexican-style chili powder (available at the supermarket)

1 tsp. ground cumin

1 tsp. sweet paprika

1 28-oz. can diced tomatoes

1½–2 cups water

2 fresh poblano chili peppers (or 1 large green bell pepper), diced

juice of 1 lime

salt and pepper

chopped cilantro for garnish

diced avocado for garnish (optional)

Sauté onions and garlic in olive oil in large heavy pot over medium-high heat until onions are soft. Add the bison meat and cook, breaking up the clumps with a large wooden spoon. When all the pink is gone, add the spices and cook about 2 minutes more. Add the tomatoes and then add water, just enough to cover. Start with 1½ cups, and then add more later if it becomes necessary. Bring to a boil, reduce heat to low and simmer, loosely covered, for 1 hour. Add poblanos and cook 30 minutes more. Remove from heat and stir in lime juice. Add salt and pepper to taste. Eat over brown rice or other grain of choice. Garnish with a sprinkling of cilantro and diced avocado.

SERVES 6

Blueberry Duck Breast

This dish is extremely simple, but seems fancy. It's a good meal for nights when you get home late and are short on time but feel like treating yourself and your family to something out of the ordinary.

Preheat oven to 375 degrees. Combine all ingredients (except duck breasts) in a blender or food processor. Puree. If duck is very fatty (it usually is), score the fat with a sharp knife (diagonally slice it), and sear the duck breast, fatty side down, in a very hot pan until it is crispy and much of the fat has drained out—about 5 minutes—then proceed as follows. Place breasts in a roasting pan or baking dish on a rack and coat each one with blueberry mixture. Cook for 25–30 minutes. Duck is best medium rare to medium, so be sure it's still pink in the center. Slice diagonally into thin strips. Fan out on plate, spoon some juices from the pan over it, and serve with Lemon Quinoa (p. 148) or Saffron Jasmine Rice (p. 145) and a salad.

SERVES 4

Note: If you desire a crispier skin, run the duck breasts under the broiler on high at the end for 1–2 minutes, but keep a careful watch so as not to burn it.

1½ lbs. duck breast (2 large or 4 small)
1½ cups blueberries
2 Tbsp. rice vinegar
1 Tbsp. honey
1/2 tsp. salt
1/2–1 tsp. pepper (I like it peppery, but it's a matter of taste)
1/4 tsp. ground nutmeg
1/4 tsp. Chinese five-spice powder
1 Tbsp. olive oil

Pomegranate Glazed Rock Cornish Game Hens

Cornish hens were one of the first dishes I learned to cook for dinner parties, back when I was a freshman in college. I thought they were the epitome of sophistication. The wonderful thing about a Rock Cornish hen, other than its charming diminutive size, is that it's all white meat. They are great birds for parties, and the following recipe is exotic yet easy to prepare. And best of all, you do almost all the work the day before, simply sticking the hens in the oven for about half an hour before your guests (or family) sit down to dine.

2 Rock Cornish Game Hens, about
     1 1/2–1 3/4 lbs. each (or 4 at about
     3/4–1 lb. each), split in half
1 cup pomegranate juice
1/2 cup honey
zest of half a lemon, cut into strips with a
     potato peeler or a small sharp knife
1/4 cup lemon juice (about 1 lemon)
1½ tsp. grated fresh ginger
4 large cloves garlic, minced
1/2 tsp. ground coriander
1/2 tsp. cinnamon
1/2 tsp. cayenne pepper
salt and pepper to taste
pomegranate seeds (optional—and
     dependent on season)

Combine all ingredients except pomegranate seeds and hens, making sure to really dilute the honey. Marinate hens in marinade, making sure each half is really well coated with the sauce and refrigerate, tightly covered, overnight (or at least 8 hours) before cooking.

Preheat oven to 450 degrees. Remove hens to a roasting pan, reserving marinade. Season hens with a little salt and pepper. While oven heats up, put marinade in a saucepan and bring to a boil, then reduce to a simmer. Just before putting hens in the oven, spoon a little marinade over them. Keep marinade at a very low simmer while cooking the hens. Baste hens with it every 10 minutes. Cook 25–35 minutes, until golden brown and juices run clear when you prick the thigh. You want the hens cooked to an internal temperature of 170–180 degrees, if that's an easier way for you to judge doneness, but note that the cooking time will depend on what size birds you bought (less time for smaller hens, more for the larger). Let rest 10 minutes before serving. To serve, plate, spoon a little of the sauce/marinade on top, sprinkle with pomegranate seeds, and enjoy. Eat with Wild Rice Pilaf with Cherries, Zucchini, and Carrots (p. 146) or Saffron Jasmine Rice (p. 145) and a light green salad.

SERVES 4

Pheasant with Apples

*Try as I might, I am just not a fan of tiny game birds. They're just too small
for me, and there's so much effort for so little meat (Rock Cornish Game Hens
being the rare exception). I like a nice hearty bird, and a full-grown pheasant is my
cup of tea. They are like chicken, but with a richer flavor. You can order 2¹/₂–3 pound
fresh pheasants online at D'Artagnan, and they'll deliver them by the next day.
The following recipe is a wonderful fall or winter dish. It's sophisticated, yet simple.
I have used coconut milk where one might traditionally use cream and
added toasted coconut to complement the dish.*

Truss the pheasants with kitchen twine so they retain their shape. Heat olive oil in large skillet over medium-high heat. Brown pheasants on all sides. You may have to do them one at a time. Preheat oven to 350 degrees. Remove pheasants from skillet once browned and reduce heat to low. Add shallots and cook, stirring, about one minute. Add apples and honey. Stir well. Bring heat back up to medium and cook about 15 minutes until apples soften up, stirring frequently. Add bay leaves, salt and pepper to taste, and transfer to a large roasting pan (the kind that has a lid). Place pheasants on top of apples. Sprinkle with a little more salt and pepper. Cover and cook 45 minutes. Remove lid and cook about 30 more minutes. Remove from oven. Transfer pheasants. Add coconut milk to apples. In a hot skillet, toast coconut about 1 minute, shaking the pan, until lightly golden. Serve pheasant carved like chicken over a bed of apples, sprinkled with the toasted coconut, and garnished with a couple of sprigs of watercress. Eat with Coconut Rice (p. 146) and a light salad.

SERVES 4

2 pheasants (2¹/₂–3 lbs. each)

1/4 cup olive oil

2 shallots, minced

8 large Granny Smith apples, peeled, cored, and cut into 8 pieces each

2 Tbsp. honey

2 bay leaves

salt and pepper

1/2 cup coconut milk (see note on p. 66 regarding coconut)

1/4 cup unsweetened shredded coconut

watercress

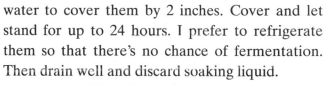

ABOUT COOKING BEANS

If you have time, you may want to consider cooking your own beans. Avoiding canned foods cuts down on the amount of metals you and your family are exposed to.

There is a fair amount of variation in cooking times for dry beans depending on their age, type, size, and moisture content; the soaking method used; and even the altitude at which they are cooked. What follows are general guidelines for dry bean preparation and cooking.

First, spread the beans out on a tray or in a colander. Sort through them, discarding any that are shriveled, discolored, or damaged. Also remove any stones, empty shells, dirt, or other debris. Rinse the beans well under cold water.

Next, the big question when cooking beans: To soak or not to soak? There is an ongoing debate about this because some feel soaking diminishes the beans' flavor. I personally like to soak my beans because it helps reduce the gas-producing sugars that lead to intestinal discomfort by about 10 percent, which I think is enough to be worth it. Soaking also cuts off about half an hour from total cooking time.

Here are three methods for soaking beans. (Lentils and split peas do not need to be soaked.)

Method 1. Place beans in a large pot and add water to cover them by 2 inches. Cover and let stand for up to 24 hours. I prefer to refrigerate them so that there's no chance of fermentation. Then drain well and discard soaking liquid.

Method 2. Place beans in a large pot, and add boiling water to cover them by 2 inches, cover, and let stand until beans have swelled to at least twice their size and have absorbed most of the water (1 2 hours). Drain and discard the soaking liquid.

Method 3. Place beans in a large pot, add water to cover them by 2 inches, and heat to boiling, then reduce heat to low and simmer for two minutes. Remove from heat, cover, and let stand about 1 hour. Drain, rinse, and discard the soaking liquid.

After soaking by whichever method you prefer, proceed to cooking. To cook, place beans in a large pot and add cold water to cover them by 2 inches. Bring beans to a boil over high heat, skimming off the foam periodically. Adding 1 Tbsp. of olive oil or canola oil helps to reduce foaming and boil overs. Once the beans have come to a boil, reduce heat to low and simmer, covered, stirring occasionally until beans are tender. Add salt if you wish toward the end of their cooking time—not earlier.

Some beans are higher in protein and antioxidants, particularly black beans and small red beans.

Cooking Dried Beans

When cooking dried beans, use the following table as a guideline. It provides the amount of water needed to cook a variety of different beans along with their approximate cooking times and yields. For additional information, see "About Cooking Beans" on page 125.

BEAN TYPE (1 CUP)	WATER	COOKING TIME	YIELD
Black	4 cups	1 ½ hours	2 cups
Black-eyed peas	3 cups	1 to 1 ½ hours	2 cups
Chick peas (garbanzo)	4 cups	3 hours	2 cups
Kidney	3 cups	1 ½ hours	2 cups
Lentils	3 cups	30 to 45 minutes	2 ¼ cups
Lima	2 cups	1 ½ hours	1 ¼ cups
Pink	3 cups	1 ½ hours	2 cups
Pinto	3 cups	1 ½ hours	2 cups
Red, small	3 cups	1 hour	2 cups
Split peas	3 cups	45 minutes	2 ¼ cups
White (navy)	3 cups	1 ½ hours	2 cups

Raf's Cuban Rice and Beans

Raf is a friend of my husband's. They used to be in a band together. Raf is a fantastic guitar player (he used to play and write with Lenny Kravitz) and a great cook. He's Cuban and makes great Cuban rice and beans. My husband wrote this recipe down without proportions or instructions on a crumpled piece of paper, so I've guessed at most of it. Traditionally, you would use a smoked ham hock, but that adds literally thousands of milligrams of unnecessary sodium, so I've omitted the meat. This recipe makes enough so that you can freeze half the beans for a later date. It also keeps well in the fridge, so feel free to make it a day in advance, and prepare the rice when you're ready to eat it. Enjoy!

Sauté onion, garlic, and bay leaf in olive oil over medium heat until onion is soft. Add green pepper, oregano, cumin, and cloves. Cook about 2 minutes. Add black beans, salt, pepper, vinegar, honey, and water. Bring to a boil, reduce heat to low and cook at a simmer, loosely covered, for about 2 hours, stirring frequently. In the last hour, cook your rice, adding the olive oil to the rice water. Brown rice usually needs about 40–50 minutes of cooking time and then sits covered another 10 minutes off the heat before fluffing with a fork. Serve with the Cuban Salad with Oranges and Red Onion (p. 52) and sliced avocado on the side.

SERVES 8

Beans:

1 large Spanish onion, diced

4 cloves garlic, minced

2 bay leaves

4 Tbsp. olive oil

1 green pepper, cut into 1/2-inch pieces

2 tsp. oregano

1 Tbsp. cumin

1/4 tsp. ground cloves

4 15- or 15.5-oz. cans black beans (Raf recommends Goya), about 6 cups

1 tsp. salt

1/4 tsp. pepper

1/4 cup red wine vinegar (or cider vinegar)

1 Tbsp. honey

2 cans (from beans) of water

Rice:

2 cups brown rice

4 cups water

salt to taste

2 Tbsp. olive oil

Polenta Pie

*Polenta Pie is a great summer dish. Serve it hot right out
of the oven, or room temperature for a picnic.*

Polenta:

4 cups water

1 cup polenta

salt to taste

Filling:

1/2 cup corn (frozen, canned, or fresh)

**1 cup The Lady from Naples Red Sauce
(p. 69) or store-bought red sauce**

**1/2 red bell pepper, sliced into
1/2-inch strips**

**1/2 green bell pepper, sliced into
1/2-inch strips**

**1 Portobello mushroom, cut into
1-inch pieces**

1/2 zucchini, cut into thin rounds

1/4 red onion, coarsely chopped

fresh basil

oregano

**2 Tbsp. olive oil, plus a little more
to oil pan**

salt and pepper

Oil a pie dish or an 8 x 8-inch cake pan with olive oil. Boil water and add polenta and salt. Cook, stirring constantly, over medium heat until thickened, about 3 minutes. Add corn, and cook, continuing to stir, about 2 more minutes. Remove from heat. Pour into the pie dish or pan and, using a wooden spoon or a rubber spatula, spread into a crust, pushing the polenta up the sides to create a rim around the edges. Chill in the refrigerator about 15 minutes. Meanwhile, preheat the oven to 400 degrees. Remove polenta after about 15 minutes and use a pastry brush to spread 1 Tbsp. olive oil all across it. Cook in upper third of oven about 30 minutes, until the crust becomes a golden brown. Remove and top the crust with red sauce, then spread out the veggies and basil, sprinkle with a little oregano, salt, and pepper, and drizzle remaining 1 Tbsp. olive oil over top. Return to oven and cook about 45 minutes. Eat with a salad.

SERVES 4

Polenta with Mushrooms

This is a great winter polenta dish. It's lovely served on its own with a salad for dinner, or as a side with roast chicken or Cornish hen.

Sauté shallots in olive oil over medium-high heat until golden. Add mushrooms, salt, pepper, and thyme to pan and cook until mushrooms are soft. Add wine and simmer until at least half of it evaporates. Add cornstarch and stir quickly to thicken sauce without making lumps. Remove from heat, stir in parsley, and cover while you make the polenta.

Boil water for polenta. When it comes to a rolling boil, pour in polenta, stirring constantly. Lower heat and cook stirring about 4 or 5 minutes until polenta reaches desired consistency. When done, you may plate it individually or spread the polenta on a platter, making a slight well in the middle, and top with mushrooms. Sprinkle with salt and freshly ground pepper. Serve hot.

MAKES 4 SERVINGS (OR 6 SIDES)

Mushroom Mixture:

2 small shallots, minced fine (or
    1 small onion)

1/3 cup olive oil

1 lb. sliced mushrooms (I like shiitake,
    but you may use morels, crimini,
    baby bellas, or white button)

1/2 tsp. salt

lots of freshly ground pepper

1 tsp. fresh thyme, or 1/2 tsp. dry

3/4 cup dry white wine

1 tsp. cornstarch

2 Tbsp. chopped parsley

Polenta:

1 cup polenta

4 cups water

salt to taste

Tip

Polenta is an Italian dish made from boiled, slow-cooked, ground cornmeal. Sometimes it is made from very finely ground yellow cornmeal, and sometimes it is made from coarse grain. Sometimes yellow and white cornmeal are blended. The method of cooking polenta doesn't really vary, but use coarse polenta if you want it thick and finely ground polenta if you want it thinner. Medium-ground polenta is suitable for most dishes. Polenta is also available ready-made.

Moroccan Vegetable Tagine

*Don't be put off by this long list of ingredients. This dish is
actually quite simple to make, and well worth any effort.*

3 Tbsp. olive oil

1 medium onion, diced

3 cloves garlic, minced

1 tsp. minced fresh ginger

1 tsp. cumin

1 tsp. paprika

1/2 tsp. cinnamon

1/2 tsp. cayenne pepper

1/2 tsp. turmeric

3 carrots, peeled and cut into
    1/2-inch pieces

2 medium turnips or half a 6-inch rutabaga,
    peeled and cut into 1/2-inch cubes

2 medium potatoes, peeled and cut into
    1/2-inch cubes

1½ cups canned tomatoes, chopped, with
    liquid (or canned crushed tomatoes)

1 cup vegetable broth (or water)

2 Tbsp. honey

2 medium or 3 small zucchini, cut into
    3/4-inch pieces

4 Tbsp. lemon juice

1 cup canned chick peas

1/2 cup raisins

2 pinches saffron

1 tsp. salt

4 Tbsp. chopped cilantro (or parsley)

Cook onion, garlic, and ginger in olive oil over medium heat in large heavy pot. Sauté 3–4 minutes until soft. Add spices (minus the salt and saffron) and cook, stirring, about 2 minutes. Add carrots, turnips/rutabaga, and potatoes. Stir to coat with spices. Add tomatoes, broth, and honey. Bring to a boil, reduce heat to low, and cook covered at a simmer about 30 minutes, stirring occasionally. Add zucchini, lemon juice, chick peas, raisins, saffron, and salt. Cover again and cook another 20–30 minutes, stirring every so often. Serve piping hot over Saffron Jasmine Rice (p. 145), millet, or brown rice, and garnish with cilantro.

SERVES 4–6

Note: *Tagine* can be any of various slow-cooked Moroccan stews often consisting of a meat (such as lamb or poultry) gently simmered with vegetables, olives, preserved lemons, tomatoes, prunes, onions, garlic, and spices like cumin, ginger, pepper, saffron, and turmeric. A tagine also refers to the earthenware cooking vessel with a cone-shaped lid in which the stews are traditionally cooked.

Sunflower Lentil Loaf

This loaf is a wholesome vegan alternative to meatloaf. You can eat it as is or with a little ketchup for a nice homey meal.

Preheat oven to 350 degrees. Sauté onion, garlic, and celery in olive oil over medium heat until soft and onion is translucent. Add sage and cook another minute or so. Remove pan from heat. Combine onion mixture with rest of ingredients, saving 2 Tbsp. of sunflower seeds to top the loaf. Put into large oiled loaf pan. Top with remaining sunflower seeds and cover with aluminum foil. Cook 20 minutes covered. Remove foil and cook 30 minutes more. When done, allow to cool completely (on a wire rack if possible). Eat with a green salad.

SERVES 6

1/2 cup + 2 Tbsp. toasted sunflower seeds (see Peanut Free Planet in Resources, p. 194, for info on buying allergen-free sunflower seeds)

1 medium onion, diced

2 cloves garlic, minced

2 stalks celery, finely chopped

1/4 cup olive oil

5 fresh sage leaves, minced fine (or 2 tsp. dried)

3 cups well-drained, cooked lentils

3 cups cooked brown rice

1/4 cup brown-rice bread crumbs, or corn-flake crumbs

2 Tbsp. oat flour

3 tsp. Ener-G Egg Replacer mixed with 4 Tbsp. enriched rice or oat milk

2 Tbsp. rice vinegar

1/2 tsp. salt

1/4 tsp. pepper

Thai Yellow Curry with Eggplant and Sweet Potato

*Thai curries are easy to make and immensely satisfying. After some experimenting,
I discovered that many are just fine when made without the traditional fish sauce present in
so much Thai food. I designed this recipe using yellow curry paste because it doesn't usually
include shrimp paste—whereas green or red curry paste very often will include peanut oil,
soy, and/or shrimp paste. Even so, be sure to read the curry paste's ingredients closely. If you
can find Kaffir Lime leaves, add 4 of them to this recipe at the same time you add the
eggplant. If you find them at a specialty Asian food market, I suggest buying a bunch and
freezing them, since you never know when you'll come across them again.*

1 Tbsp. coconut oil (see note on
   p. 66 regarding coconut)

1 medium onion, diced (1½ cups)

2 tsp. minced or grated ginger

1 heaping Tbsp. yellow curry paste

1 13.5-oz. can coconut milk (see note
   on p. 66 regarding coconut)

1 cup water

1 large sweet potato, peeled and cut into
   1½-inch chunks (about 3 cups)

1 medium eggplant, quartered lengthwise,
   and sliced into ½-inch-thick pieces
   (about 4 cups)

4 Kaffir Lime leaves (optional)

1/4 cup lime juice

1 tsp. grated lime zest

2 tsp. honey

salt

1/4 cup cilantro or Thai basil, chopped

Heat coconut oil in a large wok or frying pan over medium-high heat. Add onion, ginger, and curry paste. Cook about 2 minutes, stirring. Add the coconut milk and water. Bring to a boil. Reduce heat to low and simmer, uncovered, for 5 minutes. Don't cover the pan or the coconut milk will curdle. Add the sweet potato and continue to simmer for 6 minutes. Add the eggplant (and Kaffir Lime leaves) and cook for 30 minutes, or until the vegetables are very tender, stirring occasionally. Add lime juice and zest, honey, and salt to taste. Remove from heat and sprinkle with chopped cilantro or Thai basil. Serve with Coconut Rice (p. 146).

SERVES 4–6

Falafel

*Falafel is a super fast and nutritious meal that is easy to prepare. It's also really
fun to make with kids. I prefer to bake my falafel instead of frying it to cut down
on the fat, and, in fact, prefer the lighter flavor. The batter can be used immediately
or stored in an airtight container in the refrigerator for several days.*

Preheat oven to 425 degrees. Line a cookie sheet with aluminum foil and spread olive oil on it. Mince garlic in food processor. Add onion to food processor. Chop. Add parsley. Blend well. Add all remaining ingredients except for oat flour. Combine. Add flour a little at a time. The batter will seem wet, but you don't want it so wet that it doesn't hold together. You should be able to form balls by wetting your hands with water and then molding, wetting your hands between each ball. Note that refrigerating the batter for at least one hour will make it easier to roll into balls. You will have enough batter to make about 16 2-inch falafel balls. Place them on the cookie sheet, pressing them down just slightly. Cook 15 minutes, turn, and cook about another 20 minutes. Serve with Lemon Tahini Dressing (p. 48), brown rice or corn tortillas, and a salad.

SERVES 4

3 Tbsp. olive oil for baking

3 cloves garlic

1 small onion

1/4 cup tightly packed parsley

2 15-oz. cans chick peas, drained
   (about 3 cups)

3/4–1 tsp. salt

2 tsp. cumin

1 tsp. turmeric

1/8 tsp. cayenne

black pepper to taste

1 Tbsp. lemon juice

1 Tbsp. olive oil

2/3 cup oat flour (or other flour),
   adding more as necessary

Four-Bean Stew

*This hearty bean stew only gets better the next day. It's rich, herbaceous, and slightly sweet,
and packs a great nutritional punch in the protein and fiber department.*

3 Tbsp. olive oil

1 large red onion, diced

4 large cloves garlic, minced

3 carrots, chopped

3 stalks celery, chopped

1 Tbsp. fresh or dried thyme

1 15-oz. can lima beans (about 1½ cups)

1 15-oz. can kidney beans (about 1½ cups)

1 15-oz. can pinto beans (about 1½ cups)

1 15-oz. can black beans (about 1½ cups)

2 Tbsp. rice vinegar (or cider vinegar
   or red wine vinegar)

1 Tbsp. honey

1 Tbsp. Dijon mustard

1 tsp. salt

1/2 tsp. pepper

4 Tbsp. chopped parsley

2 cups water

juice of 1 lime

Sauté onion and garlic in olive oil in large pot over medium heat until soft. Add carrots and celery. Soften. Add thyme. Cook a minute or so. Add beans (do not drain them), vinegar, honey, mustard, salt, pepper, half of the parsley, and water. Bring to a boil, reduce to a simmer over low heat and cook, loosely covered, for 2 hours, stirring every 20 minutes or so. Remove from heat after 2 hours; add lime juice and the rest of the parsley. Eat with a light green salad and Basic Biscuits (p. 20).

SERVES 6

Millet Marranca

Traditional versions of this dish call for mushrooms, but I decided to up the protein by adding navy beans instead. This simple casserole covers all your nutritional bases in one.

Combine millet and water in a saucepan. Bring to a boil over medium-high heat, reduce to low and simmer, covered, about 20 minutes until tender. Remove from heat, and fluff with a fork. Set aside, loosely covered. Meanwhile, heat 2 Tbsp. olive oil in a large sauté pan over medium heat. Add onion and cook until soft, about 5 minutes. Add the cauliflower and garlic and cook about 15 minutes more, until cauliflower is tender when pricked with a fork. Meanwhile, preheat oven to 350 degrees. Oil a 9 x 13- or 10 x 12-inch pan with 2 Tbsp. olive oil. When cauliflower has cooked 15 minutes, remove from heat and add parsley, salt, pepper, and cayenne pepper. Combine lemon juice and the navy beans with the millet, mixing well, but gently. Add the cauliflower mixture to the millet mixture. Then press into the oiled baking pan, smoothing down the top. Sprinkle all over with paprika. Bake about 30 minutes until it becomes slightly golden on top.

SERVES 6–8

1½ cups raw millet

3 ¾ cups water

4 Tbsp. olive oil (divided)

2 cups onion, diced

1 large cauliflower, cut into small
    1-inch pieces

3 large cloves garlic, minced

1/3 cup tightly packed chopped parsley

1 tsp. kosher salt

freshly ground pepper

1/4 tsp. cayenne pepper

1/4 cup lemon juice

1 15-oz. can navy beans, drained
    (about 1½ cups)

sweet paprika for the top

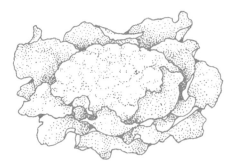

Ratatouille

Ratatouille is an eggplant casserole originally from Provence. It is extremely versatile—can be eaten hot or cold, over rice, alongside pasta, with roast chicken, or just on its own—the list goes on and on. It's even better days two and three, so feel free to make it in advance to let the flavors meld, if you wish.

1/4 cup olive oil

2 cloves garlic, minced

1 large onion, halved and thinly sliced

1 medium eggplant (about 1 lb.), cut into
   1½-inch cubes

6 small or 4 medium zucchini, cut into
   1/2-inch rounds

2 medium-size green peppers, cut into
   1-inch pieces

4 large or 6 medium tomatoes, coarsely
   chopped

1/4 cup chopped fresh parsley

1/2 tsp. dried thyme

1/2 tsp. salt

1/4 tsp. pepper

1/4 cup tightly packed, chopped fresh basil

Cook garlic and onion in olive oil over medium heat in a large heavy pot until soft, about 7 minutes. Add eggplant and zucchini. Cover and cook over medium heat for 10 minutes, stirring occasionally. Add peppers, cover, and cook 5 minutes more. Add tomatoes, parsley, thyme, salt, and pepper. Cover and cook over low heat about 20 minutes, until all vegetables are tender but not mushy. Remove from heat, stir in chopped basil, and adjust salt and pepper to taste. Serve hot or cold.

SERVES 4

Stuffed Cabbage

Stuffed cabbage is a traditional Eastern European dish. I've modernized and westernized it in the recipe on the opposite page by making it completely vegan, but for those not yet converted to vegetarian cuisine, trust me, you won't miss the meat. This recipe borrows from one for sweet and sour meatballs given to me by my husband's Grandma Lily. I modified her recipe for the sauce and paired it with the cabbage for a delightful mouthwatering treat. This dish is even better the second day, so if you have leftovers, you're in luck!

Boil a large pot of water. Cut out the core of the cabbage, using a small paring knife. You want to keep the cabbage intact, just getting rid of the tough center at the base of the cabbage. Drop the cabbage into the boiling water and boil for about 5 minutes, until the leaves start to separate and become tender. Keep the water boiling and, using tongs, remove the large outer leaves one at a time, placing them in a colander to drain. You should have about 12–14 large leaves. Let dry on paper towels. Meanwhile, boil the remaining center of the cabbage about 2 more minutes, then remove it to drain and cool. Using a paring knife, shave down the tough rib on the back of each large leaf (it's at the bottom). If it still seems at all tough, you may remove the bottom of the rib altogether by cutting out an upside-down V. Set leaves aside for stuffing. Chop the leftover center of the cabbage until it's fine. You should have about 2 cups of chopped cabbage—1 cup for stuffing and 1 cup for sauce.

To make sauce, combine onion, lemon juice, honey, tomato paste, water, salt and pepper. Bring to a boil, add 1 cup chopped cabbage, reduce heat, and simmer about 30 minutes.

Meanwhile make stuffing for cabbage. Sauté onion in olive oil over medium heat. When soft, add carrot, garlic, coriander, and cinnamon. Cook until soft, about 3 more minutes. Add water and bring to a boil. Cover, reduce heat, and cook about 3 minutes more. Remove from heat. Combine onion mixture with rice, currants (or raisins), chick peas, remaining cup of chopped cabbage, cider vinegar, salt, and pepper.

Preheat oven to 350 degrees. Cover bottom of a large baking pan (9 x 13- or 10 x 12-inch) with sauce. To stuff leaves, lay them rib side down. Place about 1/3 cup stuffing inside, fold in both sides, and roll up from the bottom to make a nice neat parcel. Place in the baking pan seam side down. Once you've stuffed all the leaves, pour remaining sauce over top. Cover with aluminum foil and bake 1¾ hours. Remove cover and bake 15 minutes more. Eat with a light green salad.

SERVES 6

1 large cabbage

Stuffing:
2 Tbsp. olive oil
1½ cups diced onion
1 carrot, diced
2 cloves garlic, minced
1/2 tsp. ground coriander
1/4 tsp. cinnamon
1/4 cup water
2 cups cooked brown rice
1/2 cup currants (or raisins)
1/2 cup cooked chick peas
2 Tbsp. cider vinegar
1/4 tsp. salt
1/8 tsp. pepper
1 cup chopped cabbage (this will come
   from the leftovers of the large cabbage
   listed above after you've boiled it)

Sauce:
1½ cups diced onion
1/2 cup lemon juice
3/4 cup honey
1 6-oz. can tomato paste
3/4 cup water
1/4 tsp. salt
1/8 tsp. pepper
1 cup chopped cabbage (this will come
   from the leftovers of the large cabbage
   listed above after you've boiled it)

Black Bean and Spinach Burritos

This is a quick, easy, high-protein, and inexpensive lunch or dinner enjoyed by young and old alike.

2 Tbsp. olive oil

1 cup diced onion (about 1 small onion)

2 large cloves garlic

2 tsp. cumin

1 tsp. chili powder

1/2 tsp. oregano

4 cups tightly packed chopped spinach (baby or regular)

2 15-oz. cans black beans, not drained (about 3 cups)

juice of 1 lime

1/4 tsp. salt

1/4 cup water

6–8 large brown rice tortillas (or follow the alternate recipe at right for soft tacos made with corn tortillas)

1/4 cup chopped cilantro

2 ripe avocados, mashed

salsa

Tip

Try making these with Food for Life Brown Rice Tortillas.

Sauté onion and garlic in olive oil over medium heat until soft, without burning garlic. Add spices. Cook a minute or two. Add spinach. Cook until wilted. Add beans, lime juice, salt, and water. Mash about half the beans with a potato masher or fork. Bring to a boil, then reduce heat to low and cook at a slow simmer for about 20–25 minutes, stirring frequently.

To assemble burritos, heat a skillet over high heat. Place the tortilla in the pan and turn after about 30 seconds. Heat 30 seconds more on the other side. You just want to warm the tortilla, not toast it. You can also warm them in a 375-degree oven for a minute or so. Next, place the warm tortilla on a plate. Spread about 1 Tbsp. mashed avocado in the center of the tortilla. Top with about 4 Tbsp. beans. Put about 1 Tbsp. salsa on top of beans and then sprinkle with chopped cilantro. Fold tortilla in on both sides. Then fold up the bottom. Lastly, fold down the top, and press lightly. The steam from the hot filling will seal the tortilla. You will have some leftover beans for later. Eat with a salad, and extra salsa if you wish. You may also serve brown rice alongside.

SERVES 6–8

Variation

For **Soft Tacos:** use 12 corn tortillas. Heat the same way you would heat the brown rice tortillas. Use the same proportions as above, except cut the beans to 2 Tbsp. per taco. Fold in half and eat the same way you eat a hard taco.

Side Dishes

I've included mostly grain, potato, and other hearty side dishes here, because I think it's pretty easy to think up vegetable dishes that are hypoallergenic, and I trust that most people are already doing that on their own. Steam, boil, roast, or sauté any vegetable of your choice and you've got that part of your dinner covered. But potato or rice side dishes, and others of that sort, traditionally use butter or cheese or other allergenic foods. So the following side-dish recipes are within the hypoallergenic guidelines of this book. As always, adapt as you see fit.

Oven Baked Sweet Potato Fries

This is another one of my recipes that first appeared in Good Housekeeping. *It's simple, addictively delicious, and serves up a hearty amount of your daily requirements for beta-carotene and vitamin C.*

Preheat oven to 475 degrees. Peel potatoes if you like. Cut in half horizontally, and then cut the halves down the middle vertically. Lay flat side down on cutting board and slice horizontally into 1/4-inch-thick steak fries. Pour olive oil on a cookie sheet. Toss potatoes with olive oil. Sprinkle with salt and pepper. Cook about 30 minutes, turning once. They are done when they've started to brown up a bit.

2 large sweet potatoes
2 Tbsp. olive oil
salt and pepper

SERVES 4

Tarragon Roast Potatoes

Tarragon is a slightly sweet herb that is excellent with roasted foods.

4 large Yukon gold or red potatoes,
    chopped into 1/2-inch pieces
2 Tbsp. chopped fresh tarragon, or
    2 tsp. dried
1 shallot, minced fine
1/3 cup olive oil
white pepper
1 Tbsp. balsamic vinegar

Preheat oven to 400 degrees. In a large baking pan, toss all ingredients, except the balsamic vinegar. Cook about 40 minutes, turning potatoes once or twice. After about 40 minutes, the potatoes should have "puffed." Turn heat down to 375 degrees and cook another 20 to 30 minutes. Potatoes are done when tender on the inside, but be careful when testing for doneness, because these little tots are very, very hot. Drizzle with balsamic vinegar.

SERVES 6–8

Potato Chips

These are a heart-healthy baked version of a favorite American side dish.
They are great with lunch or dinner, or even as an after-school snack.

2 large russet potatoes, cut into
    1/8-inch rounds
2 Tbsp. olive or canola oil
salt
pepper (optional)

Preheat oven to 475 degrees. Toss sliced potatoes with olive oil and sprinkle with salt. Lay out in one layer on a cookie sheet. Cook about 30–40 minutes, turning once, until crispy golden brown. You may wish to sprinkle them with a little more salt and pepper. Eat hot (but careful, they're really hot on the inside).

SERVES 4

New Potatoes with Parsley

*I like this savory, herbaceous side dish hot or at room temperature. It's great
with just about any kind of grilled or roasted poultry or meat.*

Cover potatoes with water in a pot and boil until tender
(15–20 minutes). Check them with a fork. Drain and toss
immediately with olive oil, chopped parsley, salt and pepper. They like a fair amount of salt. Serve hot.

SERVES 4–6

2 lbs. new potatoes (halved if larger
    than 1 inch)
1/2 cup chopped parsley
1/4 cup olive oil
salt and pepper

Mashed Potatoes

*Mashed potatoes are my number one comfort food. They are extremely
versatile due to their mild flavor, and pair up well with just about anything.*

Cook potatoes in water to cover thoroughly, about 15–20
minutes. Make sure they're really soft. Drain, and use an
electric mixer to combine with rice milk, olive oil, and salt.
Beat until fluffy.

SERVES 4

3 large baking potatoes (Idaho, etc.), cubed
3/4 cup enriched rice milk
3 Tbsp. olive oil
1/2 tsp. salt
pepper

Variation

For added flavor, add 3 cloves roasted garlic, or
2 Tbsp. parsley, or both.

Holiday Orange Sweet Potato Bake

My mother made this every year either for Thanksgiving or Christmas. It's one of my favorite foods. It tastes very fancy, but is incredibly easy to make. So easy that you may choose to make it more than once a year for holidays. In addition to this recipe, which makes enough to feed a crowd, I have also included an everyday version (see page at right) for smaller gatherings. This dish is even better the next day rewarmed, so you can always make it a day early for holidays to save yourself cooking everything at once. It takes about half an hour to rewarm at 350 degrees.

8 large sweet potatoes (best to use yams, which have a rich orange color)

8 Tbsp. canola oil

1½ tsp. cinnamon, plus more to sprinkle at end

5 Tbsp. maple sugar

2½–2¾ cups orange juice

1 large orange, sliced into very thin rounds or half-moons (you may need more than one orange)

Peel sweet potatoes and cut into 1-inch chunks. Place in large pot and cover with water. Boil about 15–20 minutes, until tender when pierced with a fork. Meanwhile, preheat oven to 350 degrees. When sweet potatoes are tender, drain. Put back in pot. With an electric beater, mix in 6 Tbsp. of the canola oil, 3 Tbsp. of the maple sugar, the 1½ tsp. cinnamon, and 2½ cups orange juice. Beat on medium speed until nice and smooth. Taste and add last 1/4 cup of orange juice if it seems too thick. Spoon whipped sweet potatoes into a lightly greased deep casserole. Smooth the top. Arrange the orange slices in a pretty pattern all across the top. Crumble last 2 Tbsp. maple sugar over top of oranges. Then drizzle with last 2 Tbsp. canola oil, and sprinkle all over with a few shakes of cinnamon. Bake about 1 hour until maple sugar becomes nicely caramelized on top and orange slices are obviously cooked and tender. Serve it really piping hot.

SERVES 12

Everyday Sweet Potato Bake

Peel sweet potatoes and cut into 1-inch chunks. Place in pot and cover with water. Boil about 15–20 minutes, until tender when pierced with a fork. Meanwhile, preheat oven to 350 degrees. When sweet potatoes are tender, drain. Put back in pot. With an electric beater, mix in 2 Tbsp. canola oil, 1 Tbsp. of the maple sugar, 1/2 tsp. cinnamon, and 3/4 cup orange juice. Beat on medium speed until nice and smooth. Taste and add last 1/4 cup of orange juice if it seems too thick. Spoon whipped sweet potatoes into a lightly greased small casserole or loaf pan. Smooth the top. Arrange the orange slices in a pretty pattern across the top. Crumble last 1/2 Tbsp. maple sugar over top of oranges and sprinkle all over with a few shakes of cinnamon. Bake about 1 hour, until maple sugar becomes nicely caramelized on top and orange slices are obviously cooked and tender.

SERVES 4

3 large sweet potatoes (best to use yams, which have a rich orange color)

2 Tbsp. canola oil

1/2 tsp. cinnamon, plus more to sprinkle at end

1½ Tbsp. maple sugar

3/4–1 cup orange juice

1/2 large orange sliced into very thin rounds or half-moons

Rosemary Garlic Fingerling Potatoes

Fingerling potatoes are best when in season when they're really, really small. But you can still find them off-season at most grocery stores. If you aren't buying them prebagged and can choose them yourself, opt for the tiny ones. They're excellent popped in your mouth whole for a little explosion of flavor, but be careful—they get extremely hot.

Preheat oven to 425 degrees. Wash and pat dry potatoes. Combine all ingredients on a cookie sheet. Cook about 30 to 40 minutes, turning once, until nice and golden. Serve at once.

SERVES 4–6

2 lbs. fingerling potatoes (cut into halves if they are big)

2 Tbsp. olive oil

2 cloves garlic

1 Tbsp. dried rosemary

salt and pepper

Herbed Jerusalem Artichokes

Jerusalem artichokes aren't really artichokes—they're the roots of the sunflower, so they're more of a sun choke. I don't think they're from Jerusalem either. But no matter what they really are, they're delicious and hearty, and way underused as far as I'm concerned. You can cook them any way you'd cook a potato; bake, fry, steam, boil, or mash them. Personally, I like to roast them in the oven with a little olive oil and herbs. They have a slightly nutty flavor and pair well with whole grains, roasted meats, or even cut up into pasta.

1½ lbs. (about 12) Jerusalem artichokes
2 Tbsp. olive oil
salt
pepper
1 tsp. dried thyme

Preheat oven to 425 degrees. Wash artichokes and cut away any bruised or brown spots. Halve or quarter them into 1-inch chunks. Toss with olive oil, sprinkle with salt, pepper, and thyme. Put on a cookie sheet or in a baking dish, and cook about 30 minutes, turning occasionally to brown up on all sides.

SERVES 4

Butternut Squash with Maple Syrup

My sons love this relatively effortless but fancy-tasting dish. It pairs up nicely with chicken, turkey, pork tenderloin, or is good just on its own as a healthy mid-afternoon snack.

1 large butternut squash
2 Tbsp. olive oil
2 Tbsp. maple syrup
sprinkle of cinnamon

Peel the squash, cut in half, and remove seeds. Cut into 1-inch chunks. Boil or steam until tender when pricked with a fork. Transfer to serving bowl, drizzle with olive oil and maple syrup, and sprinkle with cinnamon to taste. Mash or leave in chunks, whichever you prefer.

SERVES 4

Acorn Squash with Cranberries (or Cherries)

This acorn squash is a beautiful festive medley of colors and flavors. It's great in the colder months, served piping hot straight out of the oven, but also tastes wonderful at room temperature in the warmer months as part of an early harvest meal.

Preheat oven to 375 degrees. Put halved acorn squash in a shallow baking dish, cut side up. Put 1 Tbsp. of cranberries (or cherries) in each half. Sprinkle with 1 Tbsp. maple sugar or honey each. Bake for 1 hour.

SERVES 4

2 medium acorn squash, halved
and deseeded
4 Tbsp. fresh or dried cranberries
(or dried cherries)
4 Tbsp. maple sugar or honey

Saffron Jasmine Rice

This dish is great with pork chops, chicken, and Venison Osso Buco (p. 118).

Sauté shallot in olive oil in medium saucepan over medium heat until soft. Add rice and stir, crumble in saffron, add water or broth, and salt to taste. Bring to a boil, reduce heat to low, cover, and cook at a simmer for 20 minutes.

SERVES 4

1 Tbsp. finely minced shallot (or onion)
1 Tbsp. olive oil
1 cup jasmine rice
1 pinch of saffron, crumbled
2 cups water or low-salt chicken broth
salt to taste

Coconut Rice

This rice is mild, easy, and great with curry dishes or spicy meats.

1½ cups basmati rice

1 14-oz. can light coconut milk (see note on page 66 regarding coconut)

1¼ cups water

1 tsp. honey

salt

1 Tbsp. chopped cilantro (optional)

1–2 Tbsp. toasted shredded coconut (optional)

Combine rice, coconut milk, water, honey, and salt in a pan. Bring to a boil, reduce heat to low, cover and simmer 20 minutes. Remove from heat and let sit covered about 5 minutes before fluffing with a fork. Serve garnished with chopped cilantro and coconut, if you wish.

SERVES 4–6

Wild Rice Pilaf with Cherries, Zucchini, and Carrots

This rice pilaf is perfect for dinner parties or special occasions, or any time you want a lovely bowl of confetti-like color on your table.

3½ cups chicken broth

1 cup wild rice

1/2 cup long-grain brown rice (jasmine, texamati, basmati, etc.)

2 bay leaves

4 sprigs fresh thyme

1 cup minced red onion

3 Tbsp. olive oil

1 carrot, diced into very small cubes

1 small zucchini, diced into very small cubes

1/2 cup dried cherries (or cranberries)

1 Tbsp. chopped parsley

salt and pepper

Bring the chicken broth to a boil in a medium pot. Stir in wild rice, brown rice, 1 bay leaf, and 2 sprigs of the thyme. Bring to a boil, reduce heat to low and simmer, covered, 20 minutes. Meanwhile, in a medium pan, sauté onion in olive oil over medium heat until they begin to soften, about 4–5 minutes. Add carrots and zucchini. Soften a few more minutes. Add the cherries, the last bay leaf, and final 2 sprigs of thyme. Cook 1–2 minutes more. Remove from heat. Once rice has cooked 20 minutes, add vegetable/fruit mixture. Stir in. Replace cover. Cook 20 minutes more for a total cooking time of 40 minutes for the rice. Remove from heat and let sit about 10 minutes. Stir in parsley, black pepper, and salt to taste.

SERVES 6–8

Brown Rice with Celery and Mushrooms

Serve this simple, earthy side dish with roast poultry or meat.

Sauté celery and onion in olive oil over medium heat until soft. Stir in thyme and cook 1 minute more. Add rice and stir to coat with olive oil. Add mushrooms and water/broth. Bring to a boil. Reduce heat to low and cook covered 45 minutes. Remove from heat and let sit 5–10 minutes. Add salt and pepper to taste.

SERVES 4

2 stalks celery, chopped

2 Tbsp. minced onion

1 Tbsp. olive oil

1/4 tsp. thyme

1 cup brown rice

8 mushrooms, sliced

2 1/4 cups water, vegetable broth, or low-salt chicken broth

salt and pepper

Curried Rice with Raisins

This fragrant dish is great as a side, or you can add a little diced chicken for a meal unto itself.

Combine rice, water and salt to taste. Bring to a boil, reduce heat to low and cook covered about 45 minutes. Remove from heat and let sit about 5–10 minutes, then fluff with a fork. Meanwhile, sauté onion over medium heat until soft. Add curry, and cook stirring about 2 minutes. Add raisins, peas, and 1 tsp. water. Stir and cook a couple of minutes until the raisins plump up a bit. Remove from heat. When rice is cooked, combine with the curry mixture. Stir to make sure it's heated through.

SERVES 6–8

1 cup brown basmati rice

2 1/4 cups water

salt

2 Tbsp. olive oil

1 medium onion, diced (1 cup)

2 tsp. curry powder

3/4 cup raisins

1/2 cup peas (optional)

1 tsp. water

Rice Pilaf

This is a tasty pilaf with an old-world flavor.

2 Tbsp. olive oil
1 large red onion, minced
1/4 tsp. cinnamon
1/4 tsp. cumin
2 tsp. honey
salt and pepper
1 cup long-grain brown rice
2 cups vegetable broth or water
1/2 cup cooked lentils
2 Tbsp. chopped parsley

Sauté onion in olive oil in medium saucepan over medium heat about 10 minutes. Stir in spices and honey and cook about 5 minutes more. Add rice. Cook, stirring, about 3–4 more minutes. Add broth/water. Bring to a boil, then reduce heat to low, cover, and cook at a simmer 45 minutes, stirring occasionally. Add lentils and cook about 15 more minutes. Toss with chopped parsley.

SERVES 4

Lemon Quinoa

Quinoa has a wonderful texture and pairs well with just about anything.
It's also very high in protein, which makes it a favorite in my house.

1 cup quinoa
2 cups water
2 Tbsp. olive oil
grated zest from half a lemon
4 tsp. lemon juice
salt

Combine all ingredients in a saucepan. Bring to a boil, reduce heat to low and cook, covered, about 12 to 15 minutes. Quinoa is done when the little white rings have separated from the grain.

SERVES 4–6

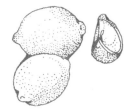

Millet with Sage and Red Bell Pepper

Millet is sort of like polenta in texture. It's very mild and makes good comfort food.
Eat it right after making, since it tends to solidify when cooled.

Combine millet with broth or water and bring to a boil. Reduce heat to low and simmer covered about 20 minutes, until water is absorbed. Remove from heat and let stand covered 10 minutes. While millet rests, sauté onion in olive oil over medium heat until it starts to soften, about 4 min - utes. Add bell pepper and cook 3 or 4 more minutes. Add sage, orange zest, and orange juice. Cook 1 minute more. Add sautéed vegetables to millet, season with salt and pep- per to taste, and serve. Add a little more olive oil if it's too thick.

SERVES 4–6

1 cup millet
2 cups vegetable broth or water
1/2 cup onion, minced
3 Tbsp. olive oil
1 bell pepper, red, orange, or yellow
   (about 1 cup chopped)
1 Tbsp. minced fresh sage or
   1/2 Tbsp. dried
1/2 tsp. grated orange zest
1 Tbsp. orange juice
salt and pepper

Polenta

Polenta is a personal favorite. I like it as is, topped with tomato sauce, or alongside
chicken, lamb, or other meats. Polenta is endlessly versatile.

Bring chicken broth to a boil. When it comes to a rolling boil, pour in polenta, stirring constantly. Lower heat and cook, stirring, about 4 or 5 minutes, until polenta reaches desired consistency. Serve drizzled with olive oil, freshly ground pepper, and sprinkled with fresh herbs.

SERVES 4–6

1 cup polenta
4 cups low-salt chicken broth or water
salt
freshly ground pepper (optional)
olive oil (optional)
parsley or basil or sage (optional)

Tip

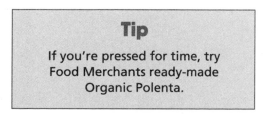

If you're pressed for time, try Food Merchants ready-made Organic Polenta.

Sausage, Dried Fruit, and Apple Stuffing

*I first made this stuffing one Christmas in Chicago, where my husband and I were living
for several months while he was doing the test run of the Broadway musical AIDA. In the
old days, Broadway shows did out-of-town test runs in Boston, but these days it's often
Chicago—which is fine by me, because I fell in love with the town. It's a real food city and
not half as cold as people like to say. I first made this stuffing in the tiny oven of our little
run-down hotel room. I cooked it in a throwaway baking pan with unpredictable oven
heat—and it turned out absolutely fabulous. We ate our Christmas dinner with fellow actor
friends, and a great time was had by all. I hope you enjoy it half as much as we do.
This recipe makes enough for plenty of leftovers, great the next day on their own
or in a sandwich (Thanksgiving on a Roll, see Sandwich Ideas, p. 64).*

8 cups cubed (1-inch) wheat-free bread

3 Tbsp. olive oil

1 Tbsp. dried thyme

salt and pepper to taste

1 lb. spicy turkey sausage

1 large sweet onion, diced (about 2 cups)

3 large cloves garlic, minced

4 stalks celery, chopped

1 tsp. dried sage, crumbled

1 Granny Smith apple, peeled, cored, and
    cut into 1/2-inch pieces

1/2 cup dried cherries or cranberries

1/2 cup dried apricots, quartered

1½ cups low-salt chicken broth

Preheat oven to 350 degrees. Toss bread cubes with 2 Tbsp. olive oil, thyme, salt, and pepper. Spread in one layer on cookie sheet. Bake about 20 minutes until lightly toasted, shaking occasionally to toast on all sides. Remove from oven and set aside. Meanwhile, remove sausage from casing and break up into clumps. Heat a heavy skillet over medium heat and add sausage. Cook until all the pink is gone. Remove to a large mixing bowl. Pour off fat if there is any remaining in skillet. Add 1 Tbsp. olive oil, onion, garlic, celery, and sage to pan, and sauté over medium heat until wilted, about 15 minutes, stirring frequently. Once wilted, add to mixing bowl with sausage. Toss. Add in bread cubes, apple, cherries, and apricots. Toss. Oil a 9 x 13-inch baking dish with olive oil. Spoon in the stuffing, and drizzle with chicken broth. Bake until crusty and golden brown, about 1 hour, tossing once or twice.

SERVES 8

Dora's Cranberry Sauce

This is my great-grandmother Dora's cranberry sauce. I've been known to eat it on its own with a spoon. It's traditionally made with walnuts, but for the purposes of this book, I've omitted them. However, if you can eat nuts without risk, add 1/2 cup of broken walnut meats in last 5 minutes of cooking. There was no recipe left by Dora, but according to my father, this is pretty close to the original stuff. The proportions can be shifted around to suit your personal taste, or you can substitute oranges for the tangerines. Note that cranberries are berries, so don't give this to a child who isn't permitted to eat berries.

Wash and pick over berries to remove any stems or spoiled berries. Put in saucepan, add water, and bring to a slow boil. While the cranberries heat up, peel 1 tangerine, remove any seeds, and chop into pieces. Wash the other tangerine in detergent and hot water to remove any traces of pesticides (if not organic). Slice the second tangerine in half, halve one-half again, and cut both quarters into thin slivers of rind with the flesh attached. The other half can be peeled and chopped, leaving out the peel. Add tangerine peel and slices to the cranberries. When the cranberries are mostly popped, add honey and simmer for about 1 hour and 15 minutes, until sauce thickens and the fruit seems "candied." Best if chilled overnight.

SERVES 8–10

1 12-oz. package of fresh cranberries
1½ cups water
2 tangerines
1½ cups honey

Cornbread and Wild Mushroom Stuffing

*This is a rich-tasting, exotic, and delicious stuffing
that's great with any kind of poultry.*

3 cups cornbread (about half a recipe from Grandmother Catherene's Cornbread, p. 21 preferably stale so it's dried out a bit)

1/2 cup diced pancetta (about 2 oz.)

4 Tbsp. olive oil

5 large shallots (both halves), minced fine

2 stalks celery, chopped into 1/4-inch pieces

1/2 lb. wild mushrooms (I like shiitake, but you could also use chanterelles or morels, quartered or cut into eighths if very large)

1 tsp. fresh thyme, chopped

1 tsp. fresh rosemary, chopped

1/4 tsp. salt

1/4 tsp. pepper

1/4 cup white wine

1/4 cup oat milk

1/3 cup low-salt chicken broth

Preheat oven to 350 degrees. Cut cornbread into 1-inch-thick pieces and place, cut side down, on a baking sheet. Either toast in toaster oven or bake in oven at 350 degrees until golden brown and dried out a bit, about 10–15 minutes—but keep an eye on it because you don't want it to burn. Remove from oven/toaster and let cool. Heat a heavy skillet over medium-high heat. Once pan is really hot, add the pancetta and cook until crispy. Remove pancetta from pan and set aside. Add olive oil to skillet, then shallots and celery. Cook, stirring occasionally, until soft, about 3 minutes. Add the mushrooms, thyme, rosemary, salt, and pepper. Cook, stirring occasionally, until slightly soft, about 4 minutes. Add white wine and cook, stirring until it's been absorbed, about 1 or 2 minutes. Add oat milk and cook about 1 minute more. Remove pan from heat. Crumble in the cornbread and add the crispy pancetta bits. Toss gently. Oil a 9 x 13-inch baking dish with olive oil. Spoon in the stuffing and drizzle with chicken broth. Bake until crusty and golden brown, about 30 minutes.

SERVES 4–6

Caramelized Onion Gravy

You may prepare the gravy base for this up to several days in advance.
You can also freeze it and defrost when ready to use.

Cook onions with olive oil over very low heat about 45 minutes to 1 hour, until soft and starting to caramelize. Don't rush this. You'll be tempted to turn up the heat, but it's the low temperature that releases and caramelizes the sugar in the onions. Stir in the rosemary, thyme, and marjoram. Then add 1 Tbsp. of the oat flour. Cook about 1 minute. Add the vinegar and honey. Cook, stirring until thickened, about 2–3 more minutes. Set aside if using later, or if serving with roast chicken or turkey (see note below). Otherwise, proceed as follows. Over medium heat, stir final 2 Tbsp. oat flour into the onions. Then add chicken broth, salt, and pepper. Simmer about 15 minutes, reducing a bit until thickened. Taste for seasonings. Serve hot with chicken or turkey and biscuits or mashed potatoes.

MAKES ABOUT 3 ½ CUPS

Note: If you are serving this with roast chicken or turkey, make the gravy in the roasting pan. To do this, remove the chicken or turkey to a platter and cover with tented alu - minum foil to keep warm. Put roasting pan over medium heat on burner. Add broth and use a wooden spoon to scrape off bits from sides of pan. Then add gravy base, flour, salt, and pepper. I like making it this way best as it adds deeper flavor.

1/4 cup olive oil
2 large Vidalia or other sweet onions,
    cut into thin slices, not diced
1 Tbsp. fresh rosemary, chopped
1 Tbsp. fresh thyme, chopped
1 tsp. fresh marjoram, chopped, or
    1/2 tsp. dried
3 Tbsp. oat flour
1/4 cup balsamic or red wine vinegar
2 Tbsp. honey
4 cups low-salt chicken broth
salt and pepper

Avocado Raita

This is a creamy alternative to the yogurt-based raita one would usually eat with spicy Indian curries. It's quite tasty, but please note that it should be eaten quickly, as it doesn't refrigerate well overnight.

1 ripe avocado

1/2 cup enriched rice milk

1/4 tsp. salt

1 small cucumber, peeled and diced
(about 1 cup)

1/4 cup chopped fresh mint or cilantro

1/2 tsp. cumin

2 tsp. canola oil

1 tsp. black mustard seeds (optional)

Combine avocado, rice milk, and salt in a food processor. Remove to a bowl. Add the cucumber, mint or cilantro, and cumin. In heavy skillet heat oil over medium heat; add mustard seeds and cook until they finish popping. This is a messy business as they pop everywhere, so use the back burner and be prepared for them to fly. Once they've finished popping, quickly pour over the avocado mixture. Stir and refrigerate to chill, about 1 hour.

MAKES ABOUT 1$\frac{1}{2}$ CUPS

ELIMINATING REFINED CANE SUGAR

When I started writing this cookbook, I still used refined cane sugar: white, brown, and confectioners' sugar. My southern grandmother never thought twice about it, and I figured if it was good enough for her, it was good enough for me.

Throughout my childhood, my parents fed me fresh organic foods out of our garden. Yet, I always had sugar-laden home-baked treats for snacks. I never considered the dietary implications of sugar, beyond what it does to your teeth, and deemed it a safe food. I used organic sugar because it wasn't bleached and continued this way until a few years ago when it became clear that I must make every calorie count. I want every bite my family puts into their mouths to have nutritive value, so I embarked on replacing refined sugar with whole foods sweeteners in every single recipe.

The results have been phenomenal. I love baking without sugar. I adore the rich flavors of honey, agave nectar, maple syrup, molasses, fruit juice, maple sugar, palm sugar, and date sugar. And there's been an added bonus, which is that I feel great. I think I have spent a good deal of my life surfing sugar highs and lows, which I am no longer experiencing. I have not felt that daily midmorning or afternoon crash since I started this. And I am never going back to cane sugar.

This choice has actually become more of an imperative given my son Lennon's hyperactivity. Sugar sends him off the wall. It makes him "spin out of control" and then get moody, often ending with tears. He is, after all, very sensitive to what he puts into his body. I find that if I keep him away from refined sugar, he stays much more even-keeled. But when they give him candy at school (despite my requests that they shouldn't), he comes home a lovable handful. So whether your concern is your teeth, energy levels, nutrition, avoiding chemicals, or simply flavor, I'd strongly suggest giving refined cane sugar the old heave-ho. Whole foods sweeteners are so much better!

SWEET THINGS

- Pudding
- Cupcakes
- Cookies
- Fruit Combos
- Cakes
- Pies

Everyone in my family has a sweet tooth. My son Lennon loves chocolate, my husband loves cupcakes, I like fruity sweets, and my youngest, Monte, loves it all.

I like to indulge us, and given that I use no refined sugar and all whole grain flours, I don't even feel guilty about it.

These desserts have been taste-tested hundreds of times, and everyone who eats them loves them, whether or not they're on a hypoallergenic diet. In addition to being allergen-free, these treats are also all vegan.

Easy Coconut Rice Pudding

This dessert is about as simple and delicious as they get. You can put it into individual dessert bowls or parfait cups for a fancy-looking cap to a meal.

1½ cups cooked brown jasmine or brown basmati rice

1 14-oz. can coconut milk (see note on p. 66 regarding coconut)

1/2 cup honey

1 tsp. vanilla extract

1¼ cups canned diced peaches, apricots, mango, or mixed fruit salad, with their own juice (8.5-oz. can)

Combine cooked rice, coconut milk, and honey in pan over medium heat. Cook, stirring frequently, until thickened, about 15 minutes. Remove from heat, stir in vanilla extract, and transfer to a serving bowl. Cover and refrigerate to chill. Once chilled, top with fruit. For a fancier presentation, spoon a little fruit into a dessert bowl or parfait cup, top with rice pudding, and then add a little more fruit.

SERVES 4–6

Banana Cupcakes

*This tasty cupcake doubles well as breakfast on mornings
when you're running out the door.*

Preheat oven to 350 degrees. Line muffin pans with 12
liners. Combine canola oil and honey in a large bowl.
Beat until smooth. Add egg replacer, banana, and vanilla
extract. Combine oat flour, barley flour, baking soda,
baking powder, and salt. Alternating, add flour mixture
and rice/oat milk to bowl. Beat until fully mixed. Pour
into muffin pan. Bake for 25 minutes. Cupcakes are done
when they've become a lovely golden color on top, and they
bounce back when pressed. Let cool well before removing
from pan. Loosen with a knife if necessary.
Eat plain or frosted.

To make the frosting, combine vegetable shortening
with honey using an electric mixer. Add vanilla extract
and rice/oat milk. Mix. Then add Better Than Milk Powder
and beat until fluffy. Frost cupcakes with a butter knife.

MAKES 12 CUPCAKES

Note: You can also make this into a layer cake by using
two round 8-inch pans and doubling the frosting.

Cupcakes:

1/2 cup canola oil

1 cup honey

3 tsp. Ener-G Egg Replacer, mixed with
    4 Tbsp. enriched rice or oat milk

1 cup mashed banana

1 tsp. vanilla extract

1 cup oat flour

1 cup barley flour

1/2 tsp. baking soda

3 tsp. double-acting baking powder

1/4 tsp. salt

1/2 cup enriched rice or oat milk

Vanilla Frosting:

1/4 cup vegetable shortening

1/4 cup honey

1 tsp. vanilla extract

2 Tbsp. enriched rice or oat milk

2/3 cup "Better Than Milk" Rice Powder

(For optional frostings, see p. 169.)

Old-Fashioned Oatmeal Cookies

This is an adaptation of my grandmother Catherene's old-fashioned oatmeal cookies.
I grew up on these cookies. They are delicious and nutritious. Note that the dough
freezes well, so you can always double the recipe and freeze half to use at a later date.

1/2 cup vegetable shortening

1/4 cup molasses

1/2 cup maple syrup

1 tsp. vanilla extract

1/2 cup + 2 Tbsp. oat flour

1/2 cup + 2 Tbsp. barley flour

1/4 tsp. salt

1/2 tsp. cinnamon

1/2 tsp. baking soda

1 tsp. double-acting baking powder

1 cup oats

1/2 cup raisins

Preheat oven to 350 degrees. Beat shortening with molasses and maple syrup in a large mixing bowl. Add vanilla extract. Combine oat flour, barley flour, salt, cinnamon, baking soda, and baking powder. Add to mixing bowl. Add oats, stir, and then add raisins.

Drop batter by heaping teaspoons onto a parchment-lined cookie sheet, and bake 10 minutes, until cookies are browning around the edges.

Let cool on cookie sheet before transferring to plate with a spatula.

MAKES ABOUT 2 DOZEN COOKIES

Variation

For a more decadent cookie, omit the raisins and add 1/4 cup shredded coconut and 1/4 cup dairy/soy-free chocolate chips.

Rolled Maple Sugar Cookies

Rolled cookies are a tasty treat that's fun to make with kids (or anyone, for that matter).
Use cookie cutters to cut out any shapes you like, and decorate accordingly.

1/2 cup vegetable shortening

3/4 cup maple sugar

1½ tsp. Ener-G Egg Replacer, mixed with
    2 Tbsp. enriched rice or oat milk

1/2 tsp. vanilla extract

1 Tbsp. enriched rice or oat milk

3/4 cup oat flour

3/4 cup barley flour

1/4 tsp. salt

1/2 tsp. baking powder

decorative toppings (optional): raisins,
    maple sugar mixed with cinnamon,
    coconut, dairy-free and soy-free choco-
    late chips

Cream shortening with maple sugar (note that maple sugar doesn't really cream, it blends). Beat in egg replacer and vanilla extract. Add 1 Tbsp. rice/oat milk. Combine oat flour, barley flour, salt, and baking powder. Add to bowl and combine thoroughly (it will be a bit stiff, but that's okay—use hands to combine if necessary). Mold into a ball, wrap in aluminum foil, and refrigerate for at least 1 hour. When ready to bake, preheat oven to 375 degrees. Remove dough from fridge. If it still seems too dry, sprinkle a few drops of water on it and work them in. Roll out dough with a floured rolling pin to 1/4-inch thickness, and use cookie cutters to cut out shapes. Decorate with raisins, maple sugar mixed with cinnamon, dairy-free chocolate chips, coconut, or whatever else you fancy. Arrange on a lightly greased cookie tray, and bake about 8 minutes. Let cool on tray before removing with a spatula or they'll break. How many you make depends on what shape and size cookie cutters you are using.

MAKES ABOUT 2 DOZEN COOKIES

Note: For basic maple sugar cookies, reduce both oat and barley flour by 2 Tbsp. each and skip the 1 hour of chilling. Just drop by teaspoons onto a lightly greased cookie sheet and bake about 8 minutes.

Chocolate Chip Cookie Bars

*These easy-to-make cookie bars are the perfect treat. Pack them in a lunch,
or serve them as an after-school snack with a chilled glass of rice milk
for dunking. They keep well in the fridge for days!*

1 ¼ cups barley flour

1 ¼ cups oat flour

1 ½ tsp. double-acting baking powder

1/4 tsp. salt

3/4 cup vegetable shortening

1 ½ cups light agave nectar

1 Tbsp. vanilla extract

3 tsp. Ener-G egg replacer mixed with
    4 Tbsp. rice milk

1 ½ cups dairy-free, soy-free chocolate
    chips (1 10 oz. bag)

Preheat oven to 350 degrees. Whisk together flours, baking powder, and salt. Set aside. Cream vegetable shortening using an electric mixer set on medium for about 2 minutes. Add agave nectar and beat until light and a little fluffy. Add vanilla extract and egg replacer. Mix. Add flour mixture, and beat on low speed until combined. Fold in chocolate chips. Grease a 9 x 9-inch baking pan and sprinkle with a little flour, tapping out any extra. Turn dough into pan, and smooth out with the back of a spoon or spatula. Bake about 35 minutes in center of oven, rotating pan once about halfway through until lightly golden. Remove from oven and let cool in pan on wire rack about 15 minutes. Cut into 16 squares. Let cool. Store in an airtight container in the fridge.

MAKES 16 BARS

Raspberry Streusel Bars

*These healthy, fruity bars are easy to make, and are great for dessert
or as an after-school snack. They're hands-on, so roll up your sleeves.*

Place rack in bottom third of oven and preheat to 350
degrees. Make Rolled Maple Sugar Cookie dough (see note
in the right-hand column). Add 1 cup oats to dough, and
use hands to knead in completely. Remove 1/2 cup of this
dough and set aside for later. Place remainder of dough in a
greased and lightly floured 9 x 13-inch or 8.5 x 12-inch baking pan. Use fingers to press down all over into a thin crust,
about 1/4 inch thick. Spread raspberry jam evenly in a thin
layer over the dough. In mixing bowl, combine remaining
1/2 cup dough with remaining 1/2 cup oats, the maple sugar,
and the cinnamon. Use fingers to break up into a crumble.
Sprinkle evenly over jam layer. Bake 25 to 30 minutes until
golden brown and jam is bubbling up around the edges.
Remove from oven and let cool about
10 minutes before slicing into bars. Let cool completely
before removing from pan to allow them to set.

MAKES 12–16 BARS

1 recipe Rolled Maple Sugar Cookies (p. 161)
   (Note: Be sure to reduce both the oat
   flour and the barley flour by 2 Tbsp.
   each, and skip the 1 hour of chilling.)
1½ cups oats
1 cup fruit-only raspberry jam
1/4 cup maple sugar
1 tsp. cinnamon

Pear Crumble

This dish is a great way to get the kids (or anyone else for that matter) to eat fruit. You can substitute just about anything for the pears—I think plums, peaches, and apples all work very well, as do strawberries and rhubarb, or mixed berries. You can use fresh fruit or frozen. Just make sure you've got enough fruit to cover the pan about two layers deep.

5 large ripe pears
1/4 cup raisins
2 Tbsp. lemon juice
1/2 cup maple syrup
1/2 tsp. cinnamon
2 Tbsp. cornstarch

Crumble Topping:
1/2 cup sweet rice flour
1/4 cup oat flour
1/4 cup barley flour
1/4 tsp. salt
1 tsp. double-acting baking powder
3/4 cup palm sugar, maple sugar, sucanat,
    or date sugar
1/4 tsp. cinnamon
1 cup old-fashioned oats
1/2 cup vegetable shortening

Preheat oven to 350 degrees. Coat an 8 x 8-inch baking dish with cooking spray. Core pears, cut into bite-sized pieces and add to dish. Toss in raisins and lemon juice. Add maple syrup, toss gently, then sprinkle in 1/2 tsp. cinnamon and the cornstarch, stirring gently to combine. To make topping, combine flours, salt, baking powder, sugar, 1/4 teaspoon cinnamon, and oats. Melt shortening (about 30 seconds in the microwave does it) and drizzle into flour mixture, stirring to combine until it has the consistency of a course granola (not paste). Spread topping evenly over pears. Bake in center of oven 40 minutes until fruit is bubbling up around the sides.

SERVES 8

Chocolate Fondue

This is a fun dessert that's loved by kids, and provides a romantic cap to a grown-up dinner.

Cut up fruit into 1-inch pieces, and de-stem strawberries. Set fruit aside. Combine chocolate chips and rice milk in saucepan over lowest possible flame. Melt chocolate, stirring constantly until smooth. Remove from heat and stir in vanilla extract. Transfer to fondue pot over low sterno flame if you have one. If not, you can set the saucepan over a bowl of warm water, or just eat quickly (my favorite choice!). You may also transfer the fondue to small ramekins for kids. Serve with fruit and fondue forks or wooden skewers, or toothpicks for kids using ramekins.

SERVES 6–8

10 oz. dairy-free, soy-free chocolate chips
1/2 cup enriched rice milk
1 tsp. vanilla extract
assorted fruit for dipping (apples, bananas, pears, strawberries, kiwis, pineapple, grapes, and peaches all work well)

Blueberry Peach Mint Fruit Salad

This is one of my all-time favorite summer desserts. My grandmother Catherene used to make it when I was a kid, and believe it or not, I preferred it to any other baked goodies I could have been served. It can actually be made with virtually any combination of fruits if blueberries and peaches are out of season, but I think the ultimate in beauty and flavor is this particular medley.

Wash and sort blueberries. Put in a bowl. You can peel the peaches, but I often leave the skin on. Chop peaches into whatever size chunks you prefer. Add to blueberries. In a small bowl, combine honey, Marsala or sherry, and lime juice. Blend with a spoon until the honey is completely dissolved. Add to the fruit. Mix in chopped mint. If you wish to omit the Marsala or sherry, substitute with more lime. If you do this, start by adding half a lime at first, and taste. Adjust to your liking. You should get 4 servings with some left over for breakfast the next day.

MAKES ABOUT 4 SERVINGS

2 pints fresh blueberries
2 ripe peaches (or nectarines)
1/2 cup honey
1/4 cup Marsala or dry sherry
juice of 1 lime
1/4 cup chopped fresh mint

Orange Layer Cake

My parents used to combine my birthday party with my brother Dylan's because they were so close together. The bonus we got was two kinds of cake; an elegant, luscious orange cake for Dylan and a hearty chocolate cake for me. These two cakes are to this day my idea of a special treat. I've created revised hypoallergenic recipes for both. Enjoy!

Cake:

1/2 cup canola oil

1 cup honey

1 tsp. vanilla extract

3 tsp. Ener-G Egg Replacer, mixed with
    4 Tbsp. orange juice

3/4 cup unsweetened applesauce

1 cup barley flour

1 cup oat flour

2 tsp. double-acting baking powder

1 tsp. baking soda

1/4 tsp. salt

1/2 cup orange juice

grated zest of 1 orange

Orange Frosting:

1/2 cup vegetable shortening

1/2 cup honey

2 tsp. vanilla extract

4 Tbsp. enriched rice or oat milk

1¹/₃ cup "Better Than Milk" Rice Powder

grated zest of 1 orange

(For optional frostings, see p. 169.)

Preheat oven to 350 degrees. Grease two 8-inch cake pans, then cover the bottom with a piece of parchment paper cut to fit, and then grease again (or use two 8-inch round no-stick springform pans and grease very lightly). Combine oil, honey, and vanilla extract in a large bowl, using an electric mixer. Add egg replacer and applesauce. Combine flours, baking powder, baking soda, and salt. Add to bowl, alternating with orange juice. Beat in orange zest. Pour into pans and bake 30 minutes until top is lightly golden and sides are pulling away from pan. When done, let pans cool on a wire rack 10–15 minutes before removing cakes. Once cooled, loosen cake from sides with a knife or spatula if necessary, turn over, tap bottom, and gently remove cake. Peel off parchment paper and flip. Let cool completely before frosting.

To make frosting, combine vegetable shortening and honey with an electric mixer. Add vanilla extract and rice/oat milk. Mix. Then add Better Than Milk Powder and beat until fluffy. Add orange zest. When cakes have cooled, put first layer on cake plate or platter and, using a spatula or wide knife, frost the top. Put second layer on top of this, then frost top and sides. You may serve this cake cold or at room temperature.

MAKES ONE 8-INCH DOUBLE-LAYER CAKE

Chocolate Layer Cake with Agave-Sweetened Chocolate Frosting

This rich chocolate cake is moist, tender, and delicious. It's the perfect birthday cake.

Preheat oven to 350 degrees. Grease two 8-inch round cake pans. Cover the bottoms with a piece of parchment paper cut to fit, then grease again and dust with cocoa powder. In the bowl of an electric mixer, whisk together oat and barley flours, cocoa powder, baking soda, baking powder, and salt. Add egg replacer, rice milk, canola oil, maple syrup, vanilla extract, and warm water, and beat on medium-low about 3 minutes until smooth, scraping down sides of bowl as necessary. Pour even amounts of batter in the two pans, smooth surface, and bake in center of oven about 45 minutes, or until cake is beginning to pull away from sides of pan and a skewer inserted into the center of the cake comes out clean. Cool the pans on a wire rack about 30 minutes. To remove the cakes, cover each pan (one at a time) with a large plate, flip over, and tap the bottom to release the cake. Peel off the parchment paper and flip back onto wire rack right-side-up. Cool the cakes completely before adding frosting.

To make the frosting, melt the chocolate and vegetable shortening in a heavy saucepan over very low heat, stirring constantly. Be careful, chocolate burns easily. Once melted, remove from heat. Combine melted chocolate mixture and the remaining ingredients in the bowl of an electric mixer. Beat on medium speed about 15 minutes until cooled and smooth.

MAKES ONE 8-INCH DOUBLE-LAYER CAKE

Cake:

1 cup + 2 Tbsp. oat flour

1 cup + 2 Tbsp. barley flour

1 ¼ cups unsweetened cocoa powder

2 ½ tsp. baking soda

1 ¼ tsp. double-acting baking powder

1 ¼ tsp. salt

3 tsp. Ener-G egg replacer mixed with
    4 Tbsp. rice milk

1 cup + 2 Tbsp. rice milk

1/2 cup + 2 Tbsp. canola oil

1 ¾ cups + 2 Tbsp. maple syrup

1 ½ tsp. vanilla extract

1 cup warm water

Agave-Sweetened Chocolate Frosting:

4 oz. unsweetened chocolate

1 cup vegetable shortening

1 cup light agave nectar

2 tsp. vanilla extract

pinch of salt

(For optional frostings, see p. 169.)

Carrot Bundt Cake

This is a not-too-sweet dense teacake packed full of beta-carotene. It's a great way to get your kids to eat vegetables. It's good as is, or you can slice and toast it.

3/4 cup canola oil

1 cup honey

3/4 cup unsweetened applesauce

1½ cups enriched rice or oat milk

1½ tsp. vanilla extract

3 cups oat flour

3 cups barley flour

3 tsp. double-acting baking powder

1/2 tsp. salt

2 tsp. cinnamon

1½ cups grated carrot, tightly packed

1 cup raisins

Preheat oven to 350 degrees. In large mixing bowl, combine canola oil, honey, applesauce, rice milk, and vanilla extract. Mix. Combine flour, baking powder, salt, and cinnamon. Add to mixing bowl, and mix well. Add carrots and raisins. Spoon cake batter into a greased and lightly floured 10-inch bundt pan. Bake in middle of oven about 1 hour and 15 minutes. Cake is done when you can insert a skewer into the thickest part of cake and it comes out clean. Remove from oven, let cool in pan about 5 minutes, and then turn out onto a wire rack to cool.

SERVES 10–12

FROSTINGS

A luscious frosting can add the perfect finishing touch to cakes, cupcakes, dessert breads, and other baked goods. All of the following recipes yield between 2 and 2 ½ cups of frosting—enough for an 8-inch double-layer cake or two dozen cupcakes (one dozen if you're piping it on). For the vegetable shortening, I recommend Spectrum Naturals Organic Shortening.

Agave-Sweetened Chocolate Frosting

4 oz. unsweetened chocolate
1 cup vegetable shortening
1 cup light agave nectar
2 tsp. vanilla extract
pinch of salt

Melt the chocolate and vegetable shortening in a heavy saucepan over very low heat, stirring constantly. Be careful, chocolate burns easily. Once melted, remove from heat. Combine melted chocolate mixture and remaining ingredients in the bowl of an electric mixer. Beat on medium speed about 15 minutes until cooled and smooth.

Vanilla Frosting

1/2 cup vegetable shortening
1/2 cup honey
2 tsp. vanilla extract
4 Tbsp. enriched rice or oat milk
1 1/3 cups "Better Than Milk" Rice Powder

Combine the vegetable shortening and honey in a bowl with an electric mixer. Add the vanilla extract and rice/oat milk, and continue to mix. Add the "Better Than Milk" Rice Powder and beat about 5 minutes until light and fluffy.

Easy Vanilla Frosting

2/3 cup vegetable shortening
1 cup honey
1 tsp. vanilla extract

Combine all of the ingredients in a bowl. Beat with an electric mixer about 5 minutes until light and fluffy.

Orange Frosting

1/2 cup vegetable shortening
1/2 cup honey
2 tsp. vanilla extract
4 Tbsp. enriched rice or oat milk
1 1/3 cups "Better Than Milk" Rice Powder
grated zest of 1 orange

Combine the vegetable shortening and honey in a bowl with an electric mixer. Add the vanilla extract and rice/oat milk, and continue to mix. Add the "Better Than Milk" Rice Powder and beat about 5 minutes until light and fluffy. Add the orange zest and stir until well-combined.

Easy Orange Frosting

2/3 cup vegetable shortening
1 cup honey
1 tsp. vanilla extract
grated zest of 1 orange

Combine all of the ingredients in a bowl. Beat with an electric mixer about 5 minutes until light and fluffy.

Apple Pie

*Apple pie is the perfect dessert; it's satisfying as a sweet, but
guilt-free since it's packed so full of fiber and vitamins.*

Double Crust (for 9-inch pie):

2 cups oat flour

1 cup barley flour

1/4 tsp. salt

1/2 cup vegetable shortening

8 Tbsp. ice water

2 Tbsp. canola oil

Filling:

6 large Granny Smith apples (or other firm,
    tart apples), peeled, cored, and cut into
    slices about 1/4 inch thick (about 16
    slices per apple)

2 Tbsp. barley or oat flour

1/2 cup honey

2 Tbsp. lemon juice

1/2 tsp. cinnamon

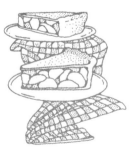

To make crust, combine flour and salt in large bowl. Add vegetable shortening, and use a wire pastry blender or two knives to cut together until the consistency of small peas. Drizzle 2 Tbsp. of the ice water around the edge. Use the wire pastry cutter or the back of a fork to work it in. Add remaining water, 2 Tbsp. at a time. Then add canola oil, 1 Tbsp. at a time, working it in. Please note that this dough will never be completely combined like cake batter. It's okay for it to be crumbly; it will bind when you roll it out. Using your hands, divide the dough in two and mound into two balls. Wrap in plastic wrap and refrigerate to chill about 30 minutes. Meanwhile, combine all of the filling ingredients, toss, and set aside. Position a rack in the lower third of the oven. Preheat oven to 425 degrees.

To roll out crusts: Once dough has chilled, remove one dough ball from fridge. Spread a sheet of wax paper on a large surface. Place dough on wax paper and cover with another sheet of wax paper. Press dough down to a disk shape. Don't worry if it cracks a bit. Using a rolling pin, roll out into a circle slightly larger than pie dish. Roll with quick strokes working outward from center, rolling as evenly as possible, so it will be the same thickness throughout. Once rolled out, gently peel off top sheet of wax paper. Put pie dish on top of rolled out dough and flip. Using your fingers, push the crust into the pie dish all the way around. Then very gently, pull off the sheet of wax paper. This is the best way I've ever found to get the crust into the pie dish without breaking or over-handling it. Prick the crust along the bottom about 6 times with the prongs of a fork. Patch as necessary. Refrigerate while you roll out the top crust. Again, place the dough ball between two sheets of wax paper (be sure to use two new sheets), press down into a disk, and roll out to slightly larger than the pie dish. Once rolled out, remove bottom crust from fridge, and spoon apple mixture into dish. Peel top sheet of wax paper off top crust. Flip carefully so it lies on top of the pie. Using your fingers, press the top crust onto the outer edge of the pie dish, all the way around. Once it's really attached all the way around, peel off the wax paper. Use fingers or a knife to remove any dough that hangs over edge of the pie dish and smooth edges. Using a sharp knife, cut about 6 slits along the top crust so that air may escape when baking. Cover edges with aluminum foil or, better yet, a pie crust shield, available at cooks' stores or online.

Cook pie at 425 degrees for 30 minutes. Slip a baking sheet underneath the pie to catch any drippings. Reduce heat to 350 degrees and cook another 30–45 minutes (40 minutes in my oven), until apple filling starts to bubble up through the slits on top and the crust is a lovely golden brown. Be sure to check your pie because ovens vary. Let cool completely on a rack for several hours so the filling really sets. If you wish to serve it warm, reheat it.

MAKES ONE 9-INCH PIE

Cherry Pie

*Cherry pie isn't really homemade unless you make it with unsweetened cherries.
Anybody can pour a couple cans of cherry pie filling into a premade crust and say they
baked a dessert, but the flavor really suffers. To find unsweetened cherries, look in the
canned fruit section at the grocery store, not the baking section. The baking section carries
the filler, which is usually made of cherries in corn syrup with lots of red dye.
I urge you to try this dessert. It's what my mother always made for me when she was
congratulating me for some accomplishment, and to this day, I still think it's special. Make it
for yourself when you feel you need a pat on the back, or for the kids when they've done
something great that deserves to be rewarded. Enjoy!*

Filling:
3 14.5-oz. cans pitted, unsweetened cher-
    ries (often called Pie Cherries)
    with liquid poured off
2 Tbsp. lime juice (or lemon juice)
1 cup maple syrup
1/4 cup minute tapioca

Crust:
9-inch double crust from Apple Pie
    recipe (p. 170)

Prepare the crust and let chill 30 minutes. In last 10 minutes, position a rack in the lower third of the oven. Preheat oven to 425 degrees. Combine cherries, lime juice, maple syrup, and tapioca, and set aside to sit about 15 minutes. Roll out dough into two circles and place one circle in the bottom of a 9-inch pie dish. Fill with cherry mixture. Top with second crust and, using a sharp knife, cut about 6 slits for air vents. If you're feeling particularly fancy, you may flute the edges. Cover edges with aluminum foil or, better yet, a pie crust shield, available at cooks' stores or online.

Bake at 425 degrees for 30 minutes. Slip a baking sheet beneath the pie to catch any drippings. Reduce heat to 350 degrees, and bake about 30–35 minutes more, or until top is golden brown, and thick juices bubble up through the slits. Let cool completely on a rack for several hours before cutting, as it needs to set.

MAKES ONE 9-INCH PIE

AFTER-SCHOOL SNACKS

- Bars, Balls, and Rolls
- Trail Mix
- Popcorn
- Fruit Delights
- Pizza
- Pretzels

After-school snacks can really be eaten any time of day, by anyone of any age. I've always been fond of them, and think they deserve their own category. For the most part, after-school snacks are different from regular sweet things because they tend to be more nutritionally packed. Also, they are easier to make and fun to cook with kids. So use your imagination. Add to the recipes here by making up your own.

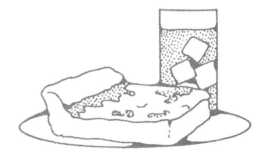

Pumpkin Seed Butter Honey Balls

*This is an easy, no-bake snack. It's so popular in my house that I have to fight
to keep my husband from eating them all before the kids or I can get to them.
I have fond memories of making peanut butter honey balls with my mother
after school. So here's my hypoallergenic version of that childhood treat.*

1/4 cup pumpkin seed butter (or sunflower
    seed butter)
1/4 cup honey
1/2 cup "Better Than Milk" Rice Powder
1/2 cup crushed Oat O's cereal (unsweet-
    ened)
1/4 cup shredded unsweetened coconut
    (see note on p. 66 regarding coconut)

Cream pumpkin seed butter and honey, then add "Better Than Milk" powder, and crushed Oat O's cereal in a large bowl. Shape into 1-inch balls. Roll balls in coconut. Chill.

MAKES 12

Crunchy Cereal Bars

1/2 cup sunflower seed butter
1/2 cup honey
3 cups crispy rice cereal
1/2 cup shredded unsweetened coconut
    (see note on p. 66 regarding coconut)
1/2 cup raisins or other dried fruit
    (chopped apricots, etc.)

Preheat oven to 350 degrees. Cream sunflower seed butter and honey together until smooth. Stir in crispy rice cereal. Then add coconut and raisins. Combine. Turn into an oiled 7 x 11-inch baking pan and press down all over. Bake 20 minutes until golden brown on top. Let cool until just warm to the touch. Cut into bars using a pizza cutter or sharp knife. Let cool completely before removing from pan.

MAKES 12 BARS

Soft Granola Bars

These soft chewy granola bars are packed full of nutritious ingredients, but they taste like a decadent cookie bar.

Preheat oven to 350 degrees. Cream honey and vegetable shortening together in a large mixing bowl. Add rest of ingredients. Mix well. Press into a well-greased 9 x 13-inch pan. Bake for about 35 minutes until golden brown on top. Let cool. Cut with a sharp knife or pizza cutter.

MAKES 12 BARS

3/4 cup honey

1/2 cup vegetable shortening

2 1/4 cups oats

3/4 cup oat flour

1/2 tsp. cinnamon

1 cup raisins

1/2 cup sunflower seeds

1/2 cup dairy-free, soy-free chocolate chips or carob chips

1 tsp. vanilla extract

1/2 cup applesauce

AFTER-SCHOOL SNACKS

Stuffed Mochi Puffs

Mochi is an amazing Japanese snack. It's made from pounded brown rice that has been pressed into a sheet. You then cut it into squares and bake it; it puffs up into the most marvelous little puffballs, crunchy on the outside, tender on the inside. The following is a great snack idea with endless possibilities. Look for mochi in the refrigeration aisle at your local health food store. It comes plain or in a variety of flavors like multigrain and cinnamon raisin. I haven't given proportions, as this is really a made-to-order treat.

mochi

dried fruit (raisins, apricots, apples, etc.)

chopped sunflower or pumpkin seeds

Preheat oven to 450 degrees. Cut mochi into 1– to 2-inch squares. Bake until they start to rise, then remove from the oven. Cut a slit across the top of each and fill with a mixture of dried fruit and chopped seeds (for example, raisins and sunflower seeds, apricots and pumpkin seeds, apples and raisins—anything). Replace tops. Then return to the oven and finish baking. Total baking time will be about 10 minutes.

Variations

- Fill mochi with fresh fruit or fruit-only jam and sesame seeds.
- Try them with your favorite seed butter (bananas and pumpkin seed butter is yummy).
- Fill mochi with applesauce mixed with cinnamon and raisins.

The Whole Foods Allergy Cookbook | **176**

Vietnamese Summer Rolls with Sweet Chili Dipping Sauce

*I have always loved the freshness of Vietnamese Summer Rolls. I much prefer
them to fried spring rolls and egg rolls. Traditionally, these are made with shrimp, peanuts,
and fish sauce, all big no-nos in my house. So I created a hypoallergenic version that I think
is equally delicious and much safer. If you want a little added crunch, usually provided
by the peanuts, you could add some chopped-up water chestnuts to the mix. You can
also substitute pork or beef for the chicken, or cut it out altogether for a vegan
summer roll. Enjoy these summer rolls winter, spring, summer, and fall!*

Puree all ingredients for dipping sauce in blender or food processor. Set aside.

Boil a pot of water. Turn off heat and add cellophane noodles. Let soak about 5 minutes until softened. Drain. Combine noodles with carrots, bean spouts, cilantro, sesame oil, lime juice, and season with salt and pepper. Set aside. Pour water into a large shallow bowl. One at a time, submerge rice paper in water for about 10 seconds to soften. Don't over-soak them or they'll fall apart. Place them on a lightly dampened towel and keep them covered while you work. To make the rolls, lay the rice paper wrapper on a plate, place a couple pieces of the torn lettuce in the bottom third of the wrapper, leaving a flap uncovered at the bottom. Put a little bit of the noodle mixture on top of the lettuce. Top with two thin strips of the chicken. Use less filling than you think you should, because if you overstuff, it will break the wrapper. Fold the bottom flap of rice paper over the filling, tuck in the left and right sides, and then fold up once. Lay 2 mint leaves on top, then tuck and roll a final time to close the whole thing up into a neat little bundle. Keep covered with a lightly damp towel until ready to eat. Arrange on a platter and serve with the dipping sauce.

MAKES 10 ROLLS

Dipping Sauce:
2 Tbsp. rice vinegar
2 Tbsp. hot water
1 Tbsp. honey
juice of half a lime
1/2 tsp. minced garlic
1/2 tsp. chili garlic sauce or paste (available in supermarkets and Asian markets)
1/4 tsp. salt

Rolls:
2 oz. cellophane noodles
1 large carrot, shredded
1 cup bean sprouts
1/4 cup chopped cilantro
2 tsp. sesame oil
juice of half a lime
salt and pepper to taste
3 cups hot (not boiling) water
10 (8½-inch) round rice paper wrappers (available in supermarkets and Asian markets)
10 Boston lettuce leaves, washed, patted dry, and torn into large pieces
1/2-lb. cooked chicken breast (steamed, boiled, or grilled), cut into thin strips
20 mint leaves

Trail Mix

Great for a snack on the go.

Oat O's cereal

raisins or other dried fruit in small pieces

sunflower seeds or pumpkin seeds

dairy-free, soy-free chocolate chips or
carob chips

shredded unsweetened coconut (see note
on p. 66 regarding coconut)

Combine equal parts of all the ingredients. Store in an airtight container or zip-top bag.

Chocolate-Covered Raisins

It's hard to find chocolate-covered raisins without butter or some form of dairy in the ingredients, so I decided to start making my own. Since raisins are fruit and chocolate is said to boost your immune system, we eat them without a trace of guilt, despite their striking resemblance to candy. Because you must work quickly, these need to be made in small batches. The following ingredients are enough for about 2 servings. If you want more, make one batch and then begin again to make a second.

1/2 cup dairy-free, soy-free chocolate chips

2 tsp. enriched rice milk

1/4 cup raisins

Cover a cookie tray with wax paper. Combine chocolate chips and rice milk in a saucepan over lowest possible heat. Melt, stirring constantly. Remove from heat. Working quickly, use a fork and skewer raisins on all its prongs. Swirl in chocolate to cover. Use your fingers to dislodge chocolate-covered raisins onto wax paper. You can either separate them for raisinettes, or drop them in clumps for clusters—both taste delicious. When finished, refrigerate to set into candy.

SERVES 2

Maple Popcorn

This is a lighter version of the buttery caramel corn we are used to. Let it dry completely so that the maple glaze hardens to candylike consistency for added crunch. Yum!

Combine maple sugar, maple syrup, and water in saucepan over medium heat. Bring to a simmer. Cook about 25 minutes until syrup hits soft ball phase (when you drip a drop into cold water it forms a soft ball).

Meanwhile, pop the popcorn by heating a heavy pan over medium-high heat, add oil to lightly coat bottom of pan, heat, then add popcorn. Cover. When it starts to pop, shake pan. Continue shaking until the popping stops. (You may also use an air popper and skip using oil completely). Pour out into a baking dish or large shallow bowl. Toss in cinnamon, and coconut (if using). When syrup is ready, drizzle popcorn and toss well. Let cool until completely dry.

SERVES 2–4

1/2 cup maple sugar
2 Tbsp. maple syrup
1/2 cup water
canola oil
1/2 cup unpopped popcorn
1 tsp. cinnamon
1/2 cup shredded unsweetened coconut (optional), (see note on p. 66 regarding coconut)

Curried Popcorn Munch

For an aromatic treat, try this recipe. If you wish to cut the oil, you can air pop your popcorn instead of pan-popping. For a sweeter treat, add currants or raisins.

Heat canola oil over medium-high heat in a heavy-bottomed pan. Add corn, cover, and shake as soon as it starts popping. Once popped, remove from heat and pour into a baking dish or large shallow bowl. Combine coconut oil, curry powder, and salt. Cook over medium heat 1 or 2 minutes until curry powder releases its lovely curry odor and salt has melted. Add pumpkin seeds to popcorn, drizzle with curry mixture, and toss well. Enjoy!

SERVES 2–4

1 Tbsp. canola oil
1/2 cup unpopped popcorn
2 Tbsp. coconut oil (see note on p. 66 regarding coconut)
1 tsp. curry powder
1/2 tsp. kosher salt
1/4 cup pumpkin seeds (optional)

Sunbutter Fruit Roll Ups

*My son Lennon loves these. They are great for an after-school snack, but he also likes them
for breakfast. They are very easy for little fingers to hold without the ingredients spilling out.
I haven't been exact with proportions because you can really just make them to order.*

brown rice or corn tortillas
sunbutter
fruit-only jam
fresh fruit (blueberries, strawberries, rasp-
　　berries, etc.)

Put a tortilla on a plate and spread a heaping spoonful
of sunbutter all over it. Then repeat with fruit-only jam of
your choice. Sprinkle with fresh fruit of your choice, and
roll up. Yum!

Fruit Nuggets

1 cup dried fruit, chopped (any combina-
　　tion you want, but I recommend using 3
　　or 4 types)
1/2 oz. unsweetened chocolate, melted
1/4 cup honey
1/3 cup crushed amaranth or oat flake
　　cereal (1 cup uncrushed)
canola oil
shredded unsweetened coconut or crushed
　　cereal for coating nuggets (see note on
　　p. 66 regarding coconut)

If using a hard dried fruit like prunes or apricots, let stand
in boiling water for 5 minutes. Drain. Put all fruit in food
processor and chop fine. Melt chocolate over very low heat,
stirring constantly. Remove pan from heat and blend in
honey until smooth. Add fruit and crushed cereal. Let cool
a bit. Put a little canola oil on hands and mold into
1½-inch balls. Roll in coconut or crushed cereal. Chill.

MAKES ABOUT 12 BALLS

Fried Bananas

*My mother always made fried bananas sautéed in butter when I was a kid.
We'd eat them for breakfast or after school as a snack. The natural sugar in
a ripe banana caramelizes and makes them slightly crunchy on the outside.
Be careful to let them cool a bit, because they are deceptively hot.*

Heat pan over medium-high flame. Add canola oil and let heat up until it starts to move a bit. Add bananas and sprinkle with a little cinnamon. Cook until golden brown on bottom, then flip with a spatula. Brown bottom. If they start to burn, turn heat down to medium.

SERVES 2

2 bananas, cut diagonally into
 3/4-inch pieces
canola oil to coat the bottom of
 a frying pan
cinnamon

Baked Apples

These are a healthy high-fiber snack for anytime of day.

Preheat oven to 350 degrees. Thoroughly wash, and then core apples, leaving bottom in tact. Place in small baking dish. Combine apple juice, honey, cinnamon, and orange zest. Whisk to dissolve honey. Pour over apples, spooning some into the center of each. Cover with aluminum foil and bake about 1¼ to 1½ hours until tender. Start checking after 1 hour to test for doneness. Serve hot or cold, in a bowl, with the syrup poured over and around them. Personally, I like them hot with vanilla rice dream frozen dessert, or cold just as is.

SERVES 4

4 apples (Gala, Braeburn, Fuji, Honey Crisp,
 or other similarly firm-fleshed apple)
1 cup apple juice
1/4 cup honey
1/4 tsp. cinnamon
2 strips orange zest, 1/2 inch thick (you can
 use a potato peeler or a small paring
 knife)

Tortilla Pizzas

This is a made-to-order sort of snack. I haven't added proportions since you can really just wing it. Below are additional suggestions for toppings. Also, you may add grilled chicken for added protein.

brown rice or corn tortillas (or some brand of gluten-free pizza crust)

pizza sauce (Trader Joe's makes a pretty good one)

finely sliced red onion or sweet onion

artichoke hearts, quartered

roasted red peppers

thinly sliced mushrooms (shiitake, white, baby bella, etc.)

Preheat oven to 450 degrees. Spread pizza sauce on tortilla. Top with onions, artichoke hearts, peppers, and mushrooms. Cook 10 minutes. Serve.

Other topping options that work well together:
- Sun-dried tomatoes, asparagus, spinach, and roasted garlic.
- Arugula, dried figs, and nitrite-free prosciutto.
- Chopped romaine lettuce, chopped tomatoes, avocado, black olives (all added after you've heated the tortilla with the sauce for 10 minutes), and drizzled with a little vinaigrette.

Soft Pretzels

*Making soft pretzels is a great rainy-day activity. You can form them into
any shape you want—traditional pretzel shape, baseball bats,
baseballs, hearts, children's initials—use your imagination.*

Preheat oven to 425 degrees. Dissolve yeast in warm water
in large bowl. In another bowl, combine rye flour and salt.
Add egg replacer and honey to yeast. Mix well. Add flour
and salt. Mix well. Flour hands and form dough into a ball.
Knead it about 20 times, turning the dough as you do so.
Divide dough into 8 parts. Roll each piece into a rope and
shape. Grease a cookie sheet with olive oil (or an allowed
vegetable cooking spray). Transfer shapes to tray. Brush
with a little olive oil, sprinkle with kosher salt, and bake for
12–15 minutes until golden brown. Serve plain or with a little deli mustard or, for a sweeter treat, mix deli mustard
with honey for honey-mustard dipping sauce.

MAKES 8 PRETZELS

1 package quick-rise dry yeast

3/4 cup warm water

2 cups rye flour (or 1 cup oat flour
    and 1 cup barley flour)

1 tsp. salt

3/4 tsp. Ener-G Egg Replacer, mixed with
    1 Tbsp. rice milk, oat milk, or water

1 tsp. honey

olive oil

kosher salt

deli mustard (optional)

honey to mix with mustard (optional)

METRIC CONVERSION TABLES

Common Liquid Conversions

Measurement	=	Milliliters
1/4 teaspoon	=	1.25 milliliters
1/2 teaspoon	=	2.50 milliliters
3/4 teaspoon	=	3.75 milliliters
1 teaspoon	=	5.00 milliliters
1 1/4 teaspoons	=	6.25 milliliters
1 1/2 teaspoons	=	7.50 milliliters
1 3/4 teaspoons	=	8.75 milliliters
2 teaspoons	=	10.0 milliliters
1 tablespoon	=	15.0 milliliters
2 tablespoons	=	30.0 milliliters

Measurement	=	Liters
1/4 cup	=	0.06 liters
1/2 cup	=	0.12 liters
3/4 cup	=	0.18 liters
1 cup	=	0.24 liters
1 1/4 cups	=	0.30 liters
1 1/2 cups	=	0.36 liters
2 cups	=	0.48 liters
2 1/2 cups	=	0.60 liters
3 cups	=	0.72 liters
3 1/2 cups	=	0.84 liters
4 cups	=	0.96 liters
4 1/2 cups	=	1.08 liters
5 cups	=	1.20 liters
5 1/2 cups	=	1.32 liters

Converting Fahrenheit to Celsius

Fahrenheit	=	Celsius
200–205	=	95
220–225	=	105
245–250	=	120
275	=	135
300–305	=	150
325–330	=	165
345–350	=	175
370–375	=	190
400–405	=	205
425–430	=	220
445–450	=	230
470–475	=	245
500	=	260

Conversion Formulas

LIQUID When You Know	Multiply By	To Determine
teaspoons	5.0	milliliters
tablespoons	15.0	milliliters
fluid ounces	30.0	milliliters
cups	0.24	liters
pints	0.47	liters
quarts	0.95	liters

WEIGHT When You Know	Multiply By	To Determine
ounces	28.0	grams
pounds	0.45	kilograms

APPENDIX

I have compiled the following information to show that a balanced nutritious diet is possible even for those who have eliminated dairy, soy, eggs, wheat, peanuts, tree nuts, shellfish, and fish. Like anyone else, you must eat a varied diet. I am not a dietitian or a nutritionist, so please consult with an expert if you have questions about your nutrition. I can only offer the benefits of my experience as an informed cook. In my estimation, the most obvious nutrients that one could potentially fall short on when following this diet are calcium, magnesium, iron, protein (if you are vegetarian or vegan), and Omega 3. The foods listed in this appendix are in compliance with the rest of the book (i.e., dairy-free, soy-free, egg-free, wheat-free, peanut-free, tree-nut-free, shellfish-free, and fish-free) except for the section on Omega-3 and Omega-6 fatty acids. I hope you find it helpful.

Calcium and Magnesium

For those on a dairy-free, shellfish-free, fish-free, and/or egg-free diet, it is very important to find alternate sources of calcium (and magnesium). *Calcium-fortified rice milk, oat milk, orange juice,* and *apple juice* provide some of this important mineral. *Calcium supplements* may also be desirable. In addition, the foods listed below are rich in calcium.

The following listings are based on a 100-gram serving (the equivalent of 3.53 oz.). The foods are listed in descending order (from the highest amount of calcium per 100-gram serving to the lowest). The amount of calcium is given in milligrams of calcium. The source of the data is the USDA Nutrient Database at http://www.nal.usda.gov/fnic/cgi-bin/nut_search.pl. The data was compiled by SoyStache.com.

Sources of Calcium (in milligrams)

Sesame seeds   975.000
Winged beans, raw   440.000
Sesame butter, tahini   426.000
Beans, white, raw   240.000
Flax seed   199.000
Beans, kidney, California red, raw   195.000
Turnip greens, raw   190.000
Dandelion greens, raw   187.000
Beans, French, raw   186.000
Beans, Great Northern, raw   175.000
Beans, small white, raw   173.000
Seaweed, kelp, raw   168.000
Beans, yellow, raw   166.000
Lotus seeds   163.000
Arugula, raw   160.000
Beans, Navy, raw   155.000
Mothbeans, raw   150.000
Seaweed, wakame, raw   150.000
Collards, raw   145.000
Figs, dried, uncooked   144.000
Beans, kidney, all types, raw   143.000
Mungo beans, raw   138.000
Parsley, raw   138.000
Yardlong beans, raw   138.000
Kale, raw   135.000
Mung beans, raw   132.000
Beans, kidney, royal red, raw   131.000
Beans, pink, raw   130.000

Wasabi, root, raw   128.000

Beans, cranberry (roman), raw   127.000

Beans, black, raw   123.000

Beans, pinto, raw   121.000

Watercress, raw   120.000

Sunflower seeds   116.000

Tomatoes, sun-dried   110.000

Chick peas (garbanzo beans, Bengal gram), raw
   105.000

Broadbeans (fava beans), raw   103.000

Mustard greens, raw   103.000

Spinach, raw   99.000

Currants, zante, dried   86.000

Rhubarb, raw   86.000

Winged beans, immature seeds, raw   84.000

Beans, kidney, red, raw   83.000

Lima beans, large, raw   81.000

Okra, raw   81.000

Seaweed, Irishmoss, raw   72.000

Seaweed, laver, raw   70.000

Lettuce, looseleaf, raw   68.000

Beans, adzuki, raw   66.000

Quinoa   60.000

Beans, pinto, immature seeds, frozen   58.000

Prickly pears, raw   56.000

Oats   54.000

Seaweed, agar, raw   54.000

Beans, pinto, immature seeds, frozen, cooked,
   boiled, drained, without salt   52.000

Chard, Swiss, raw   51.000

Lentils, raw   51.000

Prunes, dried, uncooked   51.000

Hyacinth-beans, immature seeds, raw   50.000

Chick peas (garbanzo beans, Bengal gram),
   cooked, boiled, without salt   49.000

Raisins, seedless   49.000

Beans, snap, green, cooked, boiled, drained, with-

out salt   46.000

Lotus root, raw   45.000

Beans, pinto, sprouted, raw   43.000

Peas, edible-podded, raw   43.000

Pumpkin and squash seed kernels   43.000

Burdock root, raw   41.000

Chicory roots, raw   41.000

Mulberries, raw   39.000

Beans, fava, in pod, raw   37.000

Beans, snap, green, raw   37.000

Lettuce, cos or romaine, raw   36.000

Figs, raw   35.000

Lima beans, immature seeds, raw   34.000

Milk, human   32.200

Sources of Magnesium

Magnesium is a mineral that helps the body absorb calcium. It's found in many foods, and if you eat a well-balanced diet, you're probably getting enough. Good sources of magnesium are *legumes, whole grains, dark green veggies, chocolate,* and *meats.*

Specific examples include *spinach, beet greens, broccoli, sunflower seeds, pumpkin seeds, dried figs, avocados, navy beans, kidney beans, black-eyed peas, garbanzo beans,* and *beef tenderloin* or *sirloin.*

Iron

For those concerned that a hypoallergenic diet won't enable them to get enough iron without eating loads of red meat, please note that diets consisting of vegetables, fruits, grains, legumes, and seeds should provide adequate iron. Consuming foods rich in vitamin C, such as orange juice, with iron-rich foods enhances the absorption of iron. Some foods are naturally rich in both iron and vitamin C, such as *broccoli, Swiss chard,* and other *dark green leafy vegetables.* Other good sources of iron include *iron-fortified cereals, enriched bread, rice, chick peas,* and *blackstrap molasses.* Another way to increase your iron intake is to cook with *cast-iron pans.*

The listings below are based on a 100-gram serving (the equivalent of 3.53 oz.). The foods are listed in descending order (from the highest amount of iron per 100-gram serving to the lowest). The amount of iron is given in milligrams of iron. The source of the data listed here is the USDA Nutrient Database at http://www.nal.usda.gov/fnic/cgi-bin/nut_search.pl. The data was compiled by SoyStache.com.

Sources of Iron (in milligrams)

Pumpkin and squash seed kernels   14.970
Sesame seeds   14.550
Winged beans, raw   13.440
Mothbeans, raw   10.850
Beans, white, raw   10.440
Beans, kidney, California red, raw   9.350
Quinoa   9.250
Tomatoes, sun-dried   9.090
Lentils, raw   9.020
Seeds, sesame butter, tahini   8.950
Seaweed, Irishmoss, raw   8.900
Beans, kidney, royal red, raw   8.700
Yardlong beans, raw   8.610
Beans, kidney, all types, raw   8.200
Beans, small white, raw   7.730
Mungo beans, raw   7.570
Lima beans, large, raw   7.510
Beans, yellow, raw   7.010
Sunflower seeds   6.770
Beans, pink, raw   6.770
Mung beans, raw   6.740
Broadbeans (fava beans), raw   6.700
Beans, kidney, red, raw   6.690
Beans, Navy, raw   6.440
Chick peas (garbanzo beans, Bengal gram), raw   6.240
Flax seeds   6.220
Parsley, raw   6.200
Beans, pinto, raw   5.880
Beans, Great Northern, raw   5.470
Beans, black, raw   5.020
Beans, cranberry (roman), raw   5.000
Beans, adzuki, raw   4.980
Oats   4.720
Lotus seeds   3.530
Beans, French, raw   3.400
Beef, variety meats and by-products, tongue, cooked, simmered   3.390
Olives, ripe, canned   3.300
Currants, zante, dried   3.260
Potatoes, raw, skin   3.240
Lentils, sprouted, raw   3.210
Lima beans, immature seeds, raw   3.140
Dandelion greens, raw   3.100
Beans, pinto, immature seeds, frozen   3.000
Chick peas (garbanzo beans, Bengal gram), cooked, boiled, without salt   2.890
Seaweed, kelp, raw   2.850
Seaweed, spirulina, raw   2.790
Beans, pinto, immature seeds, frozen, cooked, boiled, drained, without salt   2.710
Spinach, raw   2.710
Persimmons, native, raw   2.500
Prunes, dried, uncooked   2.480
Lima beans, immature seeds, cooked, boiled, drained, without salt   2.450
Beef, ground, regular, cooked, broiled, medium

2.440
Figs, dried, uncooked   2.230
Pumpkin leaves, raw   2.220
Seaweed, wakame, raw   2.180
Lamb, domestic, leg, whole (shank and sirloin), separable lean only, trimmed to 1/4-inch fat, choice, cooked, roasted   2.120
Beans, navy, sprouted, cooked, boiled, drained, without salt   2.110
Leeks (bulb and lower leaf portion), raw   2.100
Raisins, seedless   2.080
Peas, edible-podded, raw   2.080
Beans, pinto, sprouted, raw   1.970
Beans, navy, sprouted, raw   1.930
Broadbeans, immature seeds, raw   1.900
Mung beans, sprouted, cooked, stir-fried   1.900
Seaweed, agar, raw   1.860
Mulberries, raw   1.850
Seaweed, laver, raw   1.800
Chard, Swiss, raw   1.800
Mushroom, oyster, raw   1.740
Garlic, raw   1.700
Kale, raw   1.700
Beans, fava, in pod, raw   1.550
Winged beans, immature seeds, raw   1.500
Broadbeans, immature seeds, cooked, boiled, drained, without salt   1.500
Peas, green, raw   1.470
Mustard greens, raw   1.460
Arugula, raw   1.460
Turkey, all classes: breast, meat and skin, cooked, roasted   1.400
Brussels sprouts, raw   1.400
Lettuce, loose leaf, raw   1.400
Fiddlehead ferns, raw   1.310
Beans, snap, green, cooked, boiled, drained, without salt   1.280

Rice, white, long-grain, regular, cooked   1.200
Avocados, raw, California   1.180
Beans, adzuki, yokan, raw   1.160
Lotus root, raw   1.160
Dates, domestic, natural and dry   1.150
Pork, fresh, leg (ham), rump half, separable lean only, cooked, roasted   1.140
Lettuce, cos or romaine, raw   1.100
Turnip greens, raw   1.100
Chicken, broilers or fryers, breast, meat and skin, cooked, roasted   1.070
Chicken, broilers or fryers, light meat, meat only, cooked, roasted   1.060
Mushrooms, raw   1.040
Beans, snap, green, raw   1.040
Wasabi, root, raw   1.030
Alfalfa seeds, sprouted, raw   0.960
Chicory greens, raw   0.900
Beans, kidney, sprouted, cooked, boiled, drained, without salt   0.890
Mushrooms, enoki, raw   0.888
Broccoli, raw   0.880
Asparagus, raw   0.870
Endive, raw   0.830
Beans, kidney, sprouted, raw   0.810
Okra, raw   0.800
Beets, raw   0.800
Burdock root, raw   0.800
Chicory roots, raw   0.800
Pumpkin, raw   0.800
Squash, zucchini, baby, raw   0.790
Potatoes, raw, flesh and skin   0.760
Hyacinth-beans, immature seeds, raw   0.740
Peppers, jalapeno, raw   0.700
Squash, winter, butternut, raw   0.700
Squash, winter, acorn, raw   0.700
Mushrooms, portobello, raw   0.600

Cabbage, raw   0.590

Parsnips, raw   0.590

Squash, winter, all varieties, raw   0.580

Raspberries, raw   0.570

Apricots, raw   0.540

Rice, brown, medium-grain, cooked   0.530

Corn, sweet, yellow and white, raw   0.520

Ginger root, raw   0.500

Carrots, raw   0.500

Lettuce, iceberg (includes crisphead types), raw   0.500

Cabbage, red, raw   0.490

Squash, summer, crookneck and straightneck, raw   0.480

Squash, summer, all varieties, raw   0.460

Peppers, sweet, yellow, raw   0.460

Peppers, sweet, red, raw   0.460

Peppers, sweet, green, raw   0.460

Tomatoes, red, ripe, raw, year round average   0.450

Cauliflower, raw   0.440

Mushrooms, shiitake, cooked, without salt   0.440

Rice, brown, long-grain, cooked   0.420

Kiwi fruit (Chinese gooseberries), fresh, raw   0.410

Squash, winter, hubbard, raw   0.400

Squash, summer, scallop, raw   0.400

Celery, raw   0.400

Radishes, oriental, raw   0.400

Cherries, sweet, raw   0.390

Strawberries, raw   0.380

Figs, raw   0.370

Pineapple, raw   0.370

Crabapples, raw   0.360

Bananas, raw   0.310

Gooseberries, raw   0.310

Squash, winter, spaghetti, raw   0.310

Lettuce, butterhead (includes Boston and bibb types), raw   0.300

Pomegranates, raw   0.300

Turnips, raw   0.300

Prickly pears, raw   0.300

Radishes, raw   0.290

Eggplant, raw   0.270

Cucumber, with peel, raw   0.260

Grapes, red or green (European type varieties, such as, Thompson seedless), raw   0.260

Carambola (starfruit), raw   0.260

Pears, raw   0.250

Onions, raw   0.220

Rhubarb, raw   0.220

Melons, cantaloupe, raw   0.210

Watercress, raw   0.200

Cranberries, raw   0.200

Collards, raw   0.190

Apples, raw, with skin   0.180

Blueberries, raw   0.170

Watermelon, raw   0.170

Nectarines, raw   0.150

Mangos, raw   0.130

Peaches, raw   0.110

Plums, raw   0.100

Tangerines (mandarin oranges), raw   0.100

Papayas, raw   0.100

Oranges, raw, California, valencias   0.090

Rice Dream   0.080

Melons, honeydew, raw   0.070

Milk, human   0.030

Protein

The following list shows you just how easy it is to get enough protein, even on a diet that eliminates soy, dairy, eggs, fish, shellfish, peanuts, and tree nuts. Between meats and poultry, legumes and seeds, I think you will find it no problem to meet your daily requirements.

The listings below are based on a 100-gram serving of each (the equivalent of 3.53 oz.). The foods are listed in descending order (from the highest amount of protein per 100-gram serving to the lowest). The amount is given in grams of protein. The source of the data is the USDA Nutrient Database at http://www.nal.usda.gov/fnic/cgi-bin/nut_search.pl. The data was compiled by SoyStache.com.

Sources of Protein (in grams)

Pork, fresh, leg (ham), rump half, separable lean only, cooked, roasted   30.940

Chicken, broilers or fryers, light meat, meat only, cooked, roasted   30.910

Chicken, broilers or fryers, breast, meat and skin, cooked, roasted   29.800

Winged beans, raw   29.650

Turkey, all classes: breast, meat and skin, cooked, roasted   28.710

Lamb, domestic, leg, whole (shank and sirloin), separable lean only, trimmed to 1/4-inch fat, choice, cooked, roasted   28.300

Lentils, raw   28.060

Broadbeans (fava beans), raw   26.120

Beans, kidney, royal red, raw   25.330

Mungo beans, raw   25.210

Seeds, pumpkin and squash seed kernels   24.540

Pumpkin and squash seed kernels   24.540

Beans, kidney, California red, raw   24.370

Yardlong beans, raw   24.330

Beef, ground, regular, cooked, broiled, medium   24.070

Mung beans, raw   23.860

Beans, kidney, all types, raw   23.580

Beans, white, raw   23.360

Beans, cranberry (roman), raw   23.030

Mothbeans, raw   22.940

Sunflower seeds   22.780

Beans, kidney, red, raw   22.530

Beans, Navy, raw   22.330

Beef, variety meats and by-products, tongue, cooked, simmered   22.110

Beans, yellow, raw   22.000

Beans, Great Northern, raw   21.860

Beans, black, raw   21.600

Lima beans, large, raw   21.460

Beans, small white, raw   21.110

Beans, pink, raw   20.960

Beans, pinto, raw   20.880

Beans, adzuki, raw   19.870

Flax seeds   19.500

Chick peas (garbanzo beans, Bengal gram), raw   19.300

Beans, French, raw   18.810

Sesame seeds   17.730

Sesame butter, tahini   17.000

Oats   16.890

Lotus seeds   15.410

Tomatoes, sun-dried   14.110

Quinoa   13.100

Beans, pinto, immature seeds, frozen   9.800

Beans, pinto, immature seeds, frozen, cooked, boiled, drained, without salt   9.310

Lentils, sprouted, raw   8.960

Chick peas (garbanzo beans, Bengal gram), cooked, boiled, without salt   8.860

Beans, fava, in pod, raw   7.920

Beans, Navy, sprouted, cooked, boiled, drained, without salt   7.070

Winged beans, immature seeds, raw   6.950

Lima beans, immature seeds, raw 6.840

Lima beans, immature seeds, cooked, boiled, drained, without salt 6.810

Garlic, raw 6.360

Beans, Navy, sprouted, raw 6.150

Seaweed, spirulina, raw 5.920

Seaweed, laver, raw 5.810

Broadbeans, immature seeds, raw 5.600

Peas, green, raw 5.420

Beans, pinto, sprouted, raw 5.250

Beans, kidney, sprouted, cooked, boiled, drained, without salt 4.830

Wasabi, root, raw 4.800

Broadbeans, immature seeds, cooked, boiled, drained, without salt 4.800

Fiddlehead ferns, raw 4.550

Milk, human 1.030

Carrots, raw 1.030

Bananas, raw 1.030

Omega 3 and Omega 6

When I first started doing research on Omega 3 and Omega 6, I had a vague idea that one should find alternate sources of Omega 3 when one is not eating fish. The more research I did, the more horrified I became to discover that I was eating almost no Omega 3 at all. I corrected that, and began taking 1–2 Tbsp. of flaxseed oil a day. I mix it with a little balsamic vinegar and have it on a salad. This is not a book on nutrition, and I'm not a nutritionist, but suffice it to say, Omega-3 oils are an essential part of our diet. Omega 3 and Omega 6 are essential fatty acids. Essential fatty acids are fats that your body cannot synthesize on its own. Unlike saturated fats or cholesterol, essential fats must be eaten in the diet. There are two types of essential fatty acids: Omega 3 (alpha-linolenic acid) and Omega-6 (linoleic acid). In the old days, our ancestors' diets were made up of roughly equal amounts of Omega 3 and 6. Today, the American diet is grossly lacking in Omega 3, and typically contains twenty to thirty times more Omega 6. This imbalance is thought to be partly responsible for a myriad of health problems, from depression to eczema and heart disease.

Usually, Americans get their Omega 3 from cold deep-water fish like salmon, trout, mackerel, herring, whitefish, anchovies, and tuna. Omega 3 also occurs in very small amounts in green leafy vegetables; in fact, up to 80 percent of the fatty acids in green leafy plants are alpha-linolenic acids, but they have only small amounts of lipids, so leafy veggies don't contribute significant amounts of Omega 3 to our diets. To meet your daily needs, you really will need to supplement with raw oil. Do not cook it, as heat will destroy its nutritive properties.

The listings below are based on 100-gram servings. The oils are listed in descending order (from the highest amount of Omega 3 per 100-gram serving to the lowest). The amount of Omega 3 is given in grams. The source of the data listed here is adapted from R. S. Bhatty's, "Nutrient composition of whole flaxseed and flaxseed meal" (*Flaxseed in Human Nutrition*, S. Cunnane & L. U. Thompson, eds. AOCS Press, 1995). I could not find any USDA nutrient data-base info on Omega 3 or Omega 6.

Because sources are so few and far between, in this one instance I've included foods that are elsewhere excluded from this book. For those allowed to eat nuts, soy, or wheat, use at your own discretion.

Sources of Omega 3 (in grams)

Flaxseed oil   53.300
Walnut oil   10.400
Canola oil (conventional)   9.200
Wheat germ oil   6.900
Soybean oil   6.800
Rice Bran oil   1.600
Corn oil   0.900
Olive oil   0.500
Butterfat   0.500
Canola oil (high oleic)   0.100

Other sources of Omega 3 include *perilla oil* (from the Asian beefsteak plant), *phytoplankton* and *algae, red and black currant seeds,* and *red and black currant seed oil, seed oils from borage and evening primrose, omega-3-enriched breads with milled flax seeds, and flax and hemp seeds.* (Note that whole flax seeds are not absorbed by the body and therefore serve only as a laxative; flax seed must be milled in order to bestow the benefits of the Omega-3 fatty acids.)

Sources of Omega 6

Omega 6 is much more prevalent in our diets, and Americans are generally not deficient.

Some examples of good sources of Omega 6 include *sunflower oil* and *safflower oil, sesame seeds* and *sunflower seeds, organ meats* and other *animal-based foods,* and *corn oil.*

RESOURCES

Organizations Providing Support, Information, and Resources for People with Allergies

American Academy of Allergy, Asthma and Immunology (AAAAI)
555 East Wells Street
Milwaukee, WI 53202
414 272-6071
www.aaaai.org

American Academy of Dermatology (AAD)
930 E. Woodfield Road
Schaumburg, IL 60173
847 330-0230
www.aad.org

American Academy of Environmental Medicine (AAEM)
6505 E. Central Avenue, #296
Wichita, KS 67206
316 684-5500
www.aaem.com

American Academy of Pediatrics (AAP)
National Headquarters:
141 Northwest Point Boulevard
Elk Grove Village, IL 60007-1098
847 434-4000
www.aap.org

Washington, DC Office:
Department of Federal Affairs
601 13th Street, NW
  Suite 400 North
Washington, DC 20005
202 347-8600
www.aap.org

American Dietetic Association (ADA)
120 S. Riverside Plaza, Suite 2000
Chicago, IL 60606-6995
800 877-1600
www.eatright.org

American Medical Association (AMA)
515 North State Street
Chicago, IL 60654
800-621-8335
www.ama-assn.org

Anaphylaxis Canada
2005 Sheppard Avenue East
  Suite 800
Toronto, Ontario M2J 5B4
Canada
416 785-5666
www.anaphylaxis.org

Asthma and Allergy Foundation of America (AAFA)
1233 20th Street, NW, Suite 402
Washington, DC 20036
800 7-ASTHMA
www.aafa.org

Food Allergy and Anaphylaxis Network (FAAN)
11781 Lee Jackson Hwy., Suite 160
Fairfax, VA 22033-3309
800 929-4040, 703 691-3179
www.foodallergy.org

Food Allergy Initiative (FAI)
1414 Avenue of the Americas, Suite 1804
New York, NY 10019
212 207-1974
www.foodallergyinitiative.org

The Jaffe Food Allergy Institute, Mount Sinai School of Medicine
Box 1198, One Gustave L. Levy Place
New York, NY 10029
212 241-5548
www.mssm.edu/jaffe_food_allergy

National Institute of Environmental Health Sciences
P.O. Box 12233
Research Triangle Park, NC 27709
919 541-3345
www.niehs.hih.gov

Parents of Children with Food Allergies (PCFA)
118 Washington Street, Suite 10
Holliston, MA 01746
508 893-6977
www.foodallergykids.org

Web Sites

AllAllergy
www. allallergy.net
The self-proclaimed gateway to all asthma, allergy, and intolerance information on the web.

AllergicChild
www.allergicchild.com

AllergyGrocer
www.allergygrocer.com
An online grocery store with a wide array of allergen-free products. A fantastic resource!

AllergyKids
www.allergykids.com
Products—lunch sacks, wristbands, stickers, etc.—designed to promote Universal Food Allergy Awareness and alert others to your child's food allergies.

AllergyMoms
www.allergymoms.com
A great resource for finding local support groups and learning tips for raising a food allergic child. Also offers a free email newsletter featuring the latest allergy-friendly products, advice, and information.

AllerNeeds
www.allerneeds.com
Sells allergen-free foods and snacks.

BabyandKidAllergies
www.babyandkidallergies.com

Cybele Pascal's blog
www.allergycookbook.blogspot.com
Ask Cybele your food allergy cooking questions, get new recipes, and share your allergy stories.

FEAST
www.seattlefoodallergy.org
This Web site has a great listing of food allergy support groups, both national and international.

FoodYouCanEat
www.foodyoucaneat.com
Recipes and food support for people with food allergies.

GoDairyFree
www.godairyfree.org
A great resource for those on a dairy-free diet.

KidsWithFoodAllergies
www.kidswithfoodallergies.org
"A World of Support." Also includes Parents of Food Allergic Kids (POFAK), a support community for parents.

PeanutAllergy.Com
www.peanutallergy.com
Bulletin boards, news, email alerts, book lists, a list of peanut-free businesses, and anaphylaxis-related products.

Peanut Free Planet
www.peanutfreeplanet.com
A great resource for peanut-free, tree nut-free products, even allergen-free sunflower seeds!

Recommended Product Lines

The following product lines have been listed to help you purchase safe ingredients/products. When available, I have also listed phone numbers and/or Web-site information. When purchasing any product, always read labels carefully, since ingredients can change overnight and without notice.

Amy Lyn's Original Flax Thins
Wheat-free, egg-free, dairy-free, yeast-free, high-fiber, high-protein crackers.

Amy's
www.amyskitchen.com
Gluten-free, casein-free kids meals; vegetarian products; complete allergen labeling.

Annie's Naturals
800 434-1234
www.anniesnaturals.com
Organic condiments; premade vegetarian/vegan foods.

Applegate Farms
www.applegatefarms.com
Organic nitrite-free bacon, luncheon meats, etc.

Arrowhead Mills, Inc.
800 749-0730
www.arrowheadmills.com
Oat, millet, barley, rye, buckwheat, and brown rice flours; corn meal; cereals and other whole grain products.

Barbara's Bakery, Inc.
www.barbarasbakery.com
Cereals, crackers, etc.

Bard's Tale Beer Company
www.bardsbeer.com
Wheat-free, gluten-free beer.

Brown Family Farm
866 254-8718
www.brownfamilyfarmmaple.com
Affordable maple sugar for baking, as well as a full array of maple products.

Cascadian Farm
800 624-4123
www.cfarm.com
Fruit-only jams; organic frozen fruits and vegetables.

Chatfield's
Cocoa, dairy-free carob chips, date sugar, etc. Also makes "Better Than Milk" rice powder under American Natural & Specialty Brands.

Citterio
800 435-8888
www.citteriousa.com
Nitrite-free prosciutto.

Crisco, The J.M. Smucker Company
330-684-3381
Crisco Canola Oil is allergen-free. Call for more information on their manufacturing practices.

D'Artagnan
800 327-8246
www.dartagnan.com
Leading purveyor of organic game and poultry in the nation; also has nitrite-free prosciutto, demi glace, fresh and dried truffles, wild mushrooms, fois gras, etc. Offers overnight shipping.

Divvies
www.divvies.com
Dairy-free, egg-free, peanut-free, tree nut-free snacks.

Eden Organic
www.edenfoods.com
Canned beans, soups, etc.

Edy's
www.edys.com
Edy's Grand Ice Cream, whole fruit sorbets.

Ener-G Foods, Inc.
800 331-5222
www.ener-g.com
Egg Replacer, rice pasta, rice crackers, rice bread, gluten-free baked items, etc.

Enjoy Life Foods
888 50-ENJOY
www.enjoylifefoods.com
Wheat-free bagels, cookies, crackers, dairy-free
and soy-free chocolate chips, etc.

Exotic Meats USA
800 680-4375
www.exoticmeats.com
An amazing product list of exotic meats that they
will ship directly to you.

Farmer's Market
www.farmersmarketfoods.com
Canned organic sweet potatoes, pumpkin,
butternut squash.

Food for Life
800 797-5090
www.foodforlife.com
Wheat and gluten-free products like brown-rice tortillas.

Fungus Among Us
www.fungusamongus.com
Organic dried mushrooms.

Garden of Eatin'
Hain Celestial Group, Inc.
800 434-4246
www.gardenofeatin.com
Organic tortilla chips.

Grainfield's
The Weetabix Company, Inc.
Corn Flakes, Crispy Rice Cereal, Oat O's, etc.

Health Valley Co.
Hain Celestial Group, Inc.
800 423-4846
Canned goods, chili, cereal, etc.

Hol-Grain
Conrad Rice Mill
www.holgrain.com
Wheat-free, gluten-free products, like brown-rice
bread crumbs.

Ian's Natural Foods
www.iansnaturalfoods.com
Allergen-free chicken nuggets, oven-baked
French fries, etc.

Imagine Foods
www.imaginefoods.com
Rice Milk, "Rice Dream" ice-cream, etc.

Kitchen Basics
www.kitchenbasics.net
Allergen-free cooking stocks (also gluten-free
and free of msg).

Lundberg Family Farms
www.lundberg.com
Brown-rice pasta, all varieties of rice, etc.

Maple Grove Farms of Vermont
800 525-2540
www.maplegrove.com
Affordable maple sugar available by the pound.

Mestemacher Breads
www.germandeli.com/mebr.html
Natural whole rye bread and wheat-free
rye bread.

Muir Glen Organic
800 624-4123
www.muirglen.com
Organic canned tomatoes, ketchup, etc.

Murray's Chicken
800 770-6347
www.murrayschicken.com
All natural poultry products.

Nature's Hilights
800 313-6454
Brown-rice pizza crusts.

Nature's Path Foods
www.naturespath.com
Organic cereals.

No Nuttin' Foods
www.nonuttin.com
Peanut-free, tree nut-free, and dairy-free granola and snacks.

NOW Foods
www.nowfoods.com
Date sugar, maple syrup, etc.

Omega Nutrition
800 661-FLAX (3529)
www.omeganutrition.com
Pumpkin seed butter, flax products, etc.

Oregon Fruit Products
800 394-9333
www.oregonfruit.com
Canned pie cherries, blueberries, etc.

Orgran Natural Foods
Roma Food Products
www.orgran.com
Vegan wheat-free products like spaghetti, cookies, "No-egg," etc.

Pacific Natural Foods
503 692-9666
www.pacificfoods.com
Oat milk, rice milk, chicken broth, vegetable broth, beef broth, mushroom broth, etc.

Penzeys Spices
800 741-7787
www.penzeys.com
My favorite spice supplier. They have incredible variety. Call or visit their Web site for a catalogue.

Perky's
www.perkysnaturalfoods.com
Gluten-free, allergen-free cereals—Perky O's, Perky's Nutty Flax, Perky's Nutty Rice.

Premium Gold Flax Products
www.flaxpremiumgold.com
Gluten-free, allergen-free flax.

Quinoa Corporation
www.quinoa.net
Quinoa pasta, grain, flakes, flour, etc.; Food Merchants ready-made gluten-free polenta.

Redbridge Beer
www.redbridgebeer.com
Wheat-free, gluten-free beer.

Ricera
www.ricerafoods.com
Rice Milk Yogurt.

Rumford
Clabber Girl Corp.
www.clabbergirl.com
Aluminum-free baking powder.

Scharffen Berger
www.scharffenberger.com/nutrit.asp
Chocolate Home Baking Bars and Natural Cocoa Powder.

Shady Maple Farm
www.shadymaple.ca
Maple sugar, maple syrup, etc.

Shiloh Farms
800 362-6832
www.shilohfarms.com
Whole grains like millet, oats, etc.

Simply Organic
www.simplyorganicfoods.com
Organic spices, herbs, and seasonings.

Spectrum Naturals
www.spectrumorganic.com
Dairy-free, soy-free vegetable shortening.

Spice Garden
www.healthwisefoods.com
All natural, non-irradiated spices.

Sungold Foods
www.sunbutter.com
Sungold SUNBUTTER.

Sunspire
Division of NSpired Natural Foods
510 686-0116
www.sunspire.com
Dairy-free, grain-sweetened chocolate chips.

Tinkyada
888 323-2388
www.ricepasta.com or www.tinkyada.com
Great rice lasagna, and other rice pastas.

Trader Joe's
www.traderjoes.com
Sunflower butter, wheat-free rye bread,
corn tortillas, etc.

Turtle Mountain
www.turtlemountain.com

So Delicious Coconut Milk Yogurt and full
line of dairy-free products.

Vermont Nut Free Chocolate Co.
www.vermontnutfree.com
Peanut-free and tree nut-free gourmet chocolates.

Walnut Acres
Hain Celestial Group, Inc.
866 4Walnut (866 492-5688)
www.walnutacres.com
Organic broth, soup, canned goods, kid's snacks, etc.

Westbrae Natural
Hain Celestial Group, Inc.
800 434-4246
www.westbrae.com
Canned beans, soups, etc.

Useful Web Sites for Locating Health Food Stores, Co-ops, and Farmers' Markets

When you are having trouble finding an ingredient at your supermarket or grocery store, a trip to your local health food store will generally do the trick. Your local yellow pages will list health food stores and, of course, the Internet now provides a wealth of information. The following sites will help guide you to a local health food store or co-op in your area. Sometimes you can order directly from the site.

Earthrise
www.earthrise.com
Lists roughly 10,000 health food stores and
nutrition centers in the United States and Canada.

Green People
www.greenpeople.org/healthfood.htm
Amazingly comprehensive list of co-ops, health food
stores, natural food stores, farmers markets, etc.

Happy Cow's Global Guide to Vegetarian Restaurants and Health Food Stores
www.happycow.net
Lists vegetarian restaurants and health food stores
throughout the world.

Local Harvest
www.localharvest.org
Locates farmers' markets, family farms, co-ops, and
other sources of sustainably grown food in your area.

Natural Health Supersite
www.anaturalway.com/supersite/toc/foods.html
A great list of natural food stores, restaurants, mail
order, and whole food direct sellers.

New Leaf Market
www.newleafcoop.com
Great links to co-ops.

Organic Consumers Association
www.organicconsumers.org/foodcoops.htm
Lists co-ops, health food stores, and natural food
stores. Also has links to specific stores for more
detailed information.

The Vegetarian Travel Guide
www.vegetarianusa.com
Good selection of links to co-ops and health
food stores.

Household Products, Hypoallergenic Vitamins, and Medicines

Abrams Royal Pharmacy
8220 Abrams Road
Dallas, TX 75231
800 458-0804
www.abramsroyalpharmacy.com
Made-to-order medicines.

Allergy Research Group/Nutricology, Inc.
4300 North Loop Road
Alameda, CA 94502
800 545-9960
www.nutricology.com
Nutritional supplement line with over 300 products designed for people with food sensitivities and allergies.

Allergy Solutions, Inc.
7 Crozerville Road
Aston, PA 19014
800 491-4300
www.allergysolutions.com
Catalog, household products, bedding, etc.

Bronson Laboratories, Inc.
600 E Quality Drive
American Fork, UT 84003-3302
800 235-3200
www.bronsononline.com
Supplements, many allergen-free, but contact for exact ingredient information.

Carlson Laboratories, Inc.
15 College Drive
Arlington Heights, IL 60004-1985
888 234-5656
www.carlsonlabs.com
Supplements, many allergen-free. Contact for exact ingredient information.

Freeda Vitamins, Inc.
47-25 34th Street 3rd Floor
Long Island City, NY 11101
800 777-3737
www.freedavitamins.com
Starch-free and sugar-free vegetarian supplements, many allergen-free. Contact for exact ingredient information.

Health Enterprises, Inc.
90 George Leven Drive
North Attleboro, MA 02760
800 633-4243
www.healthenterprises.com
Medical alert bracelets, necklaces, cards, etc.

MedicAlert Foundation
2323 Colorado Avenue
Turlock, CA 95382
888 633-4298
www.medicalert.com
Medical alert bracelets, cards, etc.; hotline.

NOW Foods
395 S. Glen Ellyn Road
Bloomingdale, IL 60108
888 669-3663
www.nowfoods.com
Hypoallergenic vitamins; some organic foods.

Puritan's Pride
1233 Montauk Highway
Oakdale, NY 11769-9001
800 645-1030
www.vitamins.com
More than 10,000 nationally advertised vitamins and health products.

The Vitamin Shoppe
Customer Care Dept.
2101 91st Street
North Bergen, NJ 07047
800 223-1216
www.vitaminshoppe.com
Supplements, many allergen-free. Contact for exact ingredient information.

Wellness, Health & Pharmaceuticals
3401 Independence Drive, Suite 231
Birmingham, AL 35209
800 227-2627
www.wellnesshealth.com
Pharmacy for custom medications free of all major allergens.

Useful Books About Food Allergies

Food Allergy Books/Magazines for Adults

Balch, James F. and Phyllis A. *Prescription for Nutritional Healing*. New York: Avery, 2000.

Barber, Marianne S. *The Parent's Guide to Food Allergies: Clear and Complete Advice from the Experts on Raising your Food Allergic Child*. New York: Owl Books, 2001.

Barnes Koerner, Celide, and Anne Munoz-Furlong. *Food Allergies: Up-to-Date Tips from the World's Foremost Nutrition Experts*. New York: John Wiley, 1998.

Collins, Lisa Cipriano. *Caring for Your Child with Severe Food Allergies: Emotional Support and Practical Advice from a Parent Who's Been There*. New York: John Wiley, 1999.

Davies, Gwynne H. *Overcoming Food Allergies*. Bath: Ashgrove Press, 1985.

Dumke, Nicolette M. *5 Years Without Food: The Food Allergy Survival Guide: How to Overcome Your Food Allergies and Recover Good Health*. Allergy Adapt Inc., 1998.

Food Allergy Network (FAN). *College Guide for Students with Food Allergies: It's Not All Pizza and Ice Cream*. Fairfax, VA: Food Allergy Network, 1999.

Living Without: The Magazine for People with Allergies and Food Sensitivities. Belvoir Media Group LLC, Norwalk, CT.

Metcalfe, Dean D., Hugh A. Sampson, and Ronald A. Simon, eds. *Food Allergy: Adverse Reactions to Foods and Food Additives*, 2nd ed. Cambridge, MA: Blackwell Science, 1997.

Vickerstaff Joneja, Janice. *Dietary Management of Food Allergies and Intolerances: A Comprehensive Guide*, 2nd ed. Burnaby, British Columbia: JA Hall, 1998.

Wedman-St Louis, Betty. *Living with Food Allergies: A Complete Guide to a Healthy Lifestyle*. Lincolnwood, IL: Contemporary Books, 1999.

Food Allergy Books for Children

Food Allergy Network (FAN). *Alexander Series: A Special Day At School, Alexander and His Pals Visit the Main Street School, Alexander Goes to a Birthday Party, Alexander Goes Trick-or-Treating, Alexander's Fun & Games Activity Book, Andrew and Maya Learn About Food Allergies, Alexander the Elephant Who Couldn't Eat Peanuts ColoringBook*. Fairfax, VA: Food Allergy Network, 1999.

Habkirk, Lauri, and Les Habkirk. *Preschoolers Guide to Peanut Allergy*. Medford, MA: PeanutAllergy.Com, 1995.

Smith, Nicole. *Allie the Allergic Elephant*. Colorado Springs, CO: Jungle Communications, Inc., 1999.

Weiner, Ellen. *Taking Food Allergies to School*. Valley Park, MO: JayJo Books, 1999.

Useful Food Allergy Cookbooks

Zevy, Aaron, and Susan Tebbutt. *No Nuts for Me!* Tampa, FL: Tumbleweed Press, 1999.

Dumke, Nicolette M. *Allergy Cooking With Ease.* Lancaster, PA: Starburst Publishers, 1992.

Emro, Rosemarie. *Bakin' Without Eggs.* New York, NY: St. Martin's Griffin, 1999.

Fleming, Alisa Marie. *Dairy Free Made Easy.* Fleming Marrs, Inc., 2006.

Food Allergy Network (FAN). *The Food Allergy News Cookbook: A Collection of Recipes from Food Allergy News and Favorite Recipes from Members of the Food Allergy Network.* Fairfax, VA: FAN, 1998.

Gioannini, Marilyn. *The Complete Food Allergy Cookbook: The Foods You've Always Loved Without the Ingredients You Can't Have.* Rocklin, CA: Prima, 1997.

Harris, Mary, and Wilma Nachsin. *"My Kid's Allergic to Everything" Dessert Cookbook.* Chicago, IL: Chicago Review Press, 1996.

Jones, Marjorie Hurt. *The Allergy Self-Help Cookbook* (revised). Rodale, 2001.

BIBLIOGRAPHY

American Academy of Pediatrics, Committee on Nutrition. "Hypoallergenic Infant Formulas." *Pediatrics*. 106(2000):346–49.

Barber, Marianne S. *The Parent's Guide to Food Allergies: Clear and Complete Advice from the Experts on Raising your Food Allergic Child*. New York: Owl Books, 2001.

Bhatty, R. S. "Nutrient composition of whole flaxseed and flaxseed meal." *Flaxseed in Human Nutrition*, S. Cunnane and L. U. Thompson, eds. Champaign, IL: AOCS Press, 1995, pp. 22–42.

The Food Allergy and Anaphylaxis Network. *Preventing or Delaying the Onset of Food Allergies in Infants*. Educational Pamphlet. www.foodallergy.org

Levi, Julie Rothschild. "Lovin' Spoonfuls: What and When to Feed Your Baby." *Living Without*. Spring, 2003:50–52.

Mofidi, Shideh. "Nutritional Management of Pediatric Food Hypersensitivity." *Pediatrics*. 111(2003):1645–53.

Sicherer, Scott H., Anne Munoz-Furlong, et al. "Symposium: Pediatric Food Allergy." *Pediatrics*. 111(2003):1591–94.

Zeiger, R. S. "Food Allergen Avoidance in the Prevention of Food Allergy in Infants and Children." *Pediatrics*. 111(2003):1662–71.

Zeiger, R. S. "Prevention of Food Allergy in Infants and Children." *Immunol Allergy Clin North Am*. 19(1999):619–46.

Meyer, Elisa. *Feeding Your Allergic Child*. New York, NY: St. Martin's Press, 1997.

GENERAL INDEX

RECIPE INDEX

NOTES

NOTES

NOTES

AUTHOR BIOGRAPHY

Cybele Pascal is an award-winning playwright and writer. She has an MFA from Columbia University and an Artists Diploma in Playwriting from the Juilliard School. She is represented by Curtis Brown, Ltd., and Rain Management Group.

In addition to her work as a writer, Cybele has had a lifelong passion for cooking and food history. She grew up on Cape Cod in a family of excellent cooks, with a large organic garden, which was harvested to cook delicious and exciting meals. She was taught to cook as a very young child by her grandmother who became a superlative home chef during the many years she lived in Italy. Cybele believes that recipes are a form of heritage and, over the years, has learned to cook dishes handed down from her Southern ancestors as well as her Eastern European great-grandmother, a famously gifted and enthusiastic cook who reputedly spent so much time at the oven she could lift out hot casseroles with her bare hands.

Cybele's eclectic food background has inspired her love for a wide range of cuisines. In addition to the recipes she learned during the fifteen years she spent working in restaurants, she is constantly expanding her repertoire. She has traveled the world extensively, making local food the focus of her trips. Food is her passion and cooking fresh, delicious, and healthy meals for her family and friends is a daily pleasure.

Cybele learned about hypoallergenic cooking firsthand when her son Lennon was diagnosed with severe food allergies and made turning family meals into delicacies her priority. She lives in Los Angeles, California, with her husband, Adam, and their sons, Lennon and Montgomery.

DEADLY HARVEST
The Intimate Relationship Between Our Health and Our Food
Geoff Bond

With an increasing number of people suffering from obesity, heart disease, and other diet-related disorders, many of us turn to fad diets in an effort to drop excess pounds or recover our health. But what if our foods were doing more harm than good, and fad diets made matters worse? *Deadly Harvest* examines how the foods we eat today have little in common with those of our ancestors, and why this fact is important to our health. It also offers a proven program to enhance health and improve longevity.

Using the latest scientific research and studies of primitive lifestyles, the author first explains the diet that our ancestors followed—one in harmony with the human species. He then describes how our present diets affect our health, leading to disorders such as cancer, diabetes, heart disease, and more. Most important, he details measures we can take to improve our diet, our health, and our quality of life.

$16.95 • 336 pages • 6 x 9-inch quality paperback • ISBN 978-0-7570-0142-0

POLITICALLY INCORRECT NUTRITION
Finding Reality in the Mire of Food Industry Propaganda
Michael Barbee, CDC

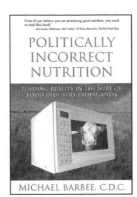

Did you know that some noncaloric artificial sweeteners can actually make you fat—or even kill you? Did you know that the overconsumption of certain soy products can upset your hormonal balance and lead to hypothyroidism? Most people didn't, until now. *Politically Incorrect Nutrition* exposes many current and widely held beliefs foisted on both consumers and health-care practitioners by well-oiled, agenda-driven food industry propaganda. It analyzes popular claims and reveals what, in fact, is healthy—and what is decidedly *unhealthy*—by exploring the most current and objective scientific data regarding good nutrition.

If you want to provide the best possible food for yourself and your family, or if you simply want to learn the truth behind the many food myths that are presented to us day after day, *Politically Incorrect Nutrition* is must reading.

$13.95 • 176 pages • 6 x 9-inch quality paperback • ISBN 978-1-890612-34-4

GMO FREE
Exposing the Hazards of Biotechnology to Ensure the Integrity of Our Food Supply
Mae-Wan Ho, PhD, and Lim Li Ching

The genetic engineering of food crops is an ecological hazard and health crisis that affects us all. Its consequences are global and potentially irrevocable. Yet the decision to use genetically modified organisms is currently being made for you by the government and major multinational corporations. To combat this practice, more than 600 scientists from 72 countries have called for a moratorium on the environmental release of GMOs. *GMO Free* is the most comprehensive resource available on the science behind this worldwide debate.

GMO Free takes a good look at the evidence scientists have compiled, and makes a strong case for a worldwide ban on GMO crops, to make way for a shift to sustainable agriculture and organic farming. It's time to take the future of your food supply and environment into your own informed hands. *GMO Free* will give you the information you need to do so.

$10.95 • 152 pages • 5.5 x 8.5-inch quality paperback • ISBN 978-1-890612-37-5

GOING WILD IN THE KITCHEN
The Fresh & Sassy Tastes of Vegetarian Cooking
Leslie Cerier

Go wild in the kitchen! Venture beyond the usual beans, grains, and vegetables to include an exciting variety of organic vegetarian fare in your meals. *Going Wild in the Kitchen,* written by expert chef Leslie Cerier, shows you how. In addition to providing helpful cooking tips and techniques, this book offers over 150 kitchen-tested recipes for taste-tempting dishes that contain such unique ingredients as edible flowers; tasty sea vegetables; wild mushrooms, berries, and herbs; and exotic ancient grains like teff, quinoa, and Chinese "forbidden" black rice. The author encourages the creative instincts of novice and seasoned cooks alike, prompting them to "go wild" in the kitchen by adding, changing, or substituting ingredients in existing recipes. To help, an extensive ingredient glossary is included, along with a wealth of helpful cooking guidelines. Lively illustrations and a complete resource list for finding organic foods completes this user-friendly cookbook.

Going Wild in the Kitchen is more than a unique cookbook—it's a recipe for inspiration. Excite your palate with this treasure-trove of distinctive, healthy, and taste-tempting recipe creations.

$16.95 • 240 pages • 7.5 x 9-inch quality paperback • ISBN 978-0-7570-0091-1

EAT SMART, EAT RAW
Creative Vegetarian Recipes for a Healthier Life
Kate Wood

As the popularity of raw vegetarian cuisine continues to soar, so does the evidence that uncooked food is amazingly good for you. From lowering cholesterol to eliminating excess weight, the health benefits of this diet are too important to ignore. Now there is another reason to go raw—taste! In *Eat Smart, Eat Raw,* cook and health writer Kate Wood not only explains how to get started, but also provides kitchen-tested recipes guaranteed to delight even the fussiest of eaters.

Eat Smart, Eat Raw begins by explaining the basics of cooking without heat. This is followed by twelve chapters offering 150 recipes for truly exceptional dishes, including hearty breakfasts, savory soups, satisfying entrées, and luscious desserts. There's even a chapter on the "almost raw." Whether you are an ardent vegetarian or just someone in search of a great meal, *Eat Smart, Eat Raw* may forever change the way you look at an oven.

$15.95 • 184 pages • 7.5 x 9-inch quality paperback • ISBN 978-0-7570-0261-8

TASTE LIFE!
ORGANIC RECIPES
Edited by Leslie Cerier

Expertly compiled and edited by Leslie Cerier—organic chef, caterer, lecturer, teacher, and cookbook writer—the mouth-watering recipes found in *Taste Life! Organic Recipes* come from discerning, health-conscious individuals all across the country. In each recipe, organic foods are used for their superior ecological benefits and high nutritional values, as well as optimal taste.

Taste Life! Organic Recipes shows that preparing meals with organic foods can result in fare that is more creative, flavorful, and, of course, healthier than nonorganic fare. Delectable, easy-to-follow recipes range from substantial dishes such as Heart-Warming Sweet Potato Pancakes, Stuffed Artichokes, and Vegetarian Chili, to sweet treats like Carob Fudge Brownies and Happy Monkey Banana Pie.

Explicit instructions—including tips for roasting corn and peppers—make this cookbook as helpful for the novice who's looking for basics, as it is for the experienced vegetarian cook who's searching for delicious new ideas.

$13.95 • 136 pages • 7 x 10-inch quality paperback • ISBN 978-1-890612-16-0

AS YOU LIKE IT COOKBOOK
Imaginative Gourmet Dishes with Exciting Vegetarian Options
Ron Pickarski

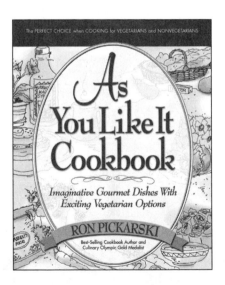

When it comes to food, we certainly like to have it our way; however, the challenge of cooking for both vegetarians and nonvegetarians is becoming more and more common. To meet that challenge, chef Ron Pickarski has written the *As You Like It Cookbook*—a unique collection of recipes designed to help you find the perfect meal for today's lifestyles.

The *As You Like It Cookbook* offers over 170 great-tasting dishes that cater to a broad range of tastes. Many of the easy-to-follow recipes are already vegetarian, and offer ingredient alternatives for meat eaters. Conversely, recipes that include meat, fish, or poultry offer nonmeat ingredient options. Vegan alternatives are provided for those who follow a strictly plant-based diet. So don't despair the next time someone asks what's for dinner. With the *As You Like It Cookbook,* a tantalizing meal—cooked exactly as your family likes it—is just minutes away.

$16.95 • 216 pages • 7.5 x 9-inch quality paperback • ISBN 978-0-7570-0013-3

GREENS & GRAINS ON THE DEEP BLUE SEA COOKBOOK
Fabulous Vegetarian Cuisine from the Holistic Holiday at Sea Cruises
Sandy Pukel and Mark Hanna

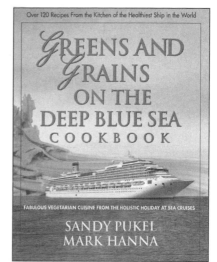

You are invited to come aboard one of America's premier health cruises. Too busy to get away? Well, even if you can't swim in the ship's pool, you can still enjoy its gourmet cuisine, because natural foods expert Sandy Pukel and master chef Mark Hanna have now put together *Greens and Grains on the Deep Blue Sea Cookbook*—a titanic collection of healthful and delicious vegetarian recipes that are among the most popular dishes served aboard the Taste of Health voyages offered through Costa Cruises.

Each of the over 200 kitchen-tested recipes in this cookbook has been created to provide not only great taste and visual appeal, but also maximum nutrition. Choose from among an innovative and distinctive selection of taste-tempting appetizers, hearty soups, sensational salads, elegant entrées, satisfying side dishes, and delectable desserts. Easy-to-follow instructions make this user-friendly cookbook an absolute delight.

Although you may not be able to walk the deck of an actual Taste of Health cruise ship, with *Greens and Grains on the Deep Blue Sea Cookbook,* you can enjoy its fabulous signature dishes whenever you so desire—in the comfort of your own home.

$16.95 • 160 pages • 7.5 x 9-inch quality paperback • ISBN 978-0-7570-0287-8

ENEMY OF THE STEAK
Vegetarian Recipes to Win Friends and Influence Meat-Eaters
Nikki and David Goldbeck

Don't blame vegetarians for starting this. Who said "real food for real people"? Aren't asparagus, carrots, and tomatoes every bit as real as . . . that other food? To answer the call to battle, best-selling authors Nikki and David Goldbeck have created a wonderfully tempting new cookbook that offers a wealth of kitchen-tested recipes—recipes that nourish the body, please the palate, and satisfy even the heartiest of appetites.

Enemy of the Steak first presents basic information on vegetarian cooking and stocking the vegetarian pantry. Then eight great chapters offer recipes for breakfast fare; appetizers and hors d'oeuvres; soups; salads; entrées; side dishes; sauces, toppings, and marinades; and desserts. Throughout the book, the Goldbecks have included practical tips and advice on weight loss, disease prevention, and other important topics. They also offer dozens of fascinating facts about why fruits and veggies are so good for you.

A perfect marriage of nutrition and the art of cooking, *Enemy of the Steak* is for everyone who loves a good healthy meal. Simply put, it's great food for smart people. If you have to take sides, you couldn't be in better company.

$16.95 • 248 pages • 7.5 x 9-inch quality paperback • ISBN 978-0-7570-0273-1

STEVIA SWEET RECIPES
Sugar-Free—Naturally

Jeffrey Goettemoeller

Stevia Sweet Recipes offers health-conscious readers over 165 kitchen-tested recipes that use Stevia—a calorie-free, nonglycemic herbal sweetener—in place of refined sugar or artificial sweeteners. Enjoy the author's many creative dishes, from healthy breakfast shakes to sensational salads to luscious desserts, while learning how to use this amazing herb in your own treasured family dishes. Soon you'll be sweetening all your foods the natural way, with Stevia.

$13.95 • 200 pages • 6 x 8.5-inch quality paperback • ISBN 978-1-890612-13-9

WHEATGRASS
Superfood for a New Millennium

Li Smith

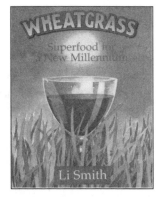

More than just a grain, wheatgrass has tremendous health and healing benefits. As a primary "sun-food," it converts the sun's rays directly into chlorophyll as well as an abundance of vitamins, minerals, amino acids, and enzymes—all of which are needed to enhance and optimize health and well-being. Wheatgrass also detoxifies and purifies the body while naturally increasing energy and restoring balance.

Wheatgrass describes the outstanding nutritive and therapeutic benefits of consuming wheatgrass juice. Written from a holistic perspective, the book explores the history of this amazing superfood and its importance within the spiritual traditions of many cultures. Included are home usage suggestions and growing instructions, as well as a cleansing and rejuvenation program that incorporates wheatgrass, fresh fruits and vegetables, fermented foods, herbs, and edible flowers. Charming illustrations, sprinkled throughout, make *Wheatgrass* as delightful as it is informative.

$10.95 • 164 pages • 5.5 x 7-inch quality paperback • ISBN 978-1-890612-10-8

JUICE ALIVE
The Ultimate Guide to Juicing Remedies

Steven Bailey, ND and Larry Trivieri, Jr.

The world of fresh juices offers a powerhouse of antioxidants, vitamins, minerals, and enzymes. The trick is knowing which juices can best serve your needs. In this easy-to-use guide, health experts Dr. Steven Bailey and Larry Trivieri, Jr. tell you everything you need to know to maximize the benefits and tastes of juice.

The book begins with a look at the history of juicing. It then examines the many components that make fresh juice truly good for you—good for weight loss and so much more. Next, it offers practical advice about the types of juices available, as well as buying and storing tips for produce. The second half of the book begins with an important chart that matches up common ailments with the most appropriate juices, followed by over 100 delicious juice recipes. Let *Juice Alive* introduce you to a world bursting with the incomparable tastes and benefits of fresh juice.

$14.95 • 272 pages • 6 x 9-inch quality paperback • ISBN 978-0-7570-0266-3